John Lydgate
MUMMINGS AND ENTERTAINMENTS

T0165898

MIDDLE ENGLISH TEXTS SERIES

GENERAL EDITOR
Russell A. Peck, University of Rochester

ASSOCIATE EDITOR
Alan Lupack, University of Rochester

ASSISTANT EDITOR
John H. Chandler, University of Rochester

ADVISORY BOARD

Theresa Coletti
University of Maryland

Michael Livingston
The Citadel

Rita Copeland
University of Pennsylvania

R. A. Shoaf
University of Florida

Susanna Fein
Kent State University

Lynn Staley
Colgate University

Thomas G. Hahn
University of Rochester

Paul E. Szarmach
The Medieval Academy of America

David A. Lawton
Washington University in St. Louis

Bonnie Wheeler
Southern Methodist University

The Middle English Texts Series is designed for classroom use. Its goal is to make available to teachers and students texts that occupy an important place in the literary and cultural canon but have not been readily available in student editions. The series does not include those authors, such as Chaucer, Langland, or Malory, whose English works are normally in print in good student editions. The focus is, instead, upon Middle English literature adjacent to those authors that teachers need in compiling the syllabuses they wish to teach. The editions maintain the linguistic integrity of the original work but within the parameters of modern reading conventions. The texts are printed in the modern alphabet and follow the practices of modern capitalization, word formation, and punctuation. Manuscript abbreviations are silently expanded, and *u/v* and *j/i* spellings are regularized according to modern orthography. Yogh (ȝ) is transcribed as *g*, *gh*, *y*, or *s*, according to the sound in Modern English spelling to which it corresponds; thorn (þ) and eth (ð) are transcribed as *th*. Distinction between the second person pronoun and the definite article is made by spelling the one *thee* and the other *the*, and final *-e* that receives full syllabic value is accented (e.g., *charité*). Hard words, difficult phrases, and unusual idioms are glossed on the page, either in the right margin or at the foot of the page. Explanatory and textual notes appear at the end of the text, often along with a glossary. The editions include short introductions on the history of the work, its merits and points of topical interest, and brief working bibliographies.

This series is published in association with the University of Rochester.

Medieval Institute Publications is a program of
The Medieval Institute, College of Arts and Sciences

 WESTERN MICHIGAN UNIVERSITY

John Lydgate

MUMMINGS AND ENTERTAINMENTS

Edited by
Claire Sponsler

TEAMS • Middle English Texts Series

MEDIEVAL INSTITUTE PUBLICATIONS
Western Michigan University
Kalamazoo

Copyright © 2010 by the Board of Trustees of
Western Michigan University

Manufactured in the United States of America

Library of Congress Cataloging-in-Publication Data

Lydgate, John, 1370?-1451?
  [Poems. Selections]
  Mummings and entertainments / John Lydgate ; edited by Claire Sponsler.
      p. cm. -- (Middle English texts series)
  Includes bibliographical references.
  ISBN 978-1-58044-148-3 (paperbound : alk. paper)
  1. Mumming. I. Sponsler, Claire II. Title.
  PR2032.S66 2010
  821'.2--dc22
                            2009050461

ISBN 978-1-58044-148-3

P 5 4 3 2 1

CONTENTS

ACKNOWLEDGMENTS

I am grateful to Derek Pearsall for his early support, to Doug Sugano for generously sharing advice gleaned from editing the N-Town plays, and to Russell Peck and his hard-working assistants for their deft guidance at the University of Rochester. The staffs of the British Library, the Bodleian Library, and the Wren Library of Trinity College, Cambridge, provided valuable assistance in accessing manuscripts. Leah Haught helped check textual notes, and John H. Chandler read through the volume and prepared the text for publication. Alan Lupack gave the manuscript a final reading and was especially helpful in refining some of the glosses. A fellowship from the National Endowment for the Humanities funded work on a monograph about Lydgate, whose findings have enriched this edition. I am also grateful to the National Endowment for its support of the Middle English Texts Series over the past decade, without which publication of this volume would not have been possible. Thanks are also due to Patricia Hollahan and Tom Krol at Medieval Institute Publications for their support of the series in which this edition appears and careful attention in seeing the volume through publication.

🌿 INTRODUCTION

John Lydgate (c. 1371–1449), monk of the great abbey of Bury St. Edmunds in Suffolk, is best known today as the author of such large-scale works as the *Fall of Princes*, the *Troy Book*, and the *Siege of Thebes*, which established him as the preeminent poet of fifteenth-century England, but he also had an active career as a writer of verses for public and private ceremonies and entertainments. Although they have been eclipsed by his longer works, these verses are of great importance for literary and theatrical history. They offer an example — rare in this period — of dramatic texts by a known writer and thus provide valuable information about how performances were commissioned, created, and disseminated in written form. They also reveal the range of Lydgate's poetic activities and his versatility, reminding us that artistic categories we now think of as discrete — writing, oral or mimetic performance, and visual display — overlapped in the fifteenth century. As Lydgate's work shows, modern terms for theatrical events — "performance," "play," "drama," and "theater" — are not particularly apt for a late medieval culture of literate orality, in which poetic verses might be read silently in private, recited aloud, painted on walls or panels, sung, mimed, or enacted — or even made part of the confectioner's art.

That blurring of boundaries poses some problems for deciding which texts should appear here, and while it would certainly be possible to expand or narrow the pool, I have decided to include in this edition only those texts that were mimetic in some way and that featured both oral and visual display. For that reason, the *Roundel for the Coronation of Henry VI*, which probably has no mimetic component, is not included, but the verses that accompanied the confectionary *soteltes* that were among the entertainments at the coronation banquet are, since they were tableau-like figures that included texts meant to be read — in all likelihood aloud as well as silently. Likewise, texts such as the *Danse Macabre*, which was requested in 1430 by John Carpenter, the town clerk of London, for inscription on the cloister walls of the Pardon churchyard at St. Paul's, or the translation of the famous Marian lament "Quis dabit," which was painted along the top of the walls of the Clopton chantry in the town of Long Melford, are omitted, since they seem to have been purely visual, without any spoken or mimetic component.[1] All seventeen of the works on the following pages, then, seem to have involved some degree of mimetic activity and show signs of the use of impersonation, action or gesture, costuming, props, oral recitation, or visual display.

Most of Lydgate's performance texts were written in a flush of energy in the late 1420s and early 1430s, when he was at the peak of his career as a public poet, with the *Troy Book* (1412–20) and the *Siege of Thebes* (1421–22) behind him and the *Fall of Princes* (1431–38) yet

---

[1] See Lydgate, *Dance of Death*, ed. Warren, and, for the Clopton verses, Gibson, "Bury St Edmunds, Lydgate, and the *N-Town Cycle*," pp. 80–81, and Trapp, "Verses by Lydgate at Long Melford," pp. 1–11 (although Trapp mistakenly refers to the poem as "The Lamentation of Mary Magdalene").

to come. Chief among them are seven mummings or disguisings, which were written for both royal and civic audiences. (The mumming for Margaret of Anjou's entry into London in 1445 is no longer viewed as part of Lydgate's canon, but is included in an appendix for interested readers.)[2] Three of the mummings were designed as Christmas entertainments for the young Henry VI and his mother Catherine of Valois, while four were created for civic occasions in London. Not surprisingly, given the historical circumstances in which they were written, most of these performances share a concern with questions about the nature of sovereignty and authority, the right of succession and legitimacy of rule, standards of behavior, and proper governance. They characteristically range widely over classical and biblical history, offering an erudite and probably intentionally edifying mix of examples drawn from Greek and Roman mythology as well as Christian writings.

The ten other items in this edition are more miscellaneous in nature. *A Procession of Corpus Christi* describes a London Corpus Christi procession and, while undated, may also have been written in the late 1420s. In 1429, Lydgate was commissioned to write verses to accompany *soteltes* for the coronation banquet of Henry VI, one of four poems he produced for the occasion (the others included a prayer, a roundel, and a balade). A few years later, Lydgate wrote another poem for a civic audience when he was commissioned by the mayor of London, John Welles, to write a commemorative description of the pageants Londoners had devised to greet Henry VI on his return to England on 21 February 1432, after two years in France.[3] At an undetermined date, Lydgate wrote the *Pageant of Knowledge*, so named by Henry MacCracken after the Latin term *pagina* that appears in the text. The meaning of the term *pagina* is ambiguous, but MacCracken thought it pointed to the presentation of the piece as a school play, like what he identified as its original by Ausonius.[4] (The unattributed *Mumming of the Seven Philosophers*, which a later hand suggestively includes as among the "Poemata Anglicana Lidgati" and which appears to have been designed for a Christmas-king performance, possibly also by schoolboys, is included in an appendix for comparison.) Another poem, *Bycorne and Chychevache*, was made for a "werthy citeseyn of London," apparently to be painted onto a wall-hanging or possibly as part of a dramatic presentation, perhaps a mumming. *Of the Sodein Fal of Princes in Oure Dayes* seems to have been similarly designed to accompany pictorial representations, processional presentation, or a mumming.[5] *The Legend of St. George* was written at the request of the armorers of London to honor their brotherhood and for the feast of Saint George; like *Bycorne and Chychevache*, the verses were

---

[2] The 1445 entry was first identified as Lydgate's by Stow in his *Annales* (1592), p. 624, based on Fabyan's account, and subsequently attributed to Lydgate by a number of critics, including MacCracken, who later reversed his opinion, after finding the verses inconsistent with Lydgate's style; Kipling argues that the use of two stanzaic forms suggests two separate poets, neither of them Lydgate ("London Pageants for Margaret of Anjou," pp. 11–12).

[3] Verses describing the London entry of Henry V in 1415 are no longer ascribed to Lydgate. The verses are reprinted as Appendix IV, pp. 191–92, at the end of the *Gesta Henrici Quinti*, a text that gives the fullest extant account of the 1415 pageants. For their attribution to Lydgate, see Withington, *English Pageantry*, 1:132 ff., and the references there.

[4] For a discussion of "pageant" as synonymous with "picture," see Edwards, "Middle English Pageant 'Picture'?"; Pearsall, *John Lydgate*, p. 183, discusses tableau presentation.

[5] See Hammond, "Two Tapestry Poems;" Pearsall believes *Sodein Fal* was intended for processional performance (*John Lydgate*, p. 180); and Robbins identifies it as a mumming (*Secular Lyrics*, p. 342).

apparently created to be painted onto a wall-hanging along with pictures, and may possibly have included some sort of enactment. *Mesure Is Tresour* also seems to have been intended to accompany portraits of the various ranks of medieval society and ends with verses seemingly spoken by a shepherd figure.

LYDGATE AND HIS MILIEU

Born in a small village in Suffolk, Lydgate spent most of his life as a monk in the nearby Benedictine abbey of Bury St. Edmunds, one of the wealthiest and most powerful monastic houses in England and a center for culture and drama.[6] The town, with a population of around four thousand in the early fifteenth century, lay inside the monastery walls and the monastery controlled most town affairs. Relations between the town and the monastery were not always without conflict: in 1327 the citizens burned down and plundered the abbey and during the 1381 rising a crowd marched on the abbey and sacked the houses of monastic officials. By 1400, the abbey at Bury had around sixty to eighty monks, with up to two hundred servants and vast estates in Suffolk and beyond.[7] Lydgate tells us in his *Testament* that he entered the abbey as a novice at the age of fifteen and was eventually ordained in 1397.[8] As a student at Bury, Lydgate would have received a standard course of instruction in grammar, logic, and philosophy; he would also have had access to the monastery's library, which held some two thousand manuscripts, including the complete comedies of Terence and eight plays by Plautus.[9]

Lydgate seems to have continued his studies at Oxford, as Derek Pearsall notes in his detailed biography of the poet, where he probably made the acquaintance of a number of eminent men — including the Prince of Wales; Richard Courtenay, chancellor of Oxford in 1406–08 and off-and-on again in 1411–13; and Edmund Lacy, the bishop of Exeter — all of whom appear to have influenced his writing.[10] At Oxford, Lydgate would have studied at Gloucester College, the house for monk-students from the southern province of the Benedictine order; he appears to have stayed for a few years, but did not take a degree.[11] A few tantalizing glimpses of Lydgate's reading and writing from this period include a

---

[6] Lydgate mentions on three occasions (*Fall of Princes*, VIII.195–96 and IX.3431–35, and *Isopes Fabules*, lines 31–32) that he was born in Lydgate (or Lidgate), a small village in Suffolk, eight miles southwest of Bury, where he was recruited as a boy to the abbey (see Pearsall, *Bio-Bibliography*, p.12).

[7] Pearsall, *Bio-Bibliography*, pp. 12–13.

[8] Pearsall, *Bio-Bibliography*, pp. 13–14.

[9] See James, "Bury St. Edmunds Manuscripts," and Thomson, "Library of Bury," pp. 617–45; for Bury's ownership of the Terence and Plautus manuscripts, see Gibson, "Bury St. Edmunds, Lydgate, and the *N-Town Cycle*," p. 63.

[10] See Pearsall, *John Lydgate*, pp. 56–57, for the letter from the Prince of Wales, probably written in 1406–08, to the abbot of Bury requesting that "J. L.," of whom he has heard good reports from "R. C." [Richard Courtenay], be allowed to stay at Oxford. Norton-Smith argues that Lydgate met Edmund Lacy at Oxford (Shirley says Lydgate wrote a translation of *Gloriosa dicta sunt de te* for him) and that along with the Prince of Wales, Lacy shaped "the direction and style of Lydgate's religious verse" (*John Lydgate: Poems*, p. 195).

[11] Pearsall, *Bio-Bibliography*, p.15. See also Dobson, "Religious Orders, 1370–1540," pp. 546–48, and Pantin, *Documents*, 3:222.

volume containing Isidore's *Synonyma*, the sermons of Hildebert of Le Mans, "Versus circiter cxiv proverbiales" and "Versus lxxiv heroici proverbiales" that Lydgate may have brought with him from the library at Bury, and his *Isopes Fabules*, which the scribe John Shirley says was "made in Oxforde."[12] As Pearsall observes, Oxford would have afforded Lydgate a degree of freedom along with chances for meeting people, while also perhaps giving him a taste for the comforts and privileges of fame and money, and thus helps explain Lydgate's subsequent career of writing on-demand for influential people on important occasions.[13]

Although it remains an open question how much time Lydgate spent away from Bury, he clearly lived an active and public life. His commissions and contacts suggest that he moved in a circuit that included the court, Oxford and its environs (such as the house of Thomas Chaucer near Oxford), and London, as well as Bury, and even traveled as far as France. During the years when most of his performance pieces for Londoners and the court were written, Lydgate held the priorate at Hatfield, a small Benedictine priory in Essex (c. 1423–30), putting him closer to London and the royal palaces of Windsor and Eltham than he would have been at Bury. Lydgate would also have had an opportunity to make contacts at Bury, which welcomed many powerful visitors and enrolled others as associates of the fraternity of the abbey (such as Richard Beauchamp, William de la Pole, and Thomas Beaufort). Henry IV and Henry V visited Bury, and Henry VI made a long stay in 1433, shortly before Lydgate finished his *Lives of Sts. Edmund and Fremund*, which was presented to the king as a gift from Abbot Curteys and the monks of St. Edmunds. Lydgate surely also knew promi-nent citizens from the town of Bury, such as John Baret, who was treasurer to the abbey and was designated co-recipient of an annuity granted to Lydgate by Henry VI in the last year of the monk's life.[14]

Lydgate's writing is usually thought of in relation to the royal court or to London, yet it should also be seen as a product of East Anglian literary and religious culture. During his lifetime, East Anglia was home to a literary scene that included the poet John Metham, author of the romance *Amoryus and Cleopes* (1448); Osbern Bokenham, the Austin friar and author of, among other things, a life of Mary Magdalene; the chronicler John Capgrave, an Austin friar and poet from Lynn; the mystics Margery Kempe (c. 1373–c. 1439) and Julian of Norwich (c. 1343–c. 1413); and Benedict Burgh, who seems to have met Lydgate in the late 1440s and admired the monk enough to finish one of his poems after Lydgate's death.[15]

---

[12] The volume is Bodley MS Laud misc. 233, and contains what appears to be Lydgate's autograph on the verso of the end flyleaf; Pearsall is skeptical of Shirley's claim that *Isopes Fabules* was "made in Oxforde" since Aesop's *Fables* was a popular Latin school text that Shirley on his own may have associated with Oxford (*Bio-Bibliography*, pp. 16–18).

[13] Pearsall, *Bio-Bibliography*, p. 16.

[14] Pearsall, *Bio-Bibliography*, pp. 37–38, argues that since the king's articles of 1421 recommended against receipt of money by individual monks, Abbot Curteys insisted on giving the grant a cloak of responsibility by having it paid jointly to Lydgate and Baret.

[15] Burgh finished *The Secrees of Old Philosoffres*, on which Lydgate was apparently at work when he died; it is not known whether Burgh completed the work on his own or was commissioned to do so by the king or by Henry de Bourgchier, count of Ewe, who with his son John was admitted to the fraternity of the abbey of Bury in 1440 (see Ord, "Account of the Entertainment," p. 70n1, and Pearsall, *Bio-Bibliography*, p. 40).

The work of these writers was encouraged and read by a thriving group of regional patrons of the arts and bibliophiles, to whom Lydgate must also have been known.[16]

The religious drama that flourished in East Anglia provides another important context for Lydgate's performance pieces. The N-Town plays, along with various saints' plays and moralities — including the Digby *Mary Magdalene*, *Mankind*, *Wisdom*, and the Croxton *Play of the Sacrament* — are evidence of the region's interest in theatrically and thematically ambitious performances that show a tolerance for reformist religious positions while also supporting orthodoxy and that speak with particular directness to the spiritual preoccupations of the prosperous middle classes. Some of these plays have been linked to Bury St. Edmunds and a number share the concerns and themes of Lydgate's dramatic writings (such as Marian devotion).[17] Although Lydgate's involvement in local dramatic activities remains undocumented, it would have been hard for him to be unaware of the region's performance traditions. His own aesthetic differs — perhaps deliberately — in a number of ways from that of the extant East Anglian plays, but his performance pieces for courtly and urban audiences nonetheless share some common ground with them, including a tendency to bend religious material to secular ends.[18]

JOHN SHIRLEY

The significance of John Shirley (c. 1366–c. 1456) for Lydgate's performances is hard to overstate. Shirley's role as a preserver and disseminator of literary texts is well known. A number of Middle English poems survive only in his manuscripts, and attributions and contexts are available for other works solely on the basis of information contained in his headings and rubrics. Shirley is especially crucial for establishing the Lydgate canon and is the sole authority for a number of the poet's minor poems, including the mummings and disguisings. Two of Shirley's anthologies are the source for almost all of the performance pieces included here. Trinity College MS R.3.20, which was compiled in the early 1430s, contains six of the mummings and disguisings as well as the *Procession of Corpus Christi*, the *Sodein Fal of Princes*, *The Legend of St. George*, and *Bycorne and Chychevache*, making it the single most important source for Lydgate's performance pieces. The *Mumming at Bishopswood* was copied into Shirley's last anthology, Bodley MS Ashmole 59, which is datable by internal evidence to between 1447 and 1449.[19] Only the *Pageant of Knowledge*, *Henry VI's Triumphal Entry into London*, and the *Soteltes* are not extant in manuscripts copied by Shirley (the two poems included in appendices are also not found in Shirlean manuscripts).

Besides preserving a record of what would otherwise be ephemeral performance pieces, Shirley also provides valuable — in many instances, almost the only — information about the auspices of the texts he copied. For Lydgate's mummings and other entertainments,

---

[16] For discussions of East Anglian women as patrons and readers, see Hanna, "Some Norfolk Women" and McNamer, "Female Authors, Provincial Setting."

[17] See Gibson, "Bury St. Edmunds, Lydgate, and the *N-Town Cycle*," esp. pp. 60–63.

[18] Some of the N-Town plays may show the influence of Lydgate, and possibly some of the morality plays in the Digby and Macro manuscripts were at one time in the possession of the abbey of Bury St. Edmunds; there is also some evidence that the abbey hosted players or minstrels (see Gibson, "Bury St. Edmunds, Lydgate, and the *N-Town Cycle*," for Lydgate's influence on the N-Town plays).

[19] For the dates of these manuscripts, see Connolly, *John Shirley*, pp. 77 and 152.

Shirley usually attempts to identify the nature of the text, describe its occasion, and give whatever other details he appears to have known about it. Recent assessments agree that, despite a few errors, Shirley's rubrics are for the most part reliable and usefully help situate Lydgate's verses in their cultural and performance contexts.[20]

Some scholars have thought that Shirley was a commercial publisher who ran a scriptorium in London, but Margaret Connolly has recently demonstrated that his scribal work was an extension of the "culture of service" formed by his career in the household of Richard Beauchamp, the earl of Warwick, with which Shirley had been associated since at least 1403.[21] As he states in the preface to the first of his three anthologies, Shirley assumed that the primary audience for his anthologies would be "bothe the gret and the commune" of that household.[22] When he copied Lydgate's verses for performance, he presumably had in mind the pleasure and instruction of those household readers, a few of whom may have seen some of the original performances for which Lydgate wrote his verses, if they had happened to be at court or in London, as would not have been unlikely given Warwick's movements and duties in the 1420s and early 1430s.

Shirley seems to have been especially eager to disseminate and support Lydgate's poetry: British Library MS Additional 16165, compiled in the late 1420s, contains fourteen pieces by Lydgate, out of some forty-five texts; Trinity R.3.20 in its current form contains twenty-six poems by Lydgate, out of approximately seventy-five (twenty-seven of the non-Lydgatian pieces are short, anonymous poems in French; the other named authors in the anthology include Chaucer, Suffolk, Hoccleve, and Brampton); and Shirley's last anthology, Bodley Ashmole 59, contains thirty-five works by Lydgate as well as verses by Gower, Scogan, and Chaucer. The high percentage of poems by Lydgate in Shirley's manuscripts may simply reflect Lydgate's literary prestige, but it may also signal a deeper attachment to the writer and his work.

It in fact seems likely that Shirley's interest in Lydgate's writing was based on personal acquaintance. They were of the same generation — Shirley was roughly the same age as Lydgate — and both men had ties to the Lancastrian affinity and to London. Records show that Shirley was in Warwick's retinue in France and England from 1403 until the late 1420s; when Warwick was appointed tutor to Henry VI in 1428, Shirley appears to have settled in London where, while still maintaining connections with the aristocratic world of Warwick, he gradually developed associations with the city's merchant class.[23] At any number of places in these years Shirley could have met Lydgate and perhaps have seen some of the performances featuring his verses. John Stow's copy of what was presumably Shirley's preface to Trinity R.3.20, now missing from that manuscript, suggests that Shirley was concerned with solidifying Lydgate's reputation and with helping him gain financial reward for his poetry,

---

[20] See Pearsall, *Bio-Bibliography*, pp. 17–18.

[21] See Connolly, *John Shirley*, pp. 191–95, for a discussion of competing views of Shirley's scribal activities and his reliability.

[22] Connolly, *John Shirley*, p. 191.

[23] For Shirley's biography, see Connolly, *John Shirley*, pp. 15–63. For Lydgate's connections with Warwick, see Pearsall, *John Lydgate*, pp. 160–71.

efforts that would be especially understandable if they were motivated by firsthand know-
ledge of the poet.[24]

PERFORMANCE

Aside from a few internal clues in the poems themselves and the details contained in
Shirley's rubrics, we have little information about how Lydgate's mummings and other
entertainments were performed. In most cases, we do not know who organized and acted in
them, or how they employed props, costuming, and music. We also do not know what role,
if any, Lydgate played in the performances or how spectators reacted.

Exactly what form the performances took is complicated by Shirley's use of a variety of
terms for the verses Lydgate wrote and the performances in which they were used, terms
that include *scripture*, *bille*, *devyse*, *lettre*, *balade*, *ordenaunce*, *momyng*, and *desguysing*. In some
cases Shirley uses several different terms to describe one text and he appears to have used
some terms — including mumming and disguising — interchangeably.[25] Interestingly, in
no instance does he refer to Lydgate's verses with the words commonly used in Middle
English to designate dramatic performance — *pley* and *game* — nor does he use the related
Latin terms *ludus* and *spectacula*. Whatever Lydgate's performance pieces were, they appar-
ently did not suggest "play" to Shirley, as Anne Lancashire has noted.[26] But contemporaries
made fewer distinctions among various kinds of performances than we do, and it is probably
best for us to think of Lydgate's verses as fitting into a broad generic category that included
various combinations of music, spoken word, impersonation, gesture or action, and special
effects.

Complete information is lacking, but we can make some reasonable guesses about who
organized and performed in Lydgate's entertainments. Although records show that traveling

---

[24] The relevant passage reads:
   "yet for all his much konnynge
   which were gret tresore to a kynge
   I meane this lidgate munke duan John
   his nobles bene spent I leue ychon
   and eke hus shylinges nyche by
   his thred bare coule woll not ly
   ellas ye lordis why nill ye se
   and reward his poverte."

[25] Westfall, *Patrons and Performance*, p. 33n21, uses "mumming" to describe a dumbshow and
"disguising" for a more elaborate performance; Wickham defines mumming as involving gift-giving
and disguising as not (*Early English Stages* 1:204–05), but A. Lancashire argues convincingly that mum-
mings and disguisings "are similar kinds of occasional entertainment, performed both at court and
elsewhere" (*London Civic Theatre*, p. 275n17), and Anglo, "Evolution," p. 7, notes that in the early six-
teenth century the terms "mask," "mumming," "pageant," and "disguising" are still being used inter-
changeably. Although Shirley seems to share that sense of interchangeability, I have followed his lead
in labeling the performances at Hertford and London "disguisings," since their length and use of
iambic pentameter couplets set them apart from the other mummings. Tiner, Carnahan, and Peterson
discuss Lydgate's texts in performance (see "'Euer aftir to be rad & song'"). For a consideration of the
difficulty of knowing what medieval texts were performed and how, see Sponsler, "Drama in the
Archives."

[26] A. Lancashire, *London Civic Theatre*, pp. 125–26.

players were present for Christmas entertainments at court in the late 1420s and that a group of stagecraft professionals based in London was apparently involved in court entertainments, the royal mummings may also have been written for performance by members of the household, possibly by the chapel royal, as Suzanne Westfall argues, to which Lydgate may have had a connection through Edmund Lacy.[27] Shirley tells us that the *Disguising at Hertford* was commissioned by John Brice, the controller of the royal household; Brice was actually the cofferer, an assistant to the controller, but would nonetheless have been responsible for organizing household entertainments. Whether or not Lydgate was present for these performances, or participated in them as presenter — as Shirley's preface to Trinity R.3.20 with its description of Lydgate as a maker of "many a roundeel and balade" that he has "sayd" "with hys sugred mouthe" suggests — he appears to have been familiar with court entertainments, as we can infer from the reference by name to the king's "some tyme tregetowre," or conjuror, John Rikhill, in the Lansdowne manuscript of Lydgate's *Dance of Death*.[28]

The entertainments Lydgate wrote for Londoners may have been performed by either hired professionals or members of the companies. Guilds seem to have encouraged some of their members to become theatrically expert, and records from the sixteenth century show professional players/minstrels as members of various London companies; parish clerks were also available for hire and were sometimes members of companies other than the Parish Clerks' Company.[29] The 1432 entry for Henry VI was probably overseen by Carpenter, the town clerk, with whom Lydgate was apparently acquainted, perhaps along with advice from the mayor and the city council as well as the royal household; it would have drawn on the expertise of artisans and entertainers in London, including a group of professionals who worked on both civic and court revelry; while Lydgate did not supply original verses for the pageants in the 1432 entry, he may have been present for the event, as is suggested by details in his commemorative description of it.[30]

Whether written for the royal household or for Londoners, Lydgate's verses were designed for festive and ceremonial occasions such as Twelfth Night, Candlemas, Christmas, and May Day. Many of the verses were apparently spoken by a presenter of some sort (sometimes described as a herald), presumably to accompany mimed action; in some cases, while the verses may have been spoken they were also visible in written form as part of the pageant, confection, wall-hanging, or mural. Songs and dancing are mentioned in some verses,

---

[27] For the existence of stagecraft professionals who worked on both city and court entertainments, see Streitberger, *Court Revels*, pp. 46–47 and 172–76; for use of the chapel royal, see Westfall, *Patrons and Performance*, pp. 34–37. According to Shirley, Lydgate was at Windsor sometime between 1414 and 1417, the years when his friend Lacy was dean of the chapel royal (see Pearsall, *Bio-Bibliography*, pp. 21–22). In the 1420s, when Lydgate's royal mummings were performed, the dean was Robert Gilbert (Griffiths, *Reign of King Henry VI*, p. 59).

[28] The preface is in BL MS Additional 29729 (presumably copied from a lost preface in R.3.20); for a transcription, see Connolly, *John Shirley*, pp. 208–211. For John Rikhill, see Lydgate, *Dance of Death*, ed. Warren, line 513. *Tregetowre* is defined by the *Promptorium Parvulorum* as a "mimus, pantomimes, joculator" (1.501).

[29] A. Lancashire, *London Civic Theatre*, p. 272n116 and n117.

[30] For the likelihood that Lydgate saw at least part of the 1432 entry, see Kipling, "Poet as Deviser," pp. 87–88.

suggesting an opening for musical entertainment as part of the performance. A number of Lydgate's verses also point to the inclusion of ritual gift-giving of the sort associated with mummings such as the one Londoners performed at the palace of Kennington for the young prince Richard in January 1377, before he became king, in which the prince was given gifts after playing a game of dice with the costumed mummers.[31] The festive and ceremonial contexts of Lydgate's mummings and entertainments remind us of the social and communal purposes for which so many early vernacular plays were designed and of their role in cementing social relationships and suggesting proper courses of action, while also providing pleasure.

STYLE

The style of Lydgate's performance pieces will be familiar to anyone who has read his longer works. Most of them (the notable exception is the *Disguising at Hertford*) are written in Lydgate's characteristic "aureate" manner that depends on the use of Latinate vocabulary and elaborate syntax to achieve an elevated artistic effect. While the pieces are sometimes difficult for modern readers and often criticized as deficient in poetic qualities, recent reevaluations have shown that Lydgate's style was eminently well suited for his aims and involves a sophisticated use of language.[32] It was also widely admired by those contemporaries who repeatedly commissioned works from him and it influenced later English writers, including the Scottish Chaucerians, and early modern poets, including Spenser and Dryden.

Nearly all of the performance pieces in this edition are short poems in rhyme royal, although two (Hertford and London) are longer compositions that feature rhymed couplets.

THE TEXT

Most of Lydgate's performance pieces were included by MacCracken in his 1934 edition of Lydgate's shorter poems, but only a few have been reprinted or reedited since then. While MacCracken's edition is for the most part reliable (although his collations are sometimes confusing or inaccurate), I have in all cases used the manuscripts as my source, checking them against MacCracken. My editions of the *Procession of Corpus Christi*, *Bycorne and Chychevache*, the *Sodein Fal of Princes*, *The Legend of St. George*, the *Procession of Corpus Christi*, and all of the mummings and disguisings except for the *Mumming at Bishopswood* (which is based on Bodley Ashmole 59) follow the readings found in Trinity R.3.20, with the exception of emendations recorded in the Textual Notes. For those pieces that were never copied by Shirley, I have been guided by MacCracken in choosing a base text: the text of the *Soteltes at the Coronation Banquet* follows British Library MS Cotton Julius B.i; *Henry VI's Triumphal Entry into London* is based on British Library MS Cotton Julius B.ii; the *Pageant of Knowledge*, on Trinity R.3.21; and *Mesure Is Tresour*, on British Library MS Harley 2255 — in all cases, emendations are indicated in the Textual Notes. In those instances in which a text exists in multiple manuscripts, I have noted substantive variants in the Textual Notes.

---

[31] See the *Anonimalle Chronicle*, pp. 102–03, and the discussions in Chambers, *Mediaeval Stage*, 1:394–95, and Wickham, *Early English Stages*, 3:49.

[32] For a sympathetic reassessment of Lydgate's syntax, see Hardman, "Lydgate's Uneasy Syntax."

A few characteristics of spelling and punctuation in Shirley's manuscripts are worth noting. Shirley seldom includes punctuation at the ends of lines, although sometimes a period or dot appears between words in mid-line, where it may signal a pause or indicate emphasis; when punctuation appears, it is usually a virgule or slash. Shirley occasionally uses a tilde at the end of headnotes and a number of poems feature an *n* (or *m*) periodically in the left margin, which is usually disregarded by editors as a scribal device since it does not always seem to indicate a break, or at least not one signaled by the sense of the text. Superscript bar lines sometimes appear to signal double letters (e.g., *roñe* = *ronne*), but at other times seem not to have a purpose. Abbreviations include *w^t* for *with*, *þ^t* for *that*, and omission of *-ro* as in *pcesse* for *processe*. Shirley's characteristic spellings include *nexst, filowyng, heer, yee, reedethe*, use of *-eo* in words such as *beon, eorlle, neode*, and *weoping*, and the periodic doubling of consonants in words such as *englisshe, frensshe*, and *affter*. His ornamental flourishes on occasion include descenders in the bottom line that are enlarged and crisscrossed; ascenders in the top line that are exaggerated in large, bold loops; and decorated running titles.[33]

In accordance with the conventions of the Middle English Texts Series, I have transcribed the scribal ampersand as *and*, thorn as *th*, and yogh as *y, g*, or *gh*, depending on the modern spelling of a word. The spellings of *u/v/w* and *i/j* have been regularized (e.g., *devise* rather than *deuise*). Words ending in a single *-e* have been marked with an accent, as in *charité*. When it refers to the second-person pronoun, *the* has been transcribed as *thee*, so as to avoid confusion with the article. Except where it conforms to modern usage, double *ff* has been transcribed as single *f* (e.g., MS *giffte* appears as *gifte*). Abbreviations and suspension marks have been quietly expanded and scribal errors corrected, but for the most part Shirley's spelling has been retained. Capitalization, word division, and punctuation follow modern practice.

---

[33] Mooney, "John Shirley's Heirs," pp. 183 and 195, and Connolly, *John Shirley*, pp. 170 and 173.

BYCORNE AND CHYCHEVACHE

[*Loo, sirs, the devise (device) of a peynted or desteyned (painted or stained) clothe for an halle, a parlour, or a chaumbre, devysed by Johan Lidegate at the request of a werthy citeseyn (worthy citizen) of London.*

[*First there shal stonde an ymage in poete-wyse (in the guise of a poet) seying thees thre (these three) balades:*

	O prudent folkes, takethe heed	*pay attention*
	And remembrethe, in youre lyves,	
	Howe this story dothe proceed	
	Of the housbandes and theyre wyves,	
5	Of theyre acorde and of theyre stryves	*quarrels*
	With lyf or deethe, which to derrain	*decide the outcome of*
	Is graunted to thees beestis tweyin.	*two beasts*

[*And thane shalle theer be purtrayed twoo beestis, oon (one) fatte another leene (lean).*

	Of Chichevache and of Bycorne	*Skinny cow; Two horns (see note)*
	Tretethe hooly this matere,	*completely*
10	Whos story hathe taught us here to forne	*before*
	Howe thees beestis, bothe in feere,	*alike*
	Have theyre pasture, as yee shal here,	*Feed on [men and women]; hear*
	Of men and wymmen, in sentence,	*truly*
	Thorugh souffraunce or thorughe inpacience.	*Through patience*

15	For this Bicorne of his nature	
	Wil noon other maner foode	
	But pacient men in his pasture;	*long-suffering*
	And Chichevache etethe wymmen goode;	*eats*
	And boothe theos beestes, by the roode,	*by the cross (a mild oath)*
20	Be fatte or leene, hit may not fayle,	*Are*
	Lyke lak or plenté of theyre vitayle.	*According to lack*

[*Thane shalle ther be pourtrayhed a fatte beest called Bycorne of the cuntrey of Bycornoys and seyne (say) thees thre balades filowing (following):*

Of Bycornoys I am Bycorne,
Ful fatte and rounde, here as I stonde,
And in maryage bonde and sworne   *bound*
25   To Chichevage, as hir husbande,
Which wil not ete on see nor lande   *Who; sea*
But pacyent wyves debonayre   *Any except; humble*
Which to hir husbandes beon nat contrayre.   *their; are not contrary*

Ful scarce, God wot, is hir vitayle,   *God knows; her food*
30   Humble wyves she fyndethe so fewe,
For alweys at the countretayle   *in reply*
Theyre tunge clappethe and dothe hewe;   *tongue flaps and cuts*
Suche meke wyves I beshrewe,   *submissive; curse*
That neyther cane at bedde ne boord   *can; table*
35   Theyre husbandes nought forbere on worde.   *one*

But my foode and my cherisshing,   *nourishment*
To telle pleynly, and not tarye,   *delay*
Ys of suche folk whiche ther living,
Dar to theyre wyves be not contrarye,   *Dare*
40   Ne frome theyre lustis dar not varye,
Nor with hem holde no chaumpartye;   *contend against them*
Alle suche my stomake wol defye!   *digest*

[*Thanne shal be pourtrayed a companye of men comyng towardes this beest Bicorne and sey
thees foure balades*:

Felawes, takethe heede and yee may see
Howe Bicorne castethe him to devoure   *intends to*
45   Alle humble men, bothe you and me,
Ther is no gayne us may socour;   *no help that can protect us*
Wo be therfore, in halle and bour,   *in manor and cottage*
To alle thees husbandes, which theyre lyves
Maken maystresses of theyre wyves.   *sovereign women*

50   Who that so doothe, this is the lawe,
That this Bycorne wol him oppresse,
And devowren in his mawe
That of his wyf makethe his maystresse;   *He who*
This wol us bring in gret distresse,
55   For we for oure humylytee
Of Bycorne shal devowred be.   *By*

We stonden pleynly in suche cas,   *We are clearly in such misfortune*
That they to us maystresses be,
We may wel sing and seyne allas!   *say*
60   That wee gaf hem the sovereynté;   *gave*

For we be thralle and they beo fre,   *in thrall; free*
Wherfore Bycorne, this cruell beste,
Wol us devowren at the leest.   *Will; in any case*

But who that cane be sovereyne,
65 And his wyf teeche and chastyse,   *teach*
That she dare not a worde geyne-seyne,   *contradict*
Nor disobeye no maner wyse,   *in any way*
Of suche a man, I cane devyse,   *say*
He stant under proteccion;   *stands*
70 Frome Bycornes jurisdiccyoun.

[Thanne shal ther be a womman devowred ypurtrayhed in the mouthe of Chichevache cryen (crying) to alle wyves and sey this balade:

O noble wyves, beothe wel ware,   *be aware*
Takethe ensaumple nowe by me,   *example*
Or ellys, afferme weel I dare,   *I dare well say*
Yee shal beo ded, yee shal not flee;   *dead*
75 Beothe crabbed, voydethe humylitee,   *spiteful; avoid*
Or Chychevache ne wol not fayle
You for to swalowe in hir entrayle.

[Thanne shal be ther purtrayhed a longe horned beest sklendre (slender) and lene (lean) with sharpe teethe and on his body nothing save skyn and boone (bone).

Chychevache, this is my name,
Hungry, megre, sklendre, and lene,   *emaciated; slender; lean*
80 To shewe my body I have gret shame,
For hunger I feele so gret teene,   *pain*
On me no fattnesse wol beo seene,
By cause that pasture I fynde noon,
Therfore I am but skyn and boon.   *skin and bones*

85 For my feding in existence   *in reality*
Is of wymmen that beon meeke,
And lyche Gresylde in pacyence,   *like*
Or more, theyre bountee for to eeke;   *virtue to enhance*
But I ful longe may goon and seeke
90 Or I cane fynde a gode repaaste   *Before; good*
Amorowe to breke with my faaste.   *In the morning*

I trowe ther beo a dere yeere   *believe; is a dearth*
Of pacyent wymmen nowe theos dayes;
Who grevethe hem with worde or chere,   *makes them (i.e., women) angry; manner*
95 Let him beware of suche assayes;   *sallies*
For it is more thane thritty Mayes   *thirty*

That I have sought frome lande to londe,
But yit oone Gresylde never I fonde.

      I fonde but oone, in al my lyve,   *life*
100   And she was deed sith go ful yore;   *dead since long ago*
      For more pasture I wil not stryve
      Nor seeche for my foode no more,   *search*
      Ne for vitayle me to enstore;   *supply*
      Wymmen beon wexen so prudent   *have grown; wise*
105   They wol no more beo pacyent.

      [*Thanne shal there be pourtrayhed after Chichevache an olde man with a baston on his bakke
      manassing the beest for the rescowing of his wyf*:[1]

      My wyf, allas, devowred is;
      Moost pacyente and mooste peysyble,   *peace-loving*
      Sheo never sayde to me amysse,
      Whome hathe nowe slayne this beest horryble,
110   And for it is an inpossyble   *impossibility*
      To fynde ever suche a wyf,
      I wil lyve sool during my lyf.   *alone*

      For nowe of nuwe for theyre prowe   *benefit*
      The wyves of ful hyegh prudence   *high*
115   Have of assent made theyre avowe,   *vow*
      For to exyle Pacyence,
      And cryed, "Wolfes heed obedyence!"[2]
      To make Chichevache fayle   *fail*
      Of hem to fynde more vitayle.   *In them*

120   Nowe Chichevache may fast longe,
      And dye for al hire cruweltee,   *their cruelty*
      Wymmen have made hemself so stronge   *themselves*
      For to outraye humylyté.   *vanquish*
      O cely housbandes! woo beon yee!   *unfortunate*
125   Suche as cane have no pacyence
      Ageyns youre wyves vyolence.   *Against*

      Yif that yee suffre, yee beo but deed,   *dead*
      This Bicorne awaytethe yowe so soore,   *cruelly*
      Eeke of youre wyves yee stonde in dreed
130   Yif yee geyne-seye hem any more;   *oppose*
      And thus yee stonde, and have doone yoore,   *for a long time*

---

[1] *...with a walking stick on his back, threatening the beast in order to rescue his wife*

[2] *And cried, "Wolf's head obedience!" (i.e., "Outlaw obedience!")*

Of lyf and deeth bytwixen tweyne,   *life; between the two*
Lynkeld in a double cheyne.   *Linked; chain*

DISGUISING AT HERTFORD

[*Nowe folowethe here the maner of a bille by wey of supplicacion putte to the Kyng holding his noble feest of Cristmasse in the Castel of Hertford as in a disguysing of the rude upplandisshe people (uneducated rural people) compleyning on hir (their) wyves, with the boystous aunswere (vigorous answer) of hir wyves, devysed by Lydegate at the request of the Countré Roullour Brys slayne at Loviers.*

Moost noble Prynce, with support of your Grace
Ther beon entred into youre royal place,
And late ecomen into youre castell,
Youre poure lieges, wheche lyke nothing weel;   *who are unhappy*
5   Nowe in the vigyle of this nuwe yeere   *(i.e., on New Year's Eve)*
Certeyne sweynes ful froward of ther chere   *commoners; in an angry mood*
Of entent comen, fallen on ther kne,   *Deliberately*
For to compleyne unto yuoure Magestee
Upon the mescheef of gret adversytee,
10   Upon the trouble and the cruweltee   *cruelty*
Which that they have endured in theyre lyves
By the felnesse of theyre fierce wyves;   *treachery*
Which is a tourment verray importable,   *unbearable*
A bonde of sorowe, a knott unremuwable.   *unremovable*
15   For whoo is bounde or locked in maryage,   *marriage*
Yif he beo olde, he fallethe in dotage.   *senility*
And yonge folkes, of theyre lymes sklendre,   *slender limbs*
Grene and lusty, and of brawne but tendre,   *muscle*
Phylosophres callen in suche aage
20   A chylde to wyve, a woodnesse or a raage.   *madness; insanity*
For they afferme ther is non eorthely stryf   *earthly strife*
May beo compared to wedding of a wyf,
And who that ever stondethe in the cas,   *is in that situation*
He with his rebecke may sing ful oft ellas!   *fiddle*
25   Lyke as theos hynes, here stonding oon by oon,   *farmers*

[*i. demonstrando vi. rusticos*   *six rustics for the showing*

He may with hem upon the daunce goon,
Leorne the traas, boothe at even and morowe,   *steps*
Of Karycantowe in tourment and in sorowe;
Weyle the whyle, ellas! that he was borne.   *Regretting all the while*
30   For Obbe the Reeve, that goothe heere al toforne,   *first*
He pleynethe sore his mariage is not meete,   *complains; pleasant*
For his wyf, Beautryce Bittersweete,

	Cast upon him an hougly cheer ful rowghe,	*angry look very harsh*
	Whane he komethe home ful wery frome the ploughe,	*weary*
35	With hungry stomake deed and paale of cheere,	*dull and pale of face*
	In hope to fynde redy his dynier;	
	Thanne sittethe Beautryce bolling at the nale,	*carousing at the tavern*
	As she that gyvethe of him no maner tale;	*has no concern for him*
	For she al day, with hir jowsy nolle,	*drunken head*
40	Hathe for the collyk pouped in the bolle,	*colic; gulped; tankard*
	And for heedaache with pepir and gynger	
	Dronk dolled ale to make hir throte cleer;	*mulled ale*
	And komethe hir hoome, whane hit drawethe to eve,	
	And thanne Robyn, the cely poure reeve,	*unfortunate*
45	Fynde noone amendes of harome ne damage,	*relief from harm*
	But leene growell, and soupethe colde potage;	*gruel; dines on cold stew*
	And of his wyf hathe noone other cheer	*hospitality*
	But cokkrowortes unto his souper.	*stale gruel*
	This is his servyce sitting at the borde,	*meal; table*
50	And cely Robyne, yif he speke a worde,	*simpleminded*
	Beautryce of him doothe so lytel rekke,	*cares so little*
	That with hir distaff she hittethe him in the nekke,	
	For a medecyne to chawf with his bloode;	*warm*
	With suche a metyerde she hathe shape him an hoode.	*yardstick; deceived him*
55	And Colyn Cobeller, folowing his felawe,	

| | [*demonstrando pictaciarium* | *a cobbler for the showing* |

	Hathe hade his part of the same lawe;	
	For by the feyth that the preost him gaf,	*faith; priest gave him*
	His wyf hathe taught him to pleyne at the staff;	*complain*
	Hir quarter-strooke were so large and rounde	
60	That on his rigge the towche was alwey founde.	*backbone*
	Cecely Soure-Chere, his owen precyous spouse,	*Sourpuss*
	Kowde him reheete whane he came to house;	*Could lay into him*
	Yif he ought spake whanne he felt peyne,	
	Ageyne oon worde, alweys he hade tweyne;[1]	
65	Sheo qwytt him ever, ther was no thing to seeche,	*She repaid*
	Six for oon of worde and strookes eeche.	*Six times for every word and stroke of his*
	Ther was no meen bytweene hem for to goone;	
	Whatever he wan, clowting olde shoone	*earned, mending old shoes*
	The wykday, pleynly this is no tale,	*On weekdays*
70	Sheo wolde on Sondayes drynk it at the nale.	
	His part was noon, he sayde not oonys nay;	*once*
	Hit is no game but an hernest play,	
	For lack of wit a man his wyf to greeve.	*displease*

---

[1] Lines 63–64: *If he spoke when he felt pain, / For every word he received two (blows)*

	Theos housbondemen, whoso wolde hem leeve,	*believe*
75	Koude yif they dourst telle in audyence	*dared; in public*
	What folowethe therof wyves to doone offence;[1]	
	Is noon so olde ne ryveld on hir face,	*wrinkled*
	Wit tong or staff but that she dare manase.	*tongue*
	Mabyle, God hir sauve and blesse,	
80	Koude yif hir list bere hereof witnesse:	*if she wanted to*
	Wordes, strookes unhappe, and harde grace	*misfortune*
	With sharpe nayles kracching in the face.	*scratching*
	I mene thus, whane the distaff is brooke,	
	With theyre fistes wyves wol be wrooke,	*satisfy their anger*
85	Blessed thoo men that cane in suche offence	*those*
	Meekly souffre, take al in pacyence,	*suffer*
	Tendure suche wyfly purgatorye.	*To endure*
	Heven for theyre meede, to regne ther in glorye,	*reward*
	God graunt al housbandes that beon in this place,	
90	To wynne so heven for His hooly grace.	*earn*
	Nexst in ordre, this bochier stoute and bolde	*butcher*

	[*demonstrando carnificem*	*a butcher for the showing*

	That killed hathe bulles and boores olde,	
	This Berthilmewe, for al his broode knyf,	
	Yit durst he never with his sturdy wyf,	
95	In no mater holde chaumpartye;	*engage in battle*
	And if he did, sheo wolde anoon defye	
	His pompe, his pryde, with a sterne thought,	
	And sodeynly setten him at nought.	*consider him worthless*
	Thoughe his bely were rounded lyche an ooke	
100	She wolde not fayle to gyf the firste strooke;	*give*
	For proude Pernelle, lyche a chaumpyoun,	
	Wolde leve hir puddinges in a gret cawdroun,	*cauldron*
	Suffre hem boylle, and taake of hem noon heede,	*Let them boil*
	But with hir skumour reeche him on the heved.	*skimming utensil hit; head*
105	Shee wolde paye him, and make no delaye,	
	Bid him goo pleye him a twenty devel wey.	*in the name of twenty devils*
	She was no cowarde founde at suche a neode,	
	Hir fist ful oft made his cheekis bleed;	
	What querell ever that he agenst hir sette,	
110	She cast hir not to dyen in his dette.	
	She made no taylle, but qwytt him by and by;	*tally*
	His quarter sowde, she payde him feythfully,	*quarterly payments*
	And his waages, with al hir best entent,	

---

[1] *What the consequence is of offending wives*

	She made therof noon assignement.	*allotment*
115	Eeke Thome Tynker with alle hees pannes olde,	

[*demonstrando the Tynker*   *a tinker for the showing*

	And alle the wyres of Banebury that he solde —	*wares*
	His styth, his hamour, his bagge portatyf —	*anvil; carrying bag*
	Bare up his arme whane he faught with his wyf.	
	He foonde for haste no better bokeller	*shield*
120	Upon his cheeke the distaff came so neer.	
	Hir name was cleped Tybot Tapister.	
	To brawle and broyle she nad no maner fer,	*quarrel; had no fear at all*
	To thakke his pilche, stoundemel, nowe and thanne,	*beat his hide, occasionally*
	Thikker thane Thome koude clowten any panne.	*Harder; strike; head*
125	Nexst Colle Tyler, ful hevy of his cheer,	*serious*
	Compleynethe on Phelyce his wyf, the wafurer.	*a maker of wafers*
	Al his bred with sugre nys not baake,	
	Yit on his cheekis sometyme he hathe a caake	
	So hoot and nuwe, or he can taken heede,	
130	That his heres glowe verray reede,	*hairs*
	For a medecyne whane the forst is colde,	*frost*
	Making his teethe to ratle, that beon oolde.	
	This is the compleynt that theos dotardes oolde	
	Make on theyre wyves, that beon so stoute and bolde.	
135	Theos holy martirs, preved ful pacyent,	
	Lowly beseching in al hir best entent,	*their*
	Unto youre noble ryal magestee	
	To graunte hem fraunchyse and also liberté,	*freedom*
	Sith they beothe fetird and bounden in maryage,	*fettered*
140	A sauf-conduyt to sauf him frome damage.	*safe-conduct; save them*
	Eeke under support of youre hyeghe renoun,	
	Graunt hem also a proteccyoun;	
	Conquest of wyves is ronne thoroughe this lande,	
	Cleyming of right to have the hyegher hande.	*Claiming the right; upper*
145	But if you list, of youre regallye,	*power*
	The Olde Testament for to modefye,	
	And that yee list asselen theyre request,	*approve*
	That theos poure husbandes might lyf in rest,	*live*
	And that theyre wyves in theyre felle might	*treacherous*
150	Wol medle amonge mercy with theyre right.	*mix mercy with*
	For it came never of nature ne raysoun,	*reason*
	A lyonesse t'oppresse the lyoun,	*lion*
	Ner a wolfesse, for al hir thyraunye,	*she wolf; tyranny*
	Over the wolf to haven the maystrye.	*mastery*
155	Ther beon nowe wolfesses moo thane twoo or three,	
	The bookys recorde, wheeche that yonder bee.	

[*i. distaves*

Seothe to this mater of mercy and of grace,
And or thees dotardes parte out of this place,   *If either; depart*
Upon theyre compleynt to shape remedye,
160   Or they beo likly to stande in jupardye.   *jeopardy*
It is no game with wyves for to pleye,
But for foolis, that gif no force to deye!   *Except; who don't care about dying*

[*Takethe heed of th'aunswer of the wyves.*

Touching the substance of this hyeghe discorde,   *high*
We six wives beon ful of oon acorde,   *one accord*
165   Yif worde and chyding may us not avaylle,   *help*
We wol darrein it in chaumpcloos by bataylle.   *decide it; tournament field*
Jupart oure right, laate or ellys raathe.   *Risk; sooner or later*
And for oure partye the worthy Wyf of Bathe
Cane shewe statutes moo than six or seven,
170   Howe wyves make hir housbandes wynne heven,   *reach heaven*
Maugré the feonde and al his vyolence;   *In spite of; devil*
For theyre vertu of parfyte pacyence   *perfect*
Partenethe not to wyves nowe-adayes,
Sauf on theyre housbandes for to make assayes.   *Except; tests*
175   Ther pacyence was buryed long agoo,
Gresyldes story recordethe pleinly soo.
It longethe to us to clappen as a mylle,   *It is our duty to chatter like a mill*
No counseyle keepe, but the trouth oute telle;
We beo not borne by hevenly influence
180   Of oure nature to keepe us in sylence.
For this is no doute, every prudent wyf
Hathe redy aunswere in al suche maner stryf.
Thoughe theos dotardes with theyre dokked berdes,   *short*
Which strowtethe out as they were made of herdes,   *stick out; flax*
185   Have ageyn hus a gret quarell nowe sette,   *against us*
I trowe the bakoun was never of hem fette,
Awaye at Dounmowe in the Pryorye.
They weene of us to have ay the maystrye;   *hope*
Ellas! theos fooles, let hem aunswere hereto;
190   Whoo cane hem wasshe, who can hem wring alsoo?
Wryng hem, yee, wryng, so als God us speed,
Til that some tyme we make hir nases bleed,   *their noses*
And sowe hir cloothes whane they beothe torent,   *torn*
And clowte hir bakkes til somme of us beo shent;   *beat; exhausted*
195   Loo, yit theos fooles, God gyf hem sory chaunce,
Wolde sette hir wyves under govvernaunce,
Make us to hem for to lowte lowe;   *bow low to them*
We knowe to weel the bent of Jackys bowe.   *too well the set of Jack's mind*

Al that we clayme, we clayme it but of right.
200 Yif they say nay, let preve it out by fight.
We wil us grounde not upon wommanhede.
Fy on hem, cowardes! When hit komethe to nede,
We clayme maystrye by prescripcyoun,   *uninterrupted possession*
Be long tytle of successyoun,
205 Frome wyf to wyf, which we wol not leese.   *lose*
Men may weel gruchche but they shal not cheese.   *complain; choose*
Custume is us for nature and usaunce   *tradition*
To set oure housbandes lyf in gret noysaunce.   *annoyance*
Humbelly byseching nowe at oon worde
210 Unto oure Liege and moost soverein Lord,
Us to defende of his regallye,   *gloss*
And of his grace susteenen oure partye,
Requering the statuyt of olde antiquytee   *Entreating*
That in youre tyme it may confermed bee.

[*The complaynte of the lewed housbandes with the cruwell aunswers of theyre wyves herde,
the kyng givethe therupon sentence and jugement.*

215 This noble Prynce, mooste royal of estate,
Having an eyeghe to this mortal debate,   *eye*
First adverting of ful hyeghe prudence,   *being heedful of; high*
Wil unavysed gyve here no sentence,
Withoute counseylle of haste to procede,   *hastily*
220 By sodeyne doome; for he takethe heede   *rash judgment*
To eyther partye as juge indifferent,   *impartial*
Seing the paryll of hasty jugement;   *peril*
Pourposithe him in this contynude stryf
To gif no sentence therof diffynytyf,
225 Til ther beo made examynacyoun
Of other partye, and inquysicyoun.
He considerethe and makethe raysoun his guyde,   *reason*
As egal juge enclyning to noo syde;   *impartial judge*
Notwithstanding he hathe compassyoun
230 Of the poure housbandes trybulacyoun,
So oft arrested with theyre wyves rokkes,   *distaffs*
Which of theyre distaves have so many knokkes;
Peysing also, in his regallye,   *Considering; sovereignty*
The lawe that wymmen allegge for theyre partye,   *on their side*
235 Custume, nature, and eeke prescripcyoun,   *title of possession*
Statuyt used by confirmacyoun,
Processe and daate of tyme oute of mynde,
Recorde of cronycles, witnesse of hir kuynde: *natural order*
Wherfore the Kyng wol al this nexste yeere
240 That wyves fraunchyse stonde hoole and entier,   *freedom*
And that no man withstonde it, ne withdrawe,

Til man may fynde some processe oute by lawe,
That they shoulde by nature in theyre lyves
Have soverayntee on theyre prudent wyves,
245   A thing unkouthe, which was never founde.   *unknown*
Let men beware therfore or they beo bounde.
The bonde is harde, whosoo that lookethe weel;   *carefully considers*
Some man were lever fetterd beon in steel,   *would rather be fettered*
Raunsoun might help his peyne to aswaage,   *assuage*
250   But whoo is wedded lyvethe ever in servage.   *servitude*
And I knowe never nowher fer ner neer   *far nor near*
Man that was gladde to bynde him prysonier,
Thoughe that his prysoun, his castell, or his holde
Wer depeynted with asure or with golde.   *decorated*

[*Explicit.*

DISGUISING AT LONDON

[*Lo here filowethe (follows) the devyse (device) of a desguysing (disguising) to fore (before) the gret estates of this lande, thane being at London, made by Lidegate Daun Johan, the Munk of Bury, of Dame Fortune, Dame Prudence, Dame Rightwysnesse (Righteousness), and Dame Fortitudo. Beholdethe, for it is moral, plesaunt, and notable. Loo, first komethe (comes) in Dame Fortune.*

Loo here this lady that yee may see,
Lady of mutabilytee,
Which that called is Fortune,
For seelde in oon she doothe contune.   *seldom does she remain the same*
5   For as shee hathe a double face,
Right so every houre and space
She chaungethe hir condycyouns,   *disposition*
Ay ful of transmutacyouns.   *changes*
Lyche as the Romans of the Roose   *as the Romance of the Rose*
10   Descryvethe hir, withouten glose,   *without lying*
And tellethe pleyne, howe that she
Hathe hir dwelling in the see,
Joyning to a bareyne roche.   *barren rock*
And on that oon syde doothe aproche
15   A lytel mountaygne lyke an yle;   *island*
Upon which lande some whyle
Ther growen fresshe floures nuwe,
Wonder lusty of theyre huwe,
Dyvers trees, with fruyte elade.   *laden with fruit*
20   And briddes, with theyre notes glaade,   *birds*
That singen and maken melodye;
In theyre hevenly hermonye   *harmony*

	Somme sing on hye, and some lowe.	
	And Zepherus theer doothe eeke blowe	
25	With his smoothe, attempree ayre.	*temperate*
	He makethe the weder clere and fayre	*weather*
	And the sesoun ful of grace.	
	But sodeynly, in lytel space,	
	Upon this place mooste ryal	*royal*
30	Ther comethe a wawe and fordoothe al.	*wave*
	First the fresshe floures glade	*cheerful*
	On theyre stalkes he dothe faade.	
	To theyre beautee he doothe wrong;	
	And thanne farweel the briddes song.	*birds'*
35	Braunche and boughe of every tree	
	She robbethe hem of hir beautee,	
	Leef and blossomes downe they falle.	
	And in that place she hathe an halle,	
	Departed and wonder desguysee.	*Multicolored; decked out*
40	Frome that oon syde, yee may see,	
	Ceryously wrought, for the noones,	*In this order; for the occasion*
	Of golde, of sylver, and of stoones,	
	Whos richesse may not be tolde.	
	But that other syde of that hoolde	*building*
45	Is ebylt in ougly wyse,	*ugly*
	And ruynous, for to devyse;	
	Daubed of clay is that doungeoun,	
	Ay in poynt to falle adoun.	*Always about to*
	That oon fayre by apparence,	
50	And that oother in existence	
	Shaken with wyndes, rayne and hayle.	
	And sodeynly ther doothe assayle	
	A raage floode that mancyoun,	*violent; mansion*
	And overflowethe it up and doun.	
55	Her is no reskous, ner obstacle	*rescue; nor defense*
	Of this ladyes habytacle.	*dwelling*
	And as hir hous is ay unstable,	
	Right so hirself is deceyvable:	
	In oo poynt she is never elyche;	*In short; constant*
60	This day she makethe a man al ryche	
	And thorughe hir mutabilytee	
	Castethe him tomorowe in povertee.	
	The proddest she can gyve a fal:	*proudest*
	She made Alexaundre wynnen al,	*conquer*
65	That noman him withstonde dare,	
	And caste him doune, er he was ware.	*before he was aware*
	So did sheo Sesar Julius:	
	She made him first victorius,	
	Thaughe to do weel sheo beo ful loothe;	*she is very reluctant*

70   Of a bakers sonne, in soothe,
      She made him a mighty emperrour,
      And hool of Roome was governour,   *of all Rome*
      Maugrey the Senaat and al theyre might;   *Despite*
      But whanne the sonne shoone mooste bright
75   Of his tryumphe, fer and neer,
      And he was corouned with laurier,   *crowned with laurel*
      Unwarly thorughe hir mortal lawe   *Without warning*
      With bodekyns he was eslawe   *daggers*
      At the Capitoyle in Consistorye,
80   Loo, after al his gret victorye.
      See, howe this lady can appalle   *subdue*
      The noblesse of theos prynces alle.   *majesty*
      She hathe two tonnys in hir celler;   *casks*
      That oon is ful of pyment cler,   *spiced wine; pure*
85   Confeit with sugre and spyces swoote   *Made; sweet*
      And manny delytable roote.   *delightful*
      But this is yit the worst of alle:
      That other tonne is ful of galle;
      Whoo taastethe oon, ther is noon oother,   *no other choice*
90   He moste taaste eeke of that tother.   *also*
      Whos sodeyne chaunges beon not soft,
      For nowe sheo can reyse oon aloft,   *raise someone up*
      Frome lowghe estate til hye degree.   *to*
      In olde storyes yee may see
95   Estates chaunge, whoo takethe keepe.   *takes heed*
      For oon Gyges, that kepte sheepe,
      Sheo made, by vertu of a ring,
      For to be made a worthy kyng;
      And by fals mourdre, I dare expresse,   *murder*
100   He came to al his worthynesse—   *attained all his honors*
      Moost odyous of alle thinges.
      And Cresus, ricchest eeke of kynges,
      Was so surquydous in his pryde,   *haughty*
      That he wende, upon noo syde   *believed*
105   Noon eorthely thing might him pertourbe,   *harm*
      Nor his ryal estate distourbe.   *royal*
      Til on a night a dreme he mette,   *he had a dream*
      Howe Juvo in the ayre him sette
      And Jubiter, he understondes,
110   Gaf him water unto his handes,
      And Phebus heelde him the towayle.   *towel*
      But of this dreme the devynayle   *meaning*
      His doughter gane to specefye,
      And fer toforne to prophesye,
115   Whiche called was Leryopee.   *(his daughter) was called Liriope*
      Sheo sayde, he shoulde anhanged bee;

	This was hir exposicyoun.	*interpretation*
	Loo, howe his pruyde was brought adoune.	*pride*
	And alle theos chaunges, yif they beo sought,	
120	This fals lady hathe hem wrought,	*(i.e., Fortune)*
	Avaled with theyre sodeyne showres	*Destroyed*
	The worthynesse of conquerroures.	*honor*
	Reede of poetes the comedyes;	*Read*
	And in dyvers tragedyes	
125	Yee shal by lamentacyouns	*as expressions of sorrow*
	Fynden theyre destruccyouns —	
	A thousande moo than I can telle — ,	*more*
	Into mescheef howe they felle	
	Downe frome hir wheel, on see and lande.	*her (i.e., Fortune's) wheel*
130	Therfore, hir malys to withstande,	*malice*
	Hir pompe, hir surquydye, hir pryde.	*haughtiness*
	Yif she wol a whyle abyde,	
	Foure ladyes shall come heer anoon,	
	Which shal hir power overgoone,	
135	And the malys eeke oppresse	
	Of this blynde, fals goddesse,	
	Yif sheo beo hardy in this place	*If she dare*
	Oonys for to shewe hir double face.	*For once*

[*Nowe komethe here the first lady of the foure, Dame Prudence.*

	Loo, heer this lady in youre presence	
140	Of poetis called is Dame Prudence,	
	The which with hir mirrour bright,	
	By the pourveyaunce of hir forsight	*By means of*
	And hir myrrour, called provydence,	
	Is strong to make resistence	
145	In hir forsight, as it is right,	
	Ageyns Fortune and al hir might.	
	For Senec seythe who that can see,	*Seneca says*
	That Prudence hathe eyeghen three,	*eyes*
	Specyally in hir lookynges	*Expressly; vision*
150	To considre three maner thinges,	
	Alweyes by goode avysement:	*with due consideration*
	Thinges passed and eeke present,	
	And thinges after that shal falle.	
	And she mot looke first of alle,	
155	And doon hir inwarde besy peyne,	*take great pains*
	Thinges present for to ordeyne	
	Avysely on every syde,	*Carefully*
	And future thinges for to provyde,	
	The thinges passed in substaunce	*in general*
160	For to have in remembraunce.	*memory*

And who thus doothe, I say that hee
Verrayly hathe yeghen three   *Truly; eyes*
Comitted unto his difence,   *defense*
The truwe myrrour of provydence.
165   Thane this lady is his guyde,
Him to defende on every syde
Ageyns Fortune goode and perverse
And al hir power for to reverse.
For fraunchysed and at liberté,   *free*
170   Frome hir power to goo free,
Stonde alle folkes, in sentence   *in fact*
Wheeche beon governed by Prudence.

[*Nowe shewethe hir (shows herself) heer the secounde lady, Dame Rigwysnesse (Righteousness)*]

Seothe here this lady, Rightwysnesse.   *See*
Of alle vertues she is pryncesse,
175   For by the scales of hir balaunces
Sheo sette hem alle in governaunces.   *them*
She puttethe asyde, it is no dreede,
Frenship, favour and al kyns meede.   *kinfolk's profit*
Love and drede she settethe at nought,
180   For rightful doome may not beo bought.   *justice*
And Rightwysnesse, who can espye,
Hathe neyther hande ner yeghe.   *eye*
She loste hir hande ful yore agoone,
For she resceyvethe gyftes noone,
185   Nother of freonde, neyther of foo.   *foe*
And she hathe lost hir sight also,
For of right sheo doothe provyde,
Nought for to looke on neyther syde,
To hyeghe estate, ner lowe degree,   *high; nor*
190   But doothe to bothen al equytee,   *what is fair*
And makethe noon excepcyoun
To neyther part, but of raysoun.   *except for a reason*
And for the pourpos of this mater   *for the sake of this account*
Of a juge yee shal heere,
195   Which never his lyf of entent   *intentionally*
Ther passed no jugement
By his lippes of falsnesse;
Of whome the story doothe expresse,
After his deethe, by acountes cleer,
200   More thane three hundrethe yeer,
His body, as is made mencyoun,
Was tourned unto corrupcyoun,   *decayed*
The story tellethe, it is no dreed;   *there is no question*
But lyche a roos, swoote and reed,   *sweet and red*

205   Mouthe and lippes werne yfounde,
       Nought corrupte, but hoole and sounde.
       For trouth is, that he did expresse   *Because of the truth that he spoke*
       In alle hees doomes of rihtwysnesse.   *judgments*
       For this lady with theos balaunce
210   Was with him of acqweyntaunce,   *Was well known to him*
       Which him made in his ententys   *intentions*
       To gyf alle rightwyse jugementis.   *impartial*
       Wherfore this lady, which yee heer see   *you see here*
       With hir balaunces of equytee,
215   Hathe the scaalis honged soo,   *Has hung the scales in such a way*
       That she hathe no thing to doo
       Never with Fortunes doublenesse.
       For ever in oon stant Rightwysnesse,
       Nowher moeving too ne froo
220   In no thing that she hathe to doo.

       [*Loo, heer komethe in nowe the thridde lady, called Fortitudo.*

       Takethe heede, this fayre lady, loo,
       Ycalled is Fortitudo,
       Whame philosophres by theyre sentence   *Whom; custom*
       Ar wonte to cleepe Magnyfysence.   *call*
225   And Fortitudo sothely sheo hight,   *truly she is called*
       Ageyns alle vyces for to fight,
       Confermed as by surtee   *by a pledge*
       Ageynst all adversytee.
       In signe wherof sheo berethe a swerde,   *As a sign*
230   That sheo of nothing is aferd.
       For comune profit also she,   *common*
       Of verray magnanymyté,   *true*
       Thinges gret doothe underfonge,   *undertake*
       Taking enpryses, wheeche beon stronge.   *deeds; mighty*
235   And moost sheo doothe hir power preove
       A communaltee for to releeve,   *a nation*
       Namely upon a grounde of trouthe;
       Thanne in hir ther is no slouthe
       For to maynteyne the goode comune.
240   And alle th'assautes of fortune,   *the assaults*
       Of verray stidfastnesse of thought   *Because of*
       Alle hir chaunges she sette at nought.   *(her, i.e., Fortune's)*
       For this vertu magnyfycence
       Thorough hir mighty excellence
245   She armed theos philosophres oolde,
       Of wordely thing that they noughte tolde:
       Recorde upon Dyogenes,   *Remember*
       On Plato, and on Socrates.

	She made Cypion of Cartage	
250	To underfongen in his aage	*in his old age*
	For comune proufyte thinges gret;	
	And for no dreed list not leet,	*And did not allow him to surrender out of fear*
	Ageynst Roome, that mighty toune,	*town*
	For to defende his regyoun.	
255	Sheo made Hector for his cytee	
	To spare for noon adversytee,	*avoid*
	But, as a mighty chaumpyoun,	
	In the defence of Troyes toun	
	To dye withouten feer or dreed.	*fear*
260	And thus this lady, who takethe heed,	
	Makithe hir chaumpyounes strong,	
	Parayllous thinges to underfong,	*Dangerous*
	Til that they theyre pourpos fyne.	*achieve their purpose*
	Recorde of the worthy nyen,	*Remember*
265	Of other eeke that weere but late,	*who lived more recently*
	I meene prynces of latter date.	
	Herry the fyft, I dare sey soo,	*Henry V*
	He might beo tolde for oon of thoo;	*counted as*
	Empryses wheeche that were bygonne	*Deeds*
270	He left not til they weere wonne.	
	And I suppose, and yowe list see,	
	That thees ladyes alle three	
	Wer of his counseyle doutelesse,	
	Force, Prudence and Rightwysnesse.	
275	Of theos three he tooke his roote,	*habit*
	To putte Fortune under foote.	
	And sith this lady, in vertu strong,	
	Soustenethe trouthe, and doothe not wrong.	
	Late hir nowe, to more and lasse,	*Let; to people of every rank*
280	Be welcome to yowe this Cristmasse.	

[*And theos edoone, komethe inne the feorthe lady, cleped Dame Feyre and Wyse Attemperaunce.*

	This feorthe lady that yee seon heer,	*fourth; you see here*
	Humble, debonayre and sadde of cheer,	*courteous; sober of look*
	Ycalled is Attemperaunce;	
	To sette al thing in governaunce	
285	And for hir sustres to provyde,	
	Vyces alle shal circumsyde,	*exterminate*
	And setten hem in stabulnesse.	*stability*
	With hir Cousin Soburnesse	*Soberness*
	She shal frome vyces hem restreyne	*restrain them*
290	And in vertu holde hir reyne,	*kingdom*
	And therinne gyf hem libertee,	*give them*
	Eschuwing alle dishonestee;	*Avoiding*

	And hem enfourmen by Prudence,	*instruct*
	For to have pacyence,	
295	Lownesse and humylytee,	
	And pruyde specyally to flee.	*pride*
	Contynence frome gloutonye,	*Restraint*
	Eschuwe deshoneste compaignye,	
	Fleen the dees and the taverne,	*Flee; dice*
300	And in soburnesse hem gouverne;	
	With hert al that ever they can,	
	In vertu loven every man;	
	Sey the best ay of entent:	*voluntarily*
	Whoo that seythe weel, doothe not repent.	
305	Detraccion and gloutouny,	
	Voyde hem frome thy companye	*Banish them*
	And al rancoure sette asuyde.	*aside*
	Be not to hasty, but ever abyde,	*too; hesitate*
	Specyally to doone vengeaunce;	
310	In aboode is no repentaunce.	*In delay*
	And in vertu whoo is thus sette,	
	Thanne beo theos sustres weel ymette;	
	And soothely, if it beo discerned,	
	Who by theos foure is thus governed —	
315	Thus I mene: that by Prudence	
	He have the myrrour of provydence.	
	For to consider thinges alle,	
	Naamely parylles, or they falle —	*perils*
	And who that have by governaunce	
320	Of Rightwysnesse the ballaunce,	
	And strongly holde in his difence	*defense*
	The swerd of hir Magnyfycence:	
	Yee beon assured frome al meschaunce,	*misfortune*
	Namely whanne that Attemperaunce	
325	Hir sustre governethe al three.	
	Frome Fortune yee may thane go free,	
	Boothe alwey in hert and thought.	
	Whyle yee beo soo, ne dreed hir nought,	
	But avoydethe hir acqweyntaunce	
330	For hir double varyaunce,	*treacherous changeableness*
	And fleothe oute of hire companye	
	And alle that beon of hir allye.	*allies*
	And yee foure susters, gladde of cheer,	
	Shoule abyde here al this yeer	
335	In this housholde at libertee;	
	And joye and al prosparytee	
	With yowe to housholde yee shoule bring.	
	And yee all foure shal nowe sing	
	With al youre hoole hert entiere	*whole heart*

340	Some nuwe songe aboute the fuyre,	*new; fire*
	Suche oon as you lykethe best;	*Such a one; like*
	Lat Fortune go pley hir wher hir list.	*Let; she wishes*

[*Explicit.*

HENRY VI'S TRIUMPHAL ENTRY INTO LONDON

[*Ordenaunces (Contrivances) for the Kyng made in the Cité of London.*

	Towarde the end of wyndy Februarie,	
	Whanne Phebus was in the Fysshe eronne,	*When the sun was in Pisces*
	Out of the synge, which called is Aquarie,	
	Newe kalendes wern entred and begonne	*(i.e., February 16)*
5	Of Marchis komyng, and the mery sonne	
	Upon a Thursday shewed his bemys briht	
	Uppon London, to make hem glade and liht.	
	The stormy reyne of alle theyre hevynesse	
	Were passed away and alle her olde grevaunce,	
10	For the sixte Herry, roote of here gladnesse,	*Henry VI*
	Theyre hertis joye, theyre worldis suffisaunce,	
	By trewe dissent crounyd kyng of Fraunce,	*rightful lineage*
	The hevene rejoysyng the day of his repayre	*return*
	Made his komyng the wedir to be so fayre.	*weather*
15	A tyme, I trowe, of God, for hym provided,	
	In alle the hevenes there was no clowde seyn,	*cloud*
	From other dayes that day was so devided,	
	And fraunchised from mistys and from reyn,	*free*
	The eyre attempred, the wyndis smoth and pleyn,	*The air was mild*
20	The citezenis thurhoute the Citee	
	Halwyd that day with grete solempnyté.	*Celebrated*
	And lyke for David, after his victorie,	
	Rejoyssed was alle Jerusalem,	
	So this Citee with laude, pris, and glorie,	*honor*
25	For joye moustred lyke the sonne beem,	*assembled*
	To geve ensample thurhout the reem;	*realm*
	Alle of assent, whoso kan conseyve,	
	Theyre noble kyng wern gladde to resseyve.	*receive*
	Theyr clothing was of colour ful covenable,	*very suitable*
30	The noble Meire cladde in reede velvette,	
	The Sheryves, the Aldermen ful notable,	*Sheriffs*
	In furred clokes, the colour skarlette;	*scarlet*

In statly wyse, when they were mette,　　　　　　　　　*assembled*
Eche oon well horsed made no delay,
35　　But with here Meire roode forth in her way.　　　　　*on their way*

The citizenis echoon of the Citee　　　　　　　　　　*each one*
In here entent that they were pure and clene,
Chees hem of white a ful feyre lyveré,　　　　　　　　*livery*
In every crafte, as yt was well sene;
40　　To showe the trouthe that they dyde mene
Toward the Kyng hadd made hem feythfully
In soundry devyses enbrowdred richely.　　　　　　　*various devices*

And forto remembre of other alyens;　　　　　　*aliens (i.e., foreigners)*
First Jeneweys, though they were straungers,　　　　*Genoese*
45　　Florentyns and the Venycyens,
And Esterlinges gladde in her maners,　　　　　*Hansa merchants*
Canveyed with sergeauntes and other officers
Estatly horsed, after the Meire rydyng,　　　　　　　*Nobly*
Passed the subbarbes to mete with the kyng.　　　　*suburbs*

50　　To the Blakeheeth whanne they dydde atteyne,
The Meire, of prudence in especyall,　　　　　　　　*Mayor*
Made hem hove in rengis tweyne,　　　　　　　　*ride in two rows*
A strete bitwene eche partye lyke a wall,
Alle cladde in white, and the moste princypall
55　　Afforn in reede with theire Meire rydyng
Tyl tyme that he sauh the kyng komyng.

Thanne with his sporys, he toke his hors anoon,　　　*spurs*
That to beholde yt was a noble siht,
How like a man he to the kyng ys goon
60　　Riht well cherid, of herte gladde and liht;
Obeying to him as him ouht of riht;　　　　　*as he ought to by right*
And after that he konnyngly abrayde,　　　*courteously began to speak*
And to the kyng evyn thus he sayde:

"Sovereyn Lorde and noble Kyng, ye be welcome out of youre Reeme of Fraunce
into this your blessed Reeme of Englond, and in speciall unto your moste notable
Citee of London, othir wyse called youre Chaumbre; We thankyng God of the
goode and gracious arenyng [disposition] of youre Croune of Fraunce. Beseching
his Mercyful Grace to sende yow prosperité and many yeers, to the comforte of alle
youre lovynge peple."

But forto tellen alle the circumstaunces,
65　　Of every thing shewed in sentence,
Noble devyses, dyvers ordenaunces
Conveyed by scripture with ful grete excellence,

Alle to declare I have noone eloquence,
Wherfore I pray to alle that shall yt rede,
70   Forto correcte where as they se nede.

First whanne he passed was the fabour   *suburb*
Entryng the Brigge of this noble town,   *London Bridge*
Ther was a pyler reysed lyke a tour   *pillar; tower*
And theron stoode a sturdy champeoun,
75   Of looke and chere sterne as a lyoun,   *manner*
His swerde up rered proudely gan manace,   *threaten*
Alle foreyn enmyes from the kyng to enchace.   *drive away*

And in defence of his estate ryall
The geaunt wolde abyde eche aventure;   *giant*
80   And alle assautes that wern marcyall,   *warlike*
For his sake he proudely wolde endure,
In tokne wherof he hadde a scripture
On eyther syde declaryng his entent,
Which seyde thus by goode avysement: *prudently*

85   "Alle tho that ben enemyes to the Kyng,   *All those who are*
I shall hem clothe with confusioun,   *clothe them*
Make him myhty with vertuous levyng   *i.e., the king*
His mortall foon to oppressen and bere adoun,   *foes*
And him to encresen as Cristis champioun,   *Christ's*
90   Alle myscheffes from hym to abrigge   *prevent*
With the grace of God at th'entryng of the Brigge."

Twoo antelopes stondying on eytheyr syde
With the armes of Englond and of Fraunce,
In tokenyng that God shal for hym provyde,
95   As he hath tytle by juste enheritaunce
To regne in pees, plenté and plesaunce;   *happiness*
Sesyng of werre, that men mow ryde or goon,   *Stopping war; so that men might*
As trewe lieges, theyre hertes made both oon.   *vassals; one*

Ferthermore, so as the Kyng gan ryde,
100   Midde of the Brigge ther was a tour on lofte,   *In the middle of*
The Lorde of Lordes beyng ay his guyde,
As He hath be and yitt wole be ful ofte;
The tour arrayed with velvettes softe,
Clothis of golde, sylke, and tapcerye,   *tapestry*
105   As apperteynyth to his regalye.   *Befitting his royalty*

And at his komyng, of excellent beauté,
Beyng of port most womanly of chere,   *demeanor*
Ther yssed oute emperesses three;   *came out*

Theyre heer dysplayed as Phebus in here spere,   *hair; their cosmic spheres*
110   With crounettes of golde and stones clere;   *coronets; bright*
At whos out komyng they gaf such a liht,   *gave off; light*
That the byholders were stonyed in theire siht.   *astonished*

The first of hem called was Nature,
As she that hath under her demeyne,   *rule*
115   Man, beeste, and foule, and every creature,
Withinne the bondys of hire goldyn cheyn;
Eke heven, and erthe, and every creature
This emperesse of custume doth enbrace;   *by custom*
And next hire komyth hire sustre called Grace.   *sister*

120   Passyng famous, and of grete reverence,   *Very*
Moste desired in all regions;
For wher that ever she with here precence,   *her*
She bryngeth gladnes to citees and touns;
Of alle well fare she holdeth the possessions,
125   For, I dar say, prosperyté in no place
No while abydith, but yf ther be grace.   *Does not long abide, unless*

In tokne that Grace shulde longe contune   *remain*
Unto the Kyng she shewed hire full benyngne;   *graciousness*
And next hire come the emperesse, Fortune,
130   Apperyng to hym with many a noble sygne,
And ryall toknes, to shewe that he was dygne,   *royal; worthy*
Of God dysposed as Grace lyst to ordeyne,
Upon his heede to were crounes tweyne.

Thes three ladyes, all of oon entent   *with one intent*
135   Three goostly giftes, hevenly and devyne,   *spiritual*
Unto the Kyng anoon they dydde present,
And to his hyhnesse they dydd anoon enclyne;
And, what they were pleynly to termyne,   *to declare plainly*
Grace gaf him first at his komyng
140   Twoo riche giftes, Sciens and Kunnyng;   *Knowledge*

Nature gaf him eke strenth and feyrenesse,   *beauty*
Forto be lovyd and dredde of every wiht;   *honored by everyone*
Fortune gaf him eke prosperité and richesse,
With this scripture apperyng in theire siht,
145   To him applyed of verrey dewe riht,   *aptly*
"First undirstonde and joyfully procede
And lange to regne" the scripture seyde in dede.   *long*

This ys to mene, whoso undirstonde ariht,
Thow shalt be Fortune have lange prosperité;   *by*

150	And be Nature thow shalt have strenth and myht,	*by*
	Forth to procede in lange felicité;	*happiness*
	And Grace also hath graunted unto thee,	
	Vertuously lange in thy ryall citee,	
	With septre and croune to regne in equyté."	

155   On the riht hande of thes emperesses
        Stoode sevyn maydenys verrey celestyall;   *truly*
        Lyke Phebus bemys shone hire goldyn tresses,   *Phebus' beams*
        Upon here heedes eche havyng a cornall,   *their heads; circlet*
        Of porte and chere semyng inmortall,   *bearing and manner*
160   In siht transendyng alle erthely creatures,
        So aungelyk they wern of theyre figures.

        Alle cladde in white, in tokne of clennesse,   *purity*
        Lyche pure virgynes as in theyre ententys,   *Like*
        Shewyng outward an hevenly fressh brihtnesse;
165   Stremed with sonys were alle their garmentis,   *Ornamented with sun rays*
        Aforne provyded for pure innocentis,
        Most columbyne of chere and of lokyng,   *demure in manner and look*
        Mekely roos up at komyng of the Kyng.

        They hadde an bawdrykes alle of safir hewe,   *wore sashes; sapphire*
170   Goynge outward gan the Kyng salewe,   *to greet*
        Hym presentyng with her giftes newe,   *their*
        Lyche as theym thouht yt was unto hem dewe,
        Which goostly giftes here in ordre sewe,   *spiritual; follow*
        Doune dessendyng as sylvere dewe fro hevyn,
175   Alle grace include withinne thes giftes sevyn;

        Thes ryall giftes ben of vertue moste
        Goostly corages, moste sovernynly delyte;   *desires*
        Thes giftes called of the Hooly Gooste,
        Outward figured ben seven dowys white,   *doves*
180   And seyying to him, lyke as clerkes write,
        "God thee fulfille with intelligence
        And with a spyryt of goostly sapience.   *wisdom*

        "God sende also unto thy moste vaylle   *benefit*
        Thee to preserve from alle hevynesse,
185   A spyrit of strenth, and of goode counsaylle,
        Of konnyng, drede, pité, and lownesse,"   *reverence; humility*
        Thus thes ladyes gan theire giftes dresse,   *offer*
        Graciously at theyre oute komyng,
        Be influence liht upon the Kyng.   *By flowing in*

190   Thes emperesses hadde on theyre lefte syde
       Other sevyne virgynes, pure and clene,
       Be attendaunce contenuelly to abyde,
       Alle cladde in white, smytte fulle of sterres shene;   *studded with shining stars*
       And to declare what they wolde mene
195   Unto the Kyng with ful grete reverence
       Thes were theire giftes shortly in sentence:

       "God thee endewe with a crowne of glorie,   *endow*
       And with septre of clennesse and pytee,   *scepter; purity*
       And with a swerde of myht and victorie,
200   And with a mantel of prudence cladde thow be,
       A shelde of feyth forto defende thee,
       An helme of helthe wrouht to thyn encrees,
       Girt with a girdyll of love and parfyte pees."   *perfect peace*

       Thes sevyn virgyns, of siht most hevenly,
205   With herte, body, and handes rejoysynge,
       And of othir cheris appered murely,   *gestures; joyfully*
       For the Kyngis gracious home komynge;
       And for gladnesse they beganne to synge,
       Moste aungelyk with hevenly armonye,   *angelic; harmony*
210   This same roundell, which I shall now specyfye:

       "Sovereyne Lorde, welcome to youre citee;
       Welcome, oure Joye, and oure Hertis Plesaunce,
       Welcome, oure Gladnesse, welcome, our Suffisaunce,   *Sufficiency*
       Welcome, welcome, riht welcome mote ye be.

215   "Syngyng toforn thy ryall Magesté,
       We say of herte, withoute variaunce,   *sincerely, without hesitation*
       Sovereyene Lorde, welcome, welcome ye be.

       "Meire, citezenis and alle the comounté,   *common people*
       At youre home komyng now out of Fraunce,
220   Be grace relevyd of theyre olde grevaunce,   *By*
       Syng this day with grete solempnyté,
       Sovereyne Lorde, welcome to youre citee."

       Thus resseyvyd, an esy paas rydyng,   *easy pace*
       The Kyng is entred into this Citee:
225   And in Cornhill anoon at his komyng,
       To done plesaunce unto his Magestee,
       A tabernacle surmountyng of beauté,
       Ther was ordeyned, be ful fresh entayle,   *of new design*
       Richely arrayed with ryall apparayle.   *furnishings*

230 This tabernacle of moste magnyficence,
    Was of his byldyng verrey imperyall   *in its construction*
    Made for the lady callyd Dame Sapience;
    Tofore whos face moste statly and ryall   *Before*
    Wern the sevyn sciences called lyberall   *Were*
235 Rounde aboute, as makyd ys memorie,
    Which nevere departed from hire consistorie.   *her court*

    First ther was Gramer, as I reherse gan,
    Chief founderesse and roote of all konnyng,
    Which hadde aforne hire olde Precian;   *Who had before her*
240 And Logyk hadde aforn hire stondyng
    Arestotyll moste clerkely dysputyng;
    And Rethoryk hadde eke in hire presence,
    Tulyus, called Mirrour of Eloquence;

    And Musyk hadde, voyde of alle discorde,
245 Boece, hire clerke, with hevenly armonye,   *Boethius; harmony*
    And instrumentis alle of oone accorde;
    Forto practyse with sugred melodye   *sweet*
    He and his scolers theyre wyttes dydde applye,
    With touche of strenges on orgons eke pleyng,
250 Theyre crafte to shewe at komyng of the Kyng;

    And Arsmetryk, be castyng of nombrarye,   *Arithmetic, through mathematics*
    Chees Pyktogeras for hire partye;   *Chose Pythagoras*
    Called chief clerke to governe hire lybrarye,
    Euclyde toke mesours be crafte of Gemetrye;   *by; Geometry*
255 And alderhyhest stode Astronomye,   *highest of all*
    Albunisar last with hire of sevyn,
    With instrumentis that rauht up into hevyn.   *reached*

    The chief pryncesse called Sapience,
    Hadde toforn hire writen this scripture:
260 "Kynges," quod she, "moste of excellence,
    By me they regne and moste in joye endure,
    For thurh my helpe, and my besy cure,
    To encrece theyre glorie and hyh renoun,
    They shull of wysdome have full possessioun."

265 And in the front of this tabernacle,
    Sapience a scripture ganne devyse
    Able to be redde withoute a spectakle,
    To yonge kynges seyynge in this wyse,
    "Understondith and lernyth of the wyse,   *learn from*
270 On riht remembryng the hyh lorde to queme,   *please*
    Syth ye be juges other folke to deme."   *Since; rule over*

Ferthermore the matere doth devyse:
The Kyng, procedying forth upon his way,
Kome to the Conduyte made in cercle wyse;
275 Whame to resseyve, ther was made no delay,   *Whom to receive*
And myddys above in ful riche array,   *in the middle*
Ther satte a childe of beauté precellying,   *surpassing*
Middis of the throne rayed lyke a kyng.   *In the middle; dressed*

Wham to governe, ther was figured tweyne,   *Whom; two*
280 A lady, Mercy, satte on his riht syde;
On his lyfte hande, yf I shall nat feyne,   *feign (lie)*
A lady, Trouthe, his domes to provyde;   *judgments*
The lady Clemens alofte dydde abyde,
Of God ordeyned in the same place
285 The Kyngis throne strongely to enbrace.

For, by the sentence of prudent Salamon,
Mercy and Riht kepyn every kyng,
And Clemencé kepte by Resoun
His myhty throne from myschief and fallyng,
290 And makith yt stronge with lange abydyng;
For I darr say thes sayde ladyes three
A kyng preserve in lange prosperytee.

Thanne stoode also afore the seyde kyng
Twoo juges with full hyh noblesse —   *nobility*
295 Eight sergeauntes echon representyng   *each one*
For comune profyte, doom and rihtwysnesse,   *common profit, justice; righteousness*
With this scripture, which I shall expresse:
"Honour of kyngys, in every mannys siht,
Of comyn custum lovith equyté and riht."   *common*

300 Kyng Davyd wrote, the Sawter berith wytnesse,   *Psalter*
"Lorde God," quod he, "thy dome geve to the Kyng,
And geve thy trouthe and thy rihtwysnesse
The Kyngis sone here in his levyng";   *King's son while he is alive*
To us declaring, as by theyre writyng,
305 That kyngis, princes, shulde aboute hem drawe   *them*
Folke that be trewe and well expert in lawe.

The Kyng forth rydyng entryd Chepe anoon,
A lusty place, a place of alle delycys;   *delights*
Kome to the Conduyt, wher, as cristall stoon,   *stone*
310 The watir ranne like welles of Paradys,
The holsome lykour, ful riche and of grete prys,   *value*
Lyke to the water of Archedeclyne,   *(see note)*
Which by miracle was turned into wyne.

Thetes, which that is of waters chief goddesse,   *Thetis*
315   Hadde of the welle power noon ne myht,
For Bachus shewed there his fulsomnesse   *abundance*
Of holsome wynes to every manere wiht;   *every sort of man*
For wyn of nature makith hertes liht,
Wherfore Bachus, at reverence of the Kyng,
320   Shewed oute his plenté at his home komyng.

Wyn is a likour of recreacioun,
That day presentyd in tokne of alle gladnesse,
Unto the Kyng of famous and hyh renoun,
From us t'exile alle manere hevynesse;   *to exile*
325   For with his komyng, the dede berith wytnesse,
Out of the londe he putte away alle trouble,
And made of newe oure joyes to be double.

Eke at thes welles there were virgyns three
Which drewe wyn up of joye and of pleasaunce,   *happiness*
330   Mercy and Grace, theyre suster eke Pyté;   *Pity*
Mercy mynystred wynes of attemperaunce,   *moderation*
Grace shedde hire likour of goode gouvernaunce,
And Pitee profered with ful goode foysoun   *bounty*
Wynes of comforte and consolacioun.

335   The wyn of Mercy staunchith by nature
The gredy thristis of cruell hastynesse,
Grace with hire likour cristallyne and pure
Deferrith vengaunce of furious woodnesse,   *anger*
And Pitee blymsith the swerde of Rithwysnesse;   *blunts; Righteousness*
340   Convenable welles, moste holsom of savour,   *Excellent*
Forto be tasted of every governour.

O! how thes welles, whoso take goode hede,
With here likours moste holsome to atame,   *their; subdue*
Afore devysed notably in dede
345   Forto accorden with the Meirys name;   *Mayor's*
Which by report of his worthy fame
That day was busy in alle his governaunce,
Unto the Kyng forto done plesaunce.   *to do*

Ther were eke treen, with leves fressh of hewe,   *trees*
350   Alle tyme of yeer, fulle of fruytes lade,   *laden*
Of colour hevynly, and ever-yliche newe,   *like*
Orenges, almondis, and the pomegernade,   *pomegranate*
Lymons, dates, theire colours fressh and glade,   *bright*
Pypyns, quynces, blaunderell to disport,   *Pippins; blaunderell (apples) to enjoy*
355   And the pomecedre corageous to recomfort;   *citron eager to invigorate*

Eke the fruytes which more comune be —
Quenynges, peches, costardes and wardouns,
And other meny ful fayre and fresh to se;   *see*
The pomewater and the gentyll ricardouns;
360   And ageyns hertes for mutygaciouns   *for relief of pains*
Damysyns, which with here taste delyte,   *Damson plums*
Full grete plenté both of blak and white.

And besydis this gracious paradys,
Alle joye and gladnesse forto multyplye,
365   Twoo olde men, full circounspecte and wyse,
There dydde appere lyke folkes of feyrye;   *fairyland*
The toon was Ennok, the tothir Elye,   *The one*
The Kyng presentyng theire giftes ful notable,   *Presenting to the king*
That God conferme his state ay to be stable.

370   The first seyde, with benynge chere,   *in a kindly manner*
Gretly desirynge his prosperyté,
That noon enemyes have in him power,
Nor that no childe by false iniquyté   *wicked person*
Parturble nevere his felicité;   *Disturb; happiness*
375   Thus olde Ennok the processe gan well telle,   *speech*
And prayd for the Kyng as he roode by the welle.

After, Elyas, with his lokkes hoore,   *gray hair*
Seyde well devoutly, lokyng on the Kyng,
"God conserve thee and kepe thee evermore,
380   And make him blessid, here in erthe levyng,
And preserve him in alle manere thyng,
And specially amongis kynges alle,
In enemyes handes that he nevere falle."

And at fronteur of thes welles clere,   *the front*
385   There was a scripture komendyng the lykour; —
"Yee shall drawe waters, with goode chere,
Oute of welles of oure Savyour,
Which have vertue to curen alle langour,
Be influence of her grete swetnesse,
390   Hertes avoydyng of alle theire hevynesse."   *Purging hearts*

Thanne from thes welles of fulsome habundaunce,   *plentiful*
With theyr lykours as eny cristall clene,   *pure as any crystal*
The Kyng roode forth, with sobre contenaunce,
Towarde a castell bilt of jaspar grene,
395   Upon whos toures the sonne shone shene,   *towers; bright*
Ther clerly shewed, by notable remembraunce,
This kyngis tytle of England and of Fraunce.

Twoo green treen ther grewe upriht,
Fro Seint Edward and fro Seint Lowys,
400   The roote ytake palpable to the siht,   *lineage; visible*
Conveyed by lynes be kyngis of grete prys;   *by; honor*
Some bare leopardes, and some bare floure-de-lys,
In nouther armes founde was there no lak,
Which the sixte Herry may now bere on his bak.

405   The pedegree be juste successioun,   *by*
As trewe cronycles trewely determyne,
Unto the Kyng ys now dessended doun
From eyther partye riht as eny lyne;   *i.e., from both lines of descent*
Upon whos heede now fresshely done shyne
410   Two riche crounes most sovereyn of plesaunce
To brynge inne pees bitwene England and France.

Upon this castell on the tothir syde
There was a tree, which sprange out of Jesse,
Ordeyned of God ful longe to abyde; —
415   Davyd crounyd first for his humylité
The braunches conveyd, as men myht se,
Lyneally and in the genologie,
To Crist Jhesu, that was born of Marie.

And why the Jesse was sette on that partye,   *there*
420   This was the cause in especyall,
For next to Paulis, I dar well specefye,
Is the partye moste chief and princypall,   *place*
Callyd of London the chirche cathederall,
Which ought of reson the devyse to excuse,
425   To alle thoo that wholde ageyn yt froune or muse.   *frown*

And fro that castell the Kyng forth gan him dresse
Toward Poulys, chief chirche of this citee,
And at Conduyt a liht, and a lyknesse
Indevysible made of the Trinité,
430   A throne compassid of his ryall see;   *encompassing*
About which, shortly to conclude,
Of hevenly aungelles wern a grete multitude;

To whom was goven a precept in scripture,   *given*
Wrete in the frontour of the hyhe stage,
435   That they shulde done theyre besy cure,   *work diligently*
To kepe the Kyng from alle damage
In his lyf here, duryng alle his age,
Hys hyh renoun to sprede and shyne ferre,   *afar*
And of his twoo reemes to sese the mortall werre.   *realms to stop*

440   And laste was wretyn in the fronterys: *in front*
       "I shall fulfille him with joye and habundaunce,
       And with lengthe of holsome yeerys,
       And I shall shewe him my helpe with alle plesaunce,
       And of his lieges feythfull obeyssaunce,   *vassals; obedience*
445   And multyplye and encrese his lyne
       And make his noblesse thurh the worlde to shyne.   *nobility throughout*

       Love of his peple, favour of alle straungers,
       In bothe his remys pees, reest, and unyté,   *realms peace; unity*
       Be influence of the nyne sperys,   *Under; [cosmic] spheres*
450   Longe to contune in his ryall see,   *continue*
       Grace to cherice the Meire and the Citee,
       Longe in his mynde to be conceyved
       With how good will, that day he was resseyved."

       Comyng to Poulis ther he liht adoun,   *St. Paul's Cathedral*
455   Entryng the chirche ful demure of chere,   *manner*
       And there to mete him with processioun
       Was the Erchebisshop, and the Chaunceller,
       Lyncoln, and Bathe, of hoole herte and entier,   *most devoutly*
       Salysbury, Norwich, and Ely,
460   In pontyficall arrayed richely.

       Ther was the Bisshop of Rouchestre also,
       The Dene of Paulys, the Chanons everychon,   *The Dean of St. Paul's*
       Of dewté as they auht to do,   *duty*
       On processioun with the Kyng to goon;
465   And thouh I kan nat reherse hem oon by oon,
       Yitt dar I say, as in theyre entent,
       To do theyre devere full trewely they ment.   *duty*

       Lyke theyre estates forth they ganne procede;
       With observaunces longyng for a kyng   *belonging to*
470   Solempnely gan him conveye in dede
       Up into the chirche with full devoute syngyng;
       And whanne he hadde made his offryng,
       The Meire, the citezenis, abode and left him nouht,   *stayed*
       Unto Westmynstre tyl they hadde him brouht;

475   Wher alle the covent, in copys richely,   *convent; copes*
       Mette with him of custume as they ouht;
       The Abbot after moste solempnely
       Amonges the relikes the septre oute souht
       Of Seint Edward, and to the Kyng it brouht;
480   Thouh it were longe, large, and of grete weyht,
       Yitt on his shuldres the Kyng bare it on heyht,   *on high*

Into the mynstre, while alle the belles ronge, *minster*
Tyl he kome to the hyh awtere; *high altar*
And full devoutly *Te Deum* ther was songe,
485 And the peple, gladde of looke and chere,
Thanked God with alle here hertes entere,
To se theire Kyng with twoo crounys shyne,
From twoo trees trewly fette the lyne. *derived*

And after that, this ys the verrey sothe, *absolute truth*
490 Unto his paleys of kyngly apparaylle,
With his lordes the Kyng forth goothe
To take his reste after his travaylle; *exertions*
And than of wysdome, that may so mych avaylle, *that is so useful*
The Meire, the citezenis, which alle this dyd se,
495 Ben home repeyred into hire citee. *Went home*

The Shereves, the Aldermen in fere, *in a group*
The Saturday alther next suyng, *On the following Saturday*
Theire Meire presented, with theyre hertes entere, *wholeheartedly*
Goodly to be resseyved of the Kyng; *received by*
500 And at Westminster confermed theire askyng, *confirmed their request*
The Meyre and they with full hole entent
Unto the Kyng a gyfte gan to present.

The which gifte they goodly have dysposyd, *planned well*
Toke an hamper of golde that shene shone, *gold casket that shone brightly*
505 A thousand pounde of golde therinne yclosyd;
And therwithall to the Kyng they goone
And fylle on knees toforn him everychoone, *fell*
Full humbly the trouthe to devyse,
And to the Kyng the Meire seyde in this wyse:

"Most Cristen Prynce and noble Kyng, the goode folke of youre moste notable Citee of London, otherwyse cleped youre Chambre (*called your Chamber*), beseching in here moste lowly wyse they mowe be recomaunded (*might be recommended*) to youre Hyhnesse and that yt kan lyke unto your Noble Grace to resseyve this lytyll gyfte, gyfyn with a goode wille of trouthe and lownesse (*allegiance and humility*), as evere eny gifte was yoven (*given*) to eny erthely prince."

510 Be gladde, O London! be gladde and make grete joye,
Citee of Citees, of noblesse precellyng, *surpassing nobility*
In thy bygynnynge called Newe Troye;
For worthynesse thanke God of alle thyng,
Which hast this day resseyved so thy Kyng *received*
515 With many a signe and many an observaunce
To encrese thy name by newe remembraunce.

Suche joye was nevere in the Consistorie,
Made for the tryumphe with alle the surplusage,   *embellishments*
Whanne Sesar Julius kam home with his victorie;
520   Ne for the conqueste of Sypion in Cartage;
As London made in every manere age,
Out of Fraunce at the home komyng
Into this citee of theyre noble Kyng.

Of sevyn thinges I preyse this citee:
525   Of trewe menyng, and feythfull observaunce,   *intentions*
Of rihtwysnesse, trouthe, and equyté,   *righteousness*
Of stablenesse ay kepte in lygeaunce;   *allegiance*
And for of vertue thow hast such suffisaunce,   *sufficiency*
In this lande here and other landes alle
530   The Kyngis Chambre of custume men thee calle.

        [*L'envoye.*   *The epilogue*

O noble Meir! be yt unto youre plesaunce,
And to alle that duelle in this citee,   *dwell*
On my rudenesse and on myn ygnoraunce,
Of grace and mercy forto have pitee,
535   My symple makyng forto take at gree;   *look with favor on*
Considre this, that in moste lowly wyse
My wille were goode forto do yow servyse.

THE LEGEND OF ST. GEORGE

[*Next nowe filowing here bygynnethe the devyse of a steyned halle of the lyf of Saint George ymagyned by Daun Johan the Munk of Bury Lydegate and made with the balades at the request of th'armorieres of London for th'onour of theyre brotherhoode and theyre feest of Saint George.*

[*The poete first declarethe:*

O yee folk that heer present be,
Wheeche of this story shal have inspeccion,
Of Saint George yee may beholde and see
His martirdome, and his passyoun;
5   And howe he is protectour and patroun,
This hooly martir, of knighthood loodsterre,   *lodestar (i.e., guide)*
To Englisshe men boothe in pees and werre.   *peace and war*

In whos honnour sithen goon ful yoore   *many years ago*
The thridde Edward of knighthoode moost entier   *third; perfect*
10   In his tyme, b'assent at Wyndesore   *by assent; Windsor*

Founded th'ordre first of the gartier,   *the order; garter*
Of worthy knightes ay frome yeere to yeere
Foure and twenty cladde in oo lyveree   *one livery*
Upon his day kepte ther solempnytee.

15   This name George by interpretacioun
Is sayde of tweyne, the first of hoolynesse,   *Is said to mean two things*
And the secound of knighthood and renoun,
As that myn Auctor lykethe for to expresse,   *Author*
The feond venqwysshing of manhoode and prowesse,   *Satan; valor*
20   The worlde, the flesshe, as Crystes owen knyght,   *own*
Wherever he roode in steel armed bright.

Capadoce, a mighty strong citee,
As the story of hym list to endyte,   *likes to say*
Ordeyned was to his natyvytee;   *birth*
25   And in his youthe he gaf himself delyte   *delight*
Frome day to day, as clerkis of him wryte,
To suwe vertue, so gynnyng his passage,   *follow; beginning*
Vyces excluding, al ryot, and oultrage.   *violence*

And Cristes feyth for to magnefye   *faith*
30   At gretter age his cuntree he forsooke,   *country*
And thoroughe his noblesse and his chyvallerye   *nobility*
Trouthe to sousteene, whoso list to looke,   *sustain, whoever cares to notice*
Many a journee he upon him tooke,   *battle*
The chirche defending with swerd of equytee,   *sword; justice*
35   The right of wydowes, and of virgynytee.

And in this whyle an aventure is falle,   *And during this time a misfortune occurred*
Importable the people to sousteene,   *Too heavy for; bear*
Amiddes the provynce whiche men Lybye calle,
In a cytee that named is Lysseene;
40   A gret dragoun, with scales silver sheene,   *silvery bright*
Horryble, dreedful, and monstruous of sight,
Tofore the citee lay boothe day and night.

The kyng, the qweene, the lordes taken heed
Of this sodeyne wooful aventure,   *unexpected; occurrence*
45   And the people fellen in gret dreed   *dread*
Consydering howe that they stonde unsure,
As they that might the mescheef not endure   *misfortune*
Maade by assaute of that felle dragoun   *the assault; evil*
By pestylence upon theyre wooful toun.   *unfortunate town*

50   But whane the conseyle of theyre toun took keep   *council; realized*
Howe that theyre peyne was intollerable,   *pain*

They senten out every day twoo sheep
To this beest foule and abhomynable,   *beast*
To staunche his hunger which was unstauncheable,
55   But whane theyre sheep by processe gan to fayle   *gradually began to fail*
They most of nuwe provyde more victaylle,   *had to provide anew*

And whanne they foonde no refuyt ne coumfort   *relief*
For the dragoun to make pourveyaunce,   *provision*
Thane they tooke by lotte other by soort   *or by turn*
60   Man or chylde, theyre vytayle to avaunce,   *their food (for the dragon) to increase*
Lyche as hit felle on by mortal chaunce
Allas, ellas, it was to gret pytee   *too great a pity*
To seen the sorowe that was in that citee.   *see; city*

The statuit made noon excepcyoun   *no*
65   Of heghe ne lowe, they stoode in so gret doute   *high nor; fear*
Touchant that monstre and that foule dragoun,   *Concerning*
Eche maner man, as it came aboute,
To be devowred, allas, they were sent oute,
Til at the last the lott in this maner
70   Fel right upon the kynges doughter deer,   *dear*

That she most nexst of necessytee   *must*
Beo so devowred, helpe may no meede,   *nothing could spare her*
But to beo sent oute of that cytee,
This cely mayde quakyng in hir dreed;   *unfortunate*
75   Upon hir hande a sheep shee did leed,
Hir fader wepte, hir moder, boothe tweyne,
And al the cytee in teerys did so reyne.   *tears*

At hir oute goyng hir fader for the noones   *occasion*
Arrayed her with al his ful might
80   In cloothe of golde with gemys and with stoones,   *gems; jewels*
Whiche shoone ful sheene ageyne the sonne bright,   *splendidly against; sun*
And on hir wey sheo mette an armed knight
Sent frome the Lord as in hir diffence   *defense*
Ageynst the dragoun to make resistence.

85   Saint George it was, Oure Ladyes owen knight,
That armed seet upon a ryal steed   *sat; royal*
Which came to socour this mayde in hir right,   *help*
Of aventure in this grete neode,   *By chance; great need*
"Ellas!" quod she, whane she takethe heed,   *noticed (him)*
90   And bade him fleen in hir mortal feer,   *flee; fear*
Lest he also with hir devowred were.

And whane he saughe of hir the maner,   *saw*
He hadde pytee and eeke compassyoun,   *pity; also*
To seen, allas, the cristal streemys cleer   *see; streams clear*
95 On hir cheekys reyne and royle adowne,   *rain and roll*
Thought he wolde beon hir Chaumpyoun,   *be her Champion*
For lyf nor deeth from hir not to depart
But in hir quarell his body to jupart.   *put at risk*

Hooly Seint George his hors smote on the syde
100 Whane he the dragoun sawe lyft up his hede, *head*
And towardes him he proudely gan to ryde
Ful lyche a knight with outen fere or dreede;   *fear*
Avysyly of witt he tooke goode heed,   *Shrewdly*
With his spere sharp and kene egrounde   *keenly honed*
105 Thoroughe the body he gaf the feonde a wownde. *fiend*

The cely mayde, knelyng on hir kne,   *unfortunate (innocent)*
Unto hir goddes maked hir preyer,
And Saint George, whane he did it see,
To hir he sayde, with debonayre cheer,   *courteous manner*
110 "Ryse up anoon, myn owen doughter deer,
Take thy girdell, and make therof a bande,
And leed this dragoun boldly in thyn hande

"Into the cyté, lyche a conqueresse,
And the dragoun meekly shall obeye."
115 And to the cytee anoon she gan hir dresse, *to make her way*
The ouggely monstre durst it not withseye, *loathsome; dared not resist it*
And Saint George the mayden gan conveye, *began to guide*
That whane the kyng hade inspeccyoun,
With palme and banner he goothe processyoun,

120 Giving to him the laude of this victorye,   *praise*
Which hathe theyre cytee delyverd out of dreed;
And Saint George, to encresce his glorye,
Pulled out a swerde and smote of his hed, *cut off his (i.e., the dragon's) head*
The people alwey taking ful goode heed, *paying close attention*
125 How God this martyr list to magnefye,   *chose to*
And him to enhaunce thorughe his chivallerye.

Thanne he made the dragoun to be drawe,
With waynes and cartes fer out of the towne, *wagons*
And after that he taught hem Crystes lawe, *them (i.e., the townsfolk)*
130 By his doctryne and predicacyoun,   *preaching*
And frome th'error by conversyoun,   *the error*
He made hem tourne, the kyng and the cyté, *them turn*
And of oon hert baptysed for to be.   *one heart*

The kyng after in honnour of Marye *afterwards*
135 And in worship of Saint George hir knight,
A ful feyre chirche gan to edefye, *very beautiful; erect*
Riche of bylding and wonder feyre of sight, *fair*
Amiddes of which ther sprang up anoon right
A plesaunt welle, with stremys cristallyne,
140 Whos drynk to seek was helthe and medecyne.

Saint George thanne enfourme gan the kyng *began to instruct*
Of foure thinges of great excellence,
First that he shoulde above al other thing
Crystes chirche have ever in reverence,
145 Worship preesthood with al his diligence,
Have mynde on poore, and first his hert enclyne *Be mindful of the poor*
Frome day to day to here servyce devyne. *their*

This same tyme, the stoory telle cane,
Ageynst Crysten ther was a thyrant sent, *the Christians; tyrant*
150 The which was called Theodacyan,
Of paynyme lawe he was a presydent, *pagan; leader*
And to destroye was hooly his entent *completely*
The feyth of Cryst, and sleen his confessours, *faith; slay*
With dyvers peynes wrought by his tormentours. *pains*

155 Whane that Saint George gan hereof take heed
Howe this thyraunt gan Crystes feyth manace, *threaten*
He of pourpos left of his knightly weede, *clothes*
And pourely cladde mette him in the face, *face to face*
Mannely cheered, fulfilled al with grace, *Brave*
160 In his presence lowde he gan to crye *loudly*
"Oon God ther is, fy on ydolatrye."

The false thyraunt by gret vyolence
Comaunded hathe anoon that he be taake, *he (i.e., St. George) be taken*
And to be broughte unto his presence;
165 Bade that he shoulde Crystes feyth forsake,
But he ne liste noo delayes maake, *he (i.e., St. George) made no delay*
Aunswerd pleynly, his lyf by deth to fyne, *Answered; life; to end*
Frome Crystes lawe no thing shall him declyne. *turn away from*

The thyraunt thanne, of verray crueltee, *out of sheer cruelty*
170 Bad that he shoulde this martir moost entier *Commanded; illustrious*
Naked beon hanged upon a galowe tree,
With scowrges beet in ful feele maner, *be beaten in a very cruel manner*
And with brondes brennyng bright and cler, *burning torches*
His sydes brent. Were not hees peynes strong? *his pains*
175 His entraylles opende, salt cast in among. *intestines*

The nexst night, Cryst to him did peere,   *appear*
And gracyously gan him to coumfort,
And beed him souffre his peynes with goode cheer,   *bid; endure*
And in no wyse himselven discoumfort,
180   For he the palme of victor schal report,   *victory*
By his souffraunce, and wynnen the laurier   *suffering; win the laurel*
Of martirdame above the sterres cleer.   *stars*

This mighty geant, Crystes chaumpyoun,   *giant*
Drank bitter venyme made b'enchauntement,   *by enchantment*
185   Crystes crosse was his proteccion,
Preserving him that he was not shent,   *harmed*
And he that made hit of ful fals entent
Saughe ageyne God he hade no puissaunce,   *Saw that against; power*
Forsooke his errour and fel in repentaunce,

190   Axethe mercy in ful humble wyse,   *Asked for mercy*
And bycame Cristen, bytwix hope and dreed.
The false juge, voyde of all justyce,
Comaunded hathe that he shuld leese his heed,   *lose his head*
And in his blood, as any roose reed,   *red rose*
195   He was baptysed, whoo that can discerne,
By deethe deserving the lyf that is eterne.   *eternal*

Thanne Dacyan, furyous and cruwel,
Gane of nuwe devysen in his teene,   *Began anew; anger*
Reysed aloft a ful large wheele,   *Raised*
200   Ful of swerdes grounden sharp and keene,
And Saint George, in his entent moost cleene,
Tourned theron in that mortal rage.   *Turned*
The wheel tobraake; he felt no damage.   *broke*

Eeke in a vessel boylling ful of leed,   *boiling; lead*
205   This hooly martir was eplounged downe,   *plunged*
He enterd in withouten feer or dreed,
The grace of God was his salvacioun,
And liche a bath of consolacioun
He founde the metal coumfortable and clere,
210   Escaping oute devoyde of al daunger.   *free of*

He was eeke brought, the story doothe devyse,
Into a temple ful of mawmetrye,   *idolatry*
Of entent to have doo sacrefyce,   *to make sacrifice*
But alle theyre goddes he knightly can defye,
215   And sodyenly oure feyth to magnefye   *faith*
A fyre frome heven was by myracle sent,
Wher thorughe the temple was till asshes brent.   *burned to ashes*

And with al this we fynden in his lyf,

Thorugh Goddes might and gracyous purveyaunce   *providence*

220   That Alexandrea of Dacyan the wyf

Forsooke ydolles and al hir fals creaunce   *idols; belief*

And became Crysten with humble attendaunce,   *devotion*

Suffred deethe, baptysed in hir bloode

For love of Him that starf upon the roode.   *died upon the cross*

225   And Dacyan thanne, by ful mortal lawe,

Comaunded hathe in open audyence,

That Saint George be thorughe the cyté drawe   *city*

And after that this was his sentence,

He to ben heveded by cruwel violence,   *to be beheaded*

230   And in his dying thus it is befalle,

He made his preyer for hem that to him calle.   *them*

"O Lord," quod he, "thou here myn orysoun   *hear my prayer*

And graunte it beo unto thee plesaunce   *pleasing*

That alle folk that have devocyoun

235   To me, O Lord, have hem in remembraunce   *remember them*

And condescende with every circumstance   *with utmost care*

Of thy mercy, O Soverein Lord moost deer

Al for my saake to heren theyre preyer."   *to hear*

And al the people being in presence,

240   A voyce was herd doune frome the hye heven,

Howe that his preyer was graunted in sentence   *in fact*

Of him that is Lord of the sterres seven.   *By*

And Dacyan, with a sodein leven   *flash*

Was brent unwarly by consumpcyoun,   *burned unexpectedly by a firey annihilation*

245   As he repayred hoome to his mansyoun.   *returned*

[*Explicit.*

MESURE IS TRESOUR

Men wryte of oold how mesour is tresour,

And of al grace ground moost principall,

Of vertuous lyfe suppoort and eek favour,

Mesour conveyeth and governyth all, —

5   Trewe examplayr and orygynall,   *exemplar*

To estaatys of hyh and lowe degree,   *high*

In ther dewe ordre, for, in especiall,   *due*

Alle thyng is weel so it in mesure be.

Mesure is roote of al good policye,

10   Sustir-germayn unto discrecioun,   *True sister*

        Of poopys, prelatys, it beryth up the partye,   *popes*

        Them to conduce in hyh perfeccioun,   *guide in high*

        To leve in preyour and in devocioun,   *live*

        Yeve good exaunple of pees and unité,

15   That al ther werkys, for shoort conclusioun,   *works*

        With trewe mesure may commendid be.   *true*

Al theyre doctryne, nor all ther hoolynesse,

        Kunnyng, language, wisdam, nor science,   *Knowledge*

        Studye on bookys, in prechyng besynesse,

20   Almesse-dede, fastyng, nor abstinence,   *Almsgiving*

        Clothe the nakyd with cost and dispence,   *an outlay of money*

        Rekne alle these vertues, compassioun, and pité,   *Reckon*

        Avayllith nought, pleynly in sentence   *in plain truth*

        But there be mesure and parfight charyté.   *perfect*

25   Myghty emperours, noble wourthy kynges,

        Pryncis, dukys, erlys, and barounnys,   *earls*

        Ther greete conquestys, ther surquedous rydynges,   *haughty cavalcades*

        But ther be mesure in ther condicyounnys,   *behavior*

        That attemperaunce conveye ther renownys,   *moderation; renown*

30   Rekne up the noblesse of every conquerour,   *Reckon; nobility*

        What availlith al ther pocessiounnyns,

        But ther ende conclude in just mesure?

Kyng Alisaundre, that gat al myddyl-erthe,   *conquered all the world*

        Affryk, Ayse, Ewrope, and eek Ynde,

35   And slowh Porrus with his dreedful swerde,   *killed; sword*

        Yit in his conquest mesure was set behynde;

        For which, ye lordys, left up your eyen blynde!   *eyes*

        The stoon of paradys was fyn of his labour,   *stone; the goal of*

        In al his conquest, have ye wel in mynde,

40   Was sett ferre bak for lak of just mesure.   *far*

Knyghthood in Grece and Troye the cité

        Took hys principlys, and next in Rome toun,   *Followed his example*

        And in Cartage, a famous gret cuntré,   *country*

        Recoord of Hanybal and wourthy Scipioun;

45   The greete debaatys and the devisioun

        Among these kyngdammys by marcial labour,

        Fynal cause of ther destruccioun,

        Was fawte of vertu and lakkyng of mesure.   *lack of virtue*

To knyghthood longith the Chirche to supporte,   *belongs the duty*

50   Wydewys, and maydenys, and poore folk to diffende,   *defend*

Men in ther ryght knyghtly to recoumfoorte,
To comoun profight nyght and day entende,   *common profit*
Ther lyf, ther good manly to dispende,   *their wealth vigorously to use*
To punysshe extorcioun, raveyne, and ech robbour,   *robbery*
55   And bryngen alle unto correccioun,
That be froward unto the just mesour.   *hostile to*

Trewe juges and sergeauntis of the lawe,
For hate or frenshippe they shal ther doomys dresse,   *deliver their judgment*
Withoute excepcioun, and ther hand withdrawe,
60   Fro meede and yiftes alle surfetys to represse;   *bribes; excess*
Holde trouthe and sustene rightwisnesse,   *righteousness*
Mercy preferre alwey tofor rigour,   *instead of strict justice*
That fals for-sweryng have there noon interesse,   *perjury; no influence*
For lak of trouthe and lak of just mesour.

65   So egally ther doomys to avaunce,   *impartially; judgments*
Of God and trouthe alwey to takyn hede,
And Cambises to have in remembraunce,
That was slayn because that he took meede
Of poore folk, the causys they shall speede,   *champion*
70   To moordre nor thefte they shal doo no favour,   *murder*
In al ther doomys of conscience to dreede,
That ryght goo not bak, equité, nor mesour.

Meyris, sherevys, aldirmen, cunstablys,   *Mayors*
Which that governe bourghes and citees,   *boroughs*
75   Kepith your fraunchise and statutys profitablys,   *privileges; profitable statutes*
That moost avayalle may to the comountees;   *citizenry*
In no wise lese nought your libertees;   *lose*
Accorde ech man with his trewe neyhbour,   *Reconcile*
As ye ar bounde to hih and lowh degrees,
80   That peys and wheyghte be kept, and just mesour.   *balance; weight*

Among yoursilf suffre noon extorcioun,
Let no wrong be doo unto the poraylle,   *poor*
On thefte and manslaughte doo execucioun,
Beth weel providid for stuff and for vitaylle;   *supplies; provisions*
85   Let no devisioun, Salamon doth counsaylle,
Withinne yoursilf holde no socour;   *find refuge*
And for a tresour which greetly may avaylle,
Among alle thyng kepe peys and just mesour.

Famous marchauntys, that ferre cuntrees ryde,
90   With al ther greete rychesse and wynnynges,   *profits*
And artificerys, that at hom abyde,   *craftsmen*
So ferre castyng in many sundry thynges,   *So skillfully crafting*

And been expert in wondirful konnyngges,   *skills*
Of dyvers craftys t'avoyden al errour;   *to avoid*
95   What may avaylle al your ymagynynges,
Withoute proporciouns of weyghte and just mesour?

Rekne up phesyk with all ther letuaryes,   *physicians; potions*
Grocerys, mercerys, with ther greet habundaunce,   *mercers*
Expert surgeyns, prudent potecaryes,   *apothecaries*
100 And all ther weyghtes peysed in ballaunce,   *weighed*
Masouns, carpenterys, of Yngelond and of Fraunce,
Bakerys, browsterys, vyntenerys, with fressh lycour,   *brewers, vintners*
All set at nought to rekne in substaunce,
Yif peys or weyghte doo lake, or just mesour.   *If scales; lack*

105 Ploughmen, carterys, with othir laborerys,
Dichers, delverys, that greet travaylle endure,   *diggers*
Which bern up all, and have doon many yeerys,   *hold up*
The staatis alle set here in portrature,   *estates*
On Goddys wyll, and also by nature,
110 Alle oon ymage divers in ther degree,
Shulde be alle oon, by recoord of Scripture,
Be large mesour of parfight charyté.

Fro yeer to yeer th'experiencce is seyn,
Ne were the plough no staat mygt endure;   *Without the plow; estate*
115 The large feeldys shulde be bareyn,
No corn upgrowe nor greyn in his verdure,   *grain in its greenness*
Man to suppoorte, nor beeste in his nature,
For which we shulde of trouthe for our socour
Wourshippe the plough, sithe every creature
120 Hath of the ploughman his lyfoode be mesour.   *livelihood by*

So as the shepperde wacchith upon ther sheep,
The hoote somyr, the coolde wynterys nyght,   *summer*
Spiritual heerdys shulde take keep
In Crystes foolde, with al ther fulle myght,
125 By vertuous doctryne as they ar holde of ryght,
To save ther sogettys fro wolvys fell rygour,   *subjects from wolves' fierce attack*
That heretikys quenche nat the lyght
Of Crystes feith nor of just mesour.

Heerdys with sheep shul walke in good pasture,
130 And toward nyght sewrly sette a foolde,   *safely*
Of Isaak and Jacob a ful pleyn figure,
That wer shepperdys whyloom be dayes oolde;   *in days of old*
Which lyk prelatys and bysshoppes as I toolde,
Th'estaatys here sett in charyté shal governe,

135   By good exaumple in heete and froostys coolde,
       That ryght and mesure shal holde up the lanterne.

       Strong as Herculees of manhood and of myght,
       I am set here to stondyn at dyfence,   *in defense*
       Wrong to represse, and to suppoorte ryght
140   With this burdoun of sturdy violence;
       But unto alle that wyl doo reverence,
       To alle the staatys sett here in portrature,
       I shall to hem make no resistence,
       That be governyd justly be mesure.

145   Among boorys, beerys, and leounnys,   *boars, bears; lions*
       Myn office is to walke in wyldirnesse,   *My job*
       Reste anyght in cavys and dongeounnys,   *dens*
       Tyl Phebus shewe a morwen his bryghtnesse   *in the morning*
       Now stonde I here to kepe in sekirnesse   *security*
150   This hows in sewyrté, with al my besy cure,   *safety*
       To letyn in folk, that of gentilnesse
       Lyst hem governe justly be mesure.   *Wish to govern themselves*

MUMMING AT BISHOPSWOOD

[Nowe here nexst folowyng ys made a balade by Lydegate, sente by a poursyvant (sent by a messenger) to the Shirreves of London, acompanyed with theire bretherne upon Mayes daye at Busshopes wod, at an honurable dyner, eche of hem bringginge his dysshe.

       Mighty Flourra, goddes of fresshe floures,   *Flora*
       Whiche clothed hast the soyle in lousty grene,   *Who has clothed; vigorous*
       Made buddes springe with hir swote showres   *her sweet*
       By influence of the sonne so sheene;   *bright*
5   To do plesaunce of entent ful clene   *To bring pleasure with completely pure intent*
       Unto th'estates wheoche that nowe sitte here,   *the estates which*
       Hathe Veere doune sent hir owen doughter dere,   *Ver (i.e., Spring); her (i.e., Flora's)*

       Making the vertue that dured in the roote,   *endured*
       Called of clerkes the vertue vegytable,   *life-giving force*
10   For to trascende, moste holsome and moste swoote,   *ascend; sweet*
       Into the crope, this saysoun so greable.   *season so pleasant*
       The bawmy lykour is so comendable   *fragrant sap*
       That it rejoythe with the fresshe moysture   *makes happy*
       Man, beeste, and foole, and every creature   *bird*

15   Which hathe repressed, swaged, and bore doune   *diminished*
       The grevous constreinte of the frostes hoore;
       And caused foolis, for joye of this saysoune,

	To cheese theire makes thane by natures loore,	*choose; mates; command*
	With al gladnesse theire courage to restore,	*desire*
20	Sitting on bowes fresshly nowe to synge	
	Veere for to salue at hir home comynge;	*greet*

Ful pleinly meninge in theire ermonye | *meaning; harmony*
Wynter is goone, whiche did hem gret payne, | *them*
And with theire swoote sugre melodye, | *sugary*
25 Thanking Nature theire goddesse sovereyne
That they nowe have no mater to compleyne | *reason*
Hem for to proygne every morwenyng | *preen; morning*
With lousty gladnesse at Phebus uprysinge. | *at the sun's rising*

And to declare the hye magnifysence | *high*
30 Howe Vere inbringethe al felicytee, | *ushers in all happiness*
After wynters mighty vyolence
Avoydinge stormys of al adversytee;
For sheo hathe brought al prosperitee | *she*
To alle th'estates of this regyoun
35 At hir comynge tofore youre hye renoun: | *before*

To the mighty prynces the palme of theire victorie;
And til knighthode nowe sheo dothe presente | *to*
Noblesse in armes, lawde, honnour, and glorie; | *Nobility in battle, praise*
Pees to the people in al hir best entente, | *Peace*
40 With grace and mercy fully to consente
That provydence of hye discressioun | *sound judgment*
Avoyde descorde and al devysyoun. | *discord; dissent*

Wynter shal passe of hevynesse and trouble,
Flowres shal springe of perfite charité, | *perfect*
45 In hertes there shal be no meninge double, | *deceitful feelings*
Buddes shal blosme of trouthe and unytee, | *unity*
Pleinly for to exyle duplicytee,
Lordes to regne in theire noble puissance, | *power*
The people obeye with feythful obeyssaunce. | *obedience*

50 Of alle estates there shal beo oone ymage,
And princes first shal ocupye the hede, | *head*
And prudent juges, to correcte outrages,
Shal trespassours constreynen under drede,
That innosentes in theire lowlyhede | *humbleness*
55 As truwe comunes may beo theire socour, | *commons (subjects); succor*
Truwly contune in theire faithful labour. | *continue*

And by the grace of Oure Lorde Jhesu
That Holly Chirche may have parseveraunce, | *may persevere*

Beo faythfull founde in al vertue,   *Be*
60   Mayre, provost, shirref, eche in his substaunce;
     And aldremen, whiche have the governaunce
     Over the people by vertue may avayle,   *succeed*
     That noone oppression beo done to the pourayle.   *poor*

     Thus as the people, of prudent pollycye,
65   Pryncis of the right shal governe,
     The Chirche preye, the juges justefye,
     And knighthode manly and prudently discerne,   *nobly*
     Til light of trouthe so clerely the lanterne:
     That rightwysnesse thorughe this regyoune   *righteousness*
70   Represse the derknesse of al extorcyoune.

     Theos be the tythinges, wheoche that Weer hathe brought.   *These; tidings; Ver*
     Troubles exylinge of wynters rude derknesse;
     Wherfore rejoye yowe in hert, wille, and thought,   *rejoice; heart*
     Somer shal folowe to yowe of al gladnesse;   *Summer*
75   And sithen sheo is mynistre of lustynesse,   *since; pleasure*
     Let hir beo welcome to yowe at hir comyng,
     Sith sheo to yowe hathe brought so glad tythinge.   *such a*

     The noble princesse of moste magnifisence,
     Qweene of al joye, of gladde suffisaunce,   *sufficiency*
80   May is nowe comen to youre Hye Excellence,
     Presenting yowe prosperous plesaunce,
     Of al welfare moste foulsome haboundance,   *plentiful abundance*
     As sheo that hathe under hir demayne   *domain*
     Of floures fresshe moste holsome and soveraine.

            [*L'envoye to alle th'estates present.*   *epilogue; the estates*

85   This Princesse hathe, by favour of nature,
     Repared ageine that wynter hathe so fade,   *that which; has so withered*
     And foolis loustely recuvre   *birds; recover*
     Theire lusty notes and theire ermonye glade,   *harmony*
     And under braunches, under plesant shade,
90   Rejoyssing thaire with many swote odoures,   *sweet*
     And Zepherus with many fresshe shoures.   *showers*

     Topyted fayre, with motleys whyte and rede,   *Covered attractively; multicolored flowers*
     Alle hilles, pleynes, and lusty bankes grene,
     And made hir bawme to fleete in every mede,   *fragrance; waft over; meadow*
95   And fury Tytane shewe oute heos tresses sheene,   *the fiery sun; his*
     And uppon busshes and hawthornes kene,   *sharp*
     The nightingale with plesant ermonye
     Colde wynter stormes nowe sheo dothe defye.

On Parnoso the lusty muses nyene,   *pleasure-loving; nine*
100   Citherra with hir sone nowe dwellis,
       This sayson singe and theire notes tuwyne   *blend*
       Of poetrye besyde the cristal wellis;   *springs*
       Calyope the dytes of hem tellis,   *stories*
       And Orpheus with heos stringes sharpe
105   Syngethe a roundell with his temperd herpe.   *harmonious harp*

       Wherfore to alle estates here present,
       This plesant tyme moste of lustynesse,
       May is nowe comen tofore yow of entent   *with the intent*
       To bringe yowe alle to joye and fresshnesse,
110   Prosparitee, welfare, and al gladnesse,
       And al that may youre Hyenesse qweeme and pleese,   *satisfy*
       In any parte or doone youre hertes eese.   *heart's ease*

MUMMING AT ELTHAM

[*Loo here begynnethe a balade made by daun John Lidegate at Eltham in Cristmasse, for a momyng tofore the Kyng and the Qwene.*

       Bachus, which is god of the glade vyne,   *who; jolly vine*
       Juno and Ceres, acorded alle theos three,   *all three together*
       Thorughe theyre power, which that is devyne,
       Sende nowe theyre giftes unto your Magestee:
5   Wyne, whete, and oyle by marchandes that here be,   *(olive) oil; merchants*
       Wheche represent unto youre Hye Noblesse   *your High Nobility*
       Pees with youre lieges, plenté and gladnesse.   *Peace; vassals, abundance*

       For theos giftes pleynly to descryve,   *fully; describe*
       Wheche in hemself designe al souffisaunce: *themselves signify complete sufficiency*
10   Pees is betokened by the grene olyve;
       In whete and oyle is foulsome haboundaunce;   *plentiful abundance*
       Wheche to youre Hyenesse for to do plesaunce,   *to please your Highness*
       They represente nowe to youre Hye Noblesse,
       Pees with youre lieges, plentee with gladnesse.

15   Ysaak, the patryark ful olde,
       Gaf his blessing with his giftes three   *Gave*
       Unto Jacobe; in Scripture it is tolde,
       Genesis yee may hit reede and see.   *You may read and see it in Genesis*
       And semblabully the Hooly Trynytee,   *similarly*
20   Youre staate blessing, sent to youre Hye Noblesse   *sends*
       Pees with youre lieges, plentee with gladnesse.

In the olyve he sendethe to yowe pees,
The Lord of Lordes, that lordshipethe every sterre,   *rules over; star*
And in youre rebelles, wheche beon now reklesse,   *who are*
25   He stint shal of Mars the cruwel werre;   *stop; cruel war*
And thane youre renoun shal shyne in londes ferre   *remote lands*
Of youre two reaumes, graunting to your Noblesse   *realms*
Pees with youre lieges, plentee and gladnesse.

For Mars that is mooste furyous and woode,   *mad*
30   Causer of stryf and desobeyssaunce,   *strife; disobedience*
Shal cesse his malice; and God that is so goode,   *cease*
Of unytee shal sende al souffysaunce.   *unity; satisfaction*
He joyne the hertes of England and of Fraunce,   *hearts*
B'assent of boothe sent to your Hye Noblesse   *By the assent of both*
35   Pees with youre lieges, plentee with gladnesse.

Juno that is goddesse of al tresore,   *treasure*
Sende eeke hir gyftes to your estate royal: *also*
Laude of knighthoode, victorie and honnour,   *Praise*
Ageyns mescreantes in actes marcyal,   *pagans; martial*
40   For Crystes feyth yee enhaunce shal;   *faith*
Repeyre ageyne, and regne in youre Noblesse,   *Return*
Pees with youre lieges, plentee and gladnesse.

And al this whyle Ceres, goddesse of corne,   *grain*
Shal where yee ryde mynistre you victayle;   *wherever; supply you provisions*
45   Provydence, hir sustre, goo byforne   *before*
And provyde, soo that no thing ne fayle;   *nothing is lacking*
Bachus also, that may so miche avayle: *who can help so much*
Alle of acorde present to youre Noblesse   *in agreement*
Pees with youre lieges, plentee with gladnesse.

50   This God, this Goddesse, of entent ful goode,   *with completely good intent*
In goodely wyse also theyre gyftes dresse   *manner; direct*
To yowe, Pryncesse, borne of Saint Lowys blood;   *St. Louis'*
Frome yowe avoyding al sorowe, al hevynesse,   *driving away; sadness*
Frome yeere to yeere in verray sikrenesse;   *in genuine security*
55   To you presenting, yif yowe list adverte,   *if it please you to notice*
Ay by encresse, joye and gladnesse of hert.   *Ever be increased*

They wol theyre gyftes with you and youres dwelle   *wish that*
Peese, unytee, plentee and haboundaunce,
So that Fortune may hem not repelle,   *not drive them away*
60   Ner hem remuwe thorughe hir varyaunce;   *Nor remove them; fickleness*
Graunting also perseveraunt constaunce;   *steadfast constancy*
To you presenting, yif yowe list adverte,
Ay by encresse, joye and gladnesse of hert.

To youre Hyenesse they gif the fresshe olyve,
65 By pees t'exyle awaye al hevynesse;   *to exile*
Prosparytee eeke during al your lyve.
And Juno sent you moost excellent ricchesse,   *riches*
Love of al people, grounded in stablenesse.
With this refrete, yif yowe list adverte,   *donation*
70 Ay by encresse joye and gladnesse of hert.

Ceres also sent foulsomenesse,   *prosperity*
Frome yeere to yeere in your court t'abyde.   *to abide*
Adversyté shal ther noon manase,   *menace no one*
But care and sorrow forever sette asyde,
75 Happe, helthe and grace chosen to be youre guyde.   *Happiness*
And with al this present, yif yee adverte,
Ay beo encresse, joye and gladnesse of hert.

[*L'envoie*   *epilogue*

Prynce excellent, of your benignytee,   *of your grace*
Takethe thees gyftes, sent to your Hye Noblesse,
80 This hyeghe feest frome theos yche three: *exalted; each of these three*
Pees with youre lieges, plentee with gladdnesse,
As Bacus, Juno and Ceres bere witnesse.   *bear*
To you, Pryncesse, also, yif yee adverte,
Ay beo encresse, joye and gladdnesse of hert.

MUMMING AT WINDSOR

[*Nowe folowethe nexst the devyse of a momyng to fore the Kyng Henry the Sixst, being in his Castell of Wyndesore, the fest of his Crystmasse holding ther, made by Lidegate daun John, the Munk of Bury; howe th'ampull and the floure delys (the ampule and the fleur-de-lys) came first to the kynges of Fraunce by myrakle at Reynes (miracle at Reims).*

Mooste noble Prynce of Cristen prynces alle,   *Christian*
To youre Hyeghnesse lat hit beo plesaunce,   *may it be pleasing*
In youre presence men may to mynde calle,   *(that) men may call to mind*
Howe that whylom oure worthy reaume of Fraunce   *formerly; realm*
5   Converted was frome theyre mescreaunce,   *misbelief (i.e., paganism)*
Whane the Lord of Lordes caste a sight   *glance*
Upon youre lande and made His grace alight.

For in the heghe, hevenly consistorye,   *high; court*
Be ful acorde of the Trynitee,   *By*
10 As in cronycles maked is memorye,
The Lord, which is called oon, twoo and thre,
His eyeghe of mercy caste on Cloudovee,   *eye; Clovis*

Shadde His grace of goostely influence　　　　　　　　　　*spiritual*
Towardes that kyng, having his advertence,　　　　　　　　*attention*

15　That he shoulde passe frome paganymes lawe　　　　　　*paganism's*
By prescyence, which that is devyne,　　　　　　*foreknowledge; divine*
His hert al hoolly and himself withdrowe　　　　　　　　　*heart*
Frome his ydooles, and alle hees rytes fyne,　　　　*idols; lavish rituals*
Whane hevenly grace did upon him shyne,
20　By meene oonly and by devoute preyer　　　　　　　　*Indirectly*
Of Saint Cloote, moost goodly and entier.　　　　　*Clotilda; sincere*

Hir hertely love, hir meditacyouns,　　　　　　　　　*heartfelt*
Hir wacche, hir fasting and hir parfyt lyf,　　　　*vigils; perfect*
Hir stedfast hoope, hir hooly orysouns,　　　　　　　*prayers*
25　Hir conversacyoun moost contemplatyf　　　　　*conduct; devout*
Stynt in Fraunce of mawmetrye the stryf,　　　*Stopped; idolatry*
Causing the lawe, moost soverein of vertue　　　*greatest in virtue*
To sprede abroode of oure Lord Jhesu.　　　　　　*far and wide*

Hir meryte caused, and hir parfit entent,　　*miraculous power; pure intent*
30　That Crystes feyth aboute ther did sprede,　　　　　　*faith*
Whane that an aungel was frome heven sent
Unto an hermyte, of parfyt lyf in deed,
Presented it, whooso can take heed;
A shelde of azure, moost soverein by devys,　　*shield; superior by design*
35　And in the feelde of golde three floure delys.　　*fleur-de-lys*

At Joye en Vale, withoute more obstacle,　　　　　*further delay*
Fel at this cas, where th'aungel doune alight,　*It so happened; the angel descended*
A place notable, chosen by myracle,
Which thorughe al Fraunce shadde his bemys light.　　*shed; beams*
40　God of his grace caste on that place a sight,
For to that reaume in passing avauntage　　　*as an excellent addition*
In thilke vale was sette that hermytage.　　*that same valley; established*

Al this came in, whooso list to seen,　　*came about, whoever desires to see*
I dare afferme it withoute any dreed,
45　By parfytnesse of the hooly qweene,　　　　　　*perfection*
Saynte Cloote, floure of wommanheed.　　　　　　*flower*
Whatever she spake, acordant was the deed:
I mene it thus, that worde and werke were oon;
It is no wonder, for wymmen soo beon echoon.　　*all women are like that*

50　Hir hoolynesse Fraunce did enlumyne　　　　　　*illuminate*
And Crystes fayth gretly magnefye.
Loo what grace doothe in wymmen shyne,
Whas assurance noman may denye.　　　　　　*Whose faithfulness*

To seye pleyne trouth nys no flaterye;   *To speak plain truth is*
55   But stabulnesse in wymmen for to fynde,
Deemethe youreself wher it komethe hem of kynde.[1]

For thorughe meeknesse, yif it be adverted,   *noted*
Of Saynte Cloote, and thorugh hir hyeghe prudence,   *high (i.e., great)*
Kyng Cloudovee was to oure feyth converted.
60   In hir ther was so entier diligence,   *such complete*
Fully devoyde of slouthe and necglygence,
Ne stynt nought, til that hir lord hathe take
The feyth of Cryst and his errour forsake.[2]

This made, the kyng that Crystes feyth tooke,   *This having happened*
65   For he was boothe manly and rightwys,   *righteous*
The three crepaudes this noble kyng forsooke,   *heraldic toads*
And in his sheelde he bare thre floure delys,   *bore*
Sent frome heven, a tresore of gret prys;   *treasure; price (i.e., value)*
After at Reynes, the story tellethe thus,   *Rheims*
70   Baptysed lowly of Saint Remigius.   *humbly*

Th'aumpolle of golde a colver brought adoune,   *The ampule; dove*
With which he was, this hooly kyng, ennoynt.   *anointed*
Gret prees ther was stonding envyroun,   *crowd; all around*
For to beholde the kyng frome poynt to poynt.   *head to toe*
75   For where as he stoode, in gret desjoynt,   *distress*
First a paynyme, by baptyme anoon right   *pagan; immediately*
Was so converted, and bekame Crystes knight.

At Reynes yit that hooly unccyoun   *still; oil*
Conserved is for a remembraunce,   *Preserved*
80   And of coustume, by revolucyoun   *custom; revelation*
Of God provyded, with due observaunce,   *By; reverence*
T'annoynte of coustume kynges wheeche in Fraunce
Joustely succeede, the story doothe us leere;[3]
Of which Sixst Henry, that nowe sittethe here,

85   Right soone shal, with Goddes hooly grace,
As he is borne by successyoun,   *next in hereditary succession*
Be weel resceyved in the same place   *well*
And by vertu of that unccyoun,   *power*

---

[1] Lines 55–56: *But as for finding steadfastness in women, / Decide for yourself whether it comes to them by nature*

[2] Lines 62–63: *She did not relent until her lord (i.e., Clovis) had adopted / Christianity and had forsaken the error of his ways*

[3] *Legitimately succeed to the throne, as the story teaches us*

Atteyne in knighthoode unto ful hye renoun
90   Resceyve his coroune, he and his successours,   *Receive; crown*
        By tytle of right, lyche hees progenytours.   *like his forefathers*

        Nowe, Royal Braunche, O Blood of Saint Lowys,   *Descendant; St. Louis*
        So lyke it nowe to thy Magnyfycence,   *So may it please*
        That the story of the flour delys
95   May here be shewed in thyne heghe presence,
        And that thy noble, royal Excellence
        Lyst to supporte, here sitting in thy see,   *Allow; on your throne*
        Right as it fell this myracle to see.   *To see this miracle just as it happened*

MUMMING FOR THE GOLDSMITHS OF LONDON

[*And nowe filowethe a lettre made in wyse of (in the style of) balade by Ledegate Daun Johan,
of a mommynge, whiche the goldesmythes of the Cité of London mommed in right fresshe and
costelé (costly) Welych (Strange) desguysings to theyre Mayre Eestfeld, upon Candelmasse day
at nyght, after souper; brought and presented unto the Mayre by an heraude cleped (herald
called) Fortune.*

        That worthy David, which that sloughe Golye,   *who slew Goliath*
        The first kyng that sprang oute of Jesse,
        Of God echosen, the bookes specefye,   *specify*
        By Samuel sette in his royal see,   *throne*
5   With twelve trybus is comen to this citee,   *tribes is come*
        Brought royal gyftes, kyngly him t'aquyte,   *to acquit himself in kingly fashion*
        The noble Mayre to seen and to vysyte.   *Mayor; see and visit*

        The first trybe, the Byble cane well telle,
        Is called Juda, the hardy, strong lyoun.   *lion*
10   Fro whos kynrede — for hit did excelle —   *From whose kindred; it*
        Cryst lyneally he came adowne,
        Which lyche David was the chaumpyoun   *Who like*
        That sloughe the tyraunt, to gete himself a prysse,   *win himself a prize*
        Man to restore ageyne to Paradys.   *again*

15   This noble David, moost mighty and moost goode,
        Is nowe descended in his estate royal,
        With alle the trybus of Jacobus blood,   *Jacob's*
        For to presenten in especial   *present especially*
        Gyftes that beon bothe hevenly and moral,   *are*
20   Apperteyning unto good gouvernaunce,   *Pertaining to*
        Unto the Mayre for to doo pleasaunce.   *Mayor; to bring pleasure*

        Frome his cytee of Jherusalem
        He is come doune of humble wille and thought;

	The arke of God, bright as the sonne beeme,	*sun's beam*
25	Into this toune he hathe goodely brought,	*town*
	Which designethe, if hit be wel sought,	*signifies*
	Grace and good eure and long prosperitee	*fortune*
	Perpetuelly to byde in this cytee.	*abide*

	O yee Levytes, which bere this lordes arke,	*Levites, who carry this lord's*
30	Doothe youre devoyre with hevenly armonye	*Do your duty; harmony*
	The gret mysterye devoutly for to marke,	
	With laude and prys the Lord to magnefye;	*praise*
	Of oon acorde shewethe your melodye,	*one; show*
	Syngethe for joye, that the arke is sent	*Sing*
35	Nowe to the Mayre with hoole and truwe entent.	*complete and true*

	Whylome this arke, abyding in the hous	*Formerly*
	Of Ebdomadon, brought in ful gret joye;	
	For in effect it was more gracyous	
	Thanne ever was Palladyone of Troye.	
40	Hit did gret gladnesse and hit did accoye	*soothe*
	Thinges contrarye and all adversytee.	
	Th'effect therof, whane David did see,	

	And fully knewe, howe God list for to blesse,	*was wont to*
	Thorughe his vertu and his mighty grace,	
45	That of gladdnesse they might nothing mysse	
	Wher hit aboode any maner spaace,	*for any length of time*
	God of his might halowed so the place.	
	Wherfore Kyng David, by gret devocion,	*great*
	Maade of this ark a feyre translacion	*fair transfer*

50	Into his hous and his palays royal,	
	Brought by the Levytes with gret solempnytee.	
	And he himself in especyal	
	Daunsed and sang of gret humylyté,	*Danced*
	And ful devoutely left his ryaltee,	*kingdom*
55	With ephod gyrt, lyche preestis of the lawe,	*Girdled with an ephod, like priests*
	To gyf ensaumple howe pryde shoulde be withdrawe	*give an example of how*

	In yche estate, who list the trouth serche,	*each; whoever wishes to; seek out*
	And to exclude al veyne ambycyoun,	*vain ambition*
	Specyally fro mynistres of the Chirche,	*Especially from ministers*
60	To whome it longethe by devocyoun,	*Whose duty it is*
	To serve God with hool defeccyoun	*complete selflessness*
	And afforne him mynistre in clennesse,	*before*
	B'ensaumple of David for al his worthynesse.	*By example*

Nowe ryse up, Lord, into thy resting place,
65 Aark of thyne hooly halowed mansyoun,
Thou aark of wisdome, of vertu and of grace,
Keepe and defende in thy proteccion
The Meyre, the citeseyns, the comunes of this toune,   *commons; town*
Called in cronycles whylome Nuwe Troye,   *chronicles; New Troy*
70 Graunte hem plenté, vertu, honnour and joye.

And for that meeknesse is a vertu feyre,   *And since*
Worthy David, with kyngly excellence,
In goodely wyse hath made his repayre,   *proper style; journey*
O noble Mayre, unto youre presence,
75 And to youre Hyeghnesse with freondly dilygence   *friendly*
This presande brought, oonly for the best,   *present*
Perpetuelly this toune to sette at rest,

Of purpoose put this aark to youre depoos,[1]
With good entent, to make youre hert light;
80 And thoo three thinges, which therinne beo cloos,   *those; enclosed*
Shal gif to yowe konnyng, grace, and might,   *knowledge*
For to gouverne with wisdome, pees, and right   *peace*
This noble cytee, and lawes suche ordeyne,   *city*
That no man shal have cause for to compleyne.   *complain*

85 A wrytt withinn shal unto you declare   *writ*
And in effect pleynly specefye,   *plainly specify*
Where yee shal punysshe and where as yee shal spare,
And howe that mercy shal rygour modefye.   *strict justice*
And youre estate also to magnefye,
90 This aark of God, to make you gracyous,
Shal stille abyde with you in youre hous.   *always*

For whyles it bydethe stille in youre presence,   *while it stays*
The hyeghe Lord shal blesse boothe yowe and youres,   *high*
Of grace, of fortune sende yowe influence
95 And of vertue alle the fresshe floures;   *flowers*
And of adversytee voyde awey the shoures,   *drive away the storms*
Sette pees and rest, welfare and unytee   *peace; unity*
Duryng youre tyme thorougheoute this cytee.   *throughout*

---

[1] *Intentionally delivered this ark into your keeping*

MUMMING FOR THE MERCERS OF LONDON

[And now filowethe a lettre made in wyse of balade by Daun Iohan, brought by a poursuyvaunt (messenger) in wyse of (in the style of) mommers desguysed to fore the Mayre of London, Eestfeld, upon the twelfethe night of Cristmasse, ordeyned ryallych by the worthy merciers, citeseyns of London.

	Moost mighty Lord, Jubyter the Greet,	*Jupiter the Great*
	Whos mansyoun is over the sonnes beem,	*sun's beam*
	Frome thens that Phebus with his fervent heet	*thence; heat*
	Reflectethe his light upon the swyft streeme	
5	Of Ewfratees towardes Jerusalem,	*the Euphrates River*
	Doune coosteying, as bookys maken mynde,	*Passing along the border; remind*
	By Lubyes landes, thorughe Ethyope and Ynde;	*Libya's; India*
	Conveyed doune, where Mars in Cyrrea	
	Hathe bylt his paleys upon the sondes rede,	*palace*
10	And she, Venus, called Cytherrea,	
	On Parnaso, with Pallas ful of drede;	
	And Parseus with his furyous steede	
	Smote on the roche where the Muses dwelle,	*Struck; rock*
	Til ther sprange up al sodeynly a welle,	*suddenly*
15	Called the welle of Calyope,	
	Mooste auctorysed amonges thees Cyryens;	*honored*
	Of which the poetes that dwelle in that cuntree.	*country*
	And other famous rethorycyens,	*rhetoricians*
	And they that cleped beon musycyens,	*who are called*
20	Ar wont to drynk of that hoolsome welle,	
	Which that alle other in vertu doothe excelle;	
	Where Bachus dwellethe besydes the ryver	
	Of ryche Thagus, the gravellys alle of gold,	*sands*
	Which gyvethe a light agens the sonne cleer,	
25	So fresshe, so sheene, that hit may not beo tolde;	*bright*
	Where Bellona hathe bylt a stately hoolde,	*castle*
	In al this worlde, I trowe, ther is noon lyche,	
	Of harde magnetis and dyamandes ryche:	*lodestones and diamonds*
	And of that welle drank some tyme Tulius	
30	And Macrobye, ful famous of prudence;	
	Ovyde also, and eeke Virgilius,	
	And Fraunceys Petrark, myrour of eloquence;	*mirror*
	Johan Bocas also, flouring in sapyence.	*flourishing in wisdom*
	Thoroughe that sugred bawme aureate	*sweet aureate balm*
35	They called weren poetes laureate.	

Oute of Surrye, by many straunge stronde,   *Syria; exotic shores*
This Jubiter hathe his lettres sent,
Thoroughe oute Europe, where he did lande,
And frome the heven came doune of entent,
40   To ravisshe shortly in sentement   *in short*
Fayre Europe, mooste renommed of fame,   *renowned*
After whame yit al Europe berethe the name.   *whom still*

And thorughe Egypte his poursuyant is comme,   *messenger*
Doune descendid by the Rede See,
45   And hathe also his right wey ynomme   *made his way*
Thoroughe valeye of the Drye Tree
By Flomme Jordan, coosteying the cuntree,   *River Jordan*
Where Jacob passed whylome with his staff,   *once*
Taking his shippe, to seylen at poort Jaff.   *sail*

50   And so forthe downe his journey can devyse,
In Aquarye whane Phebus shoon ful sheene,
Forthe by passing the gret gulf of Venyse;   *Venice*
And sayled forthe soo al the ryver of Geene;   *Genoa*
In which see regnethe the mighty qweene,
55   Called Cyrses, goddesse of waters salte,
Where nymphes syng, hir honnour to exalte.

And ther he saughe, as he gan approche,   *saw*
Withinne a boote a fissher drawe his nette   *boat*
On the right syde of a crystal rooche;   *rock*
60   Fisshe was ther noon, for the draught was lette.[1]
And on th'oon syde ther were lettres sette
That sayde in Frenshe this raysoun: *Grande travayle*;   *this reason: Great effort*
This aunswere nexst in ordre: *Nulle avayle*.   *Nothing avails*

Thanne seyling forthe bysyde many a rokk,   *sailing*
65   He gane ful fast for to haaste him doune
Thoroughe the daunger and streytes of Marrokk,   *straits of Gibraltar*
Passing the parayllous currant of Arragoun;   *perilous; Aragon (i.e., Spain)*
So foorthe by Spaygne goyng envyroun,   *Spain; around*
Thorougheout the Raas and rokkes of Bretaygne,   *Brittany*
70   The Brettyssshe See til that he did atteyne   *English Channel*

Thoroughe thilk sakk, called of Poortland;   *Portland*
And towardes Caleys holding his passage,   *Calais*
Left Godwyn sandes, by grace of Goddes hand —
Havyng his wynde to his avauntage,

---

[1] *There were no fish, since the drawing of the net was hindered*

75   The weder cleer, the stormes left hir raage —   *weather*
          Entryng the see of Brutes Albyon,
          Nowe called Themse thoroughe al this regyon.   *Thames [River]*

          And in a feeld, that droughe in to the eest,   *that lay towards*
          Besyde an ylande, he saughe a shippe unlade   *island; unloaded*
80   Which hade sayled ful fer towarde the West;

          The caban peynted with floures fresshe and glaade,   *delightful*
          And lettres Frenshe, that feynt nyl ne faade: *did not dim or fade*
          Taunt haut e bas que homme soyt,
          Touz ioures regracyer dieux doyt.[1]

85   And in a boote on that other syde   *boat*
          Another fissher droughe his nette also,   *drew*
          Ful of gret fisshe (Neptunus was his guyde),
          With so gret plentee, he nyst what til do.   *did not know what to do*
          And ther were lettres enbrouded not fer froo,   *embroidered nearby*
90   Ful fresshly wryten this worde: *grande peyne*;   *great pain*
          And cloos acording with this resoun: *grande gayne.*[2]

          The noble yllande, where he saughe this sight,   *island*
          Gaf unto him a demonstracion,
          Taught him also by the poolys light,   *the pole's (i.e., lodestar's) light*
95   He was not fer frome Londones towne.
          And with a floode the pursuyaunt came downe,
          Left the water, and at Thems stronde,   *Thames' shore*
          With owte aboode, in haaste he came to lande,   *delay*

          Where certayne vesselles nowe by the anker ryde.   *anchor*
100   Hem to refresshe and to taken ayr,   *To refresh themselves*
          Certein estates, wheche purveye and provyde
          For to vysyte and seen the noble Mayr   *visit*
          Of this cytee and maken theyre repayr   *make their way*
          To his presence, or that they firther flitte,   *before they go further*
105   Under supporte, that he wol hem admytte.   *With his permission; will admit them*

OF THE SODEIN FAL OF PRINCES IN OURE DAYES

[*Here folowen seven balades made by Daun John Lydegate of the sodeine fal of certain Princes of Fraunce and Englande nowe late in oure dayes.*

---

[1] Lines 83–84: *However high or low a man may be, / He should always be grateful to God*

[2] *And closely linked with this phrase: great gain*

Beholde this gret prynce Edwarde the Secounde,
Which of divers landes lord was and kyng,
But so governed was he, nowe, understonde,
By suche as caused foule his undoying,   *wickedly*
5   For trewly to telle yowe withoute lesing,   *lying*
He was deposed by al the rewmes assent,   *realm's*
In prisoun murdred with a broche in his foundament.   *poker; rectum*

Se howe Richard, of Albyon the kyng,
Which in his tyme ryche and glorious was,
10   Sacred with abyt, with corone, and with ring,   *habit*
Yit fel his fortune so, and eke his cas,   *fate*
That yvel counseyle rewled him so, elas!
For mystreting lordes of his monarchye,
He feyne was to resigne and in prysone dye.   *was obliged to*

15   Lo Charles, of noble Fraunce the kyng,
Taken with seknesse and maladye,
Which left him never unto his eonding,   *death*
Were it of nature or by sorcerye,
Unable he was for to governe or guye   *guide*
20   His reaume, which caused such discencyon,   *realm; strife*
That fallen it is to gret destruccion.

So nowe this lusty Duc of Orlyaunce,
Which floured in Parys in chivallerie,   *flourished*
Brother to Charles, the kyng of Fraunce:
25   His yong hert thought never to dye,
But for he used the synne of lecherye,   *sin*
His cosin to assent was ful fayene,   *glad*
That he in Parys was murdred and foule slayne.

Of Edward the Thridde Thomas his sone,
30   Of Gloucestre Duc, Constable of England,
Which to love trouth was ever his wone,   *custom*
Yet notwithstonding his entent of trouthe,
He murdred was at Caleys, that was routhe,   *a pity*
And he to God and man moste acceptable,
35   And to the comune profit moste favorable.

Lo here this Eorlle and Duc of Burgoyne bothe,
Oon of the douspiers and deen of Fraunce,   *One; twelve peers; dean*
Howe fortune gan his prosparité to loothe,
And made him putte his lyf in suche balance   *life*
40   That him n'avayled kyn nor allyaunce,   *That neither kinfolk nor alliances could help him*
That for his mourder he mortherd was and slayne,   *(i.e., of Louis, duke of Orléans)*
Of whos deth th'Ermynakes were fayne.   *the Armagnacs; happy*

This Duc of Yrland, of England Chaumburleyn.
Which in plesaunce so he ledde his lyf,   *pleasure*
45   Tyl fortune of his welth hade disdeyn,
That causeles he parted was frome his wyf,   *without just cause*
Which grounde was of gret debate and stryf,   *Which was ground for*
And his destruccion, if I shal not lye,
For banned he was, and did in meschef dye.   *affliction*

PAGEANT OF KNOWLEDGE

[*Septem sunt gradus magnatum.*   *There are seven levels of magnates*

Thys world ys born up by astates sevyn,   *seven estates*
Prynces ordeynyd to susteyn the ryght,
Prestes to pray, the justyces to deme evyn,   *judge impartially*
Marchauntes in sellyng to do trouthe in weyght,   *weigh honestly*
5   For comon profyte fyghte shal the knyght,   *common profit*
Plowman in tylthe, the laborer in travayll.   *tilling*
Artyfycers diligent day and nyght.   *Craftsmen*
The ryche her almes to parte with the porayll.   *their; share with the poor*

[*Officia dictorum magnatum.*   *Duties of the said magnates*

Pryncys. To us longeth prestys to governe,   *belongs [the right]*
10   **Presthode**. And we be bounde to lyve in parfytnes.   *perfection*
Juges. Betwene ryght and wrong our office doth dyscerne.
Merchantes. In bying and sellyng we shall do no falsnes.
Knyghthode. We shull defende trouthe and ryghtwysnes.   *righteousness*
Plowman. Our occupacion to tyll and sowe the lond,
15   **Werkemen**. And by our labour we voyden idylnes.   *avoid*
Rycheman. We delyver our almes with our hond.   *hand*

[*Explicit.*

[*Septem Pagine sequntur sapiencie.*   *Here follow seven pageants on wisdom*

[*Prima de Prudencia.*   *The first is about Prudence*

Thynges passyd remembre and well dyvyde,   *past*
Thynges present consider and well governe,
For thynges commyng prudently provyde,
20   Peyse matyrs or thou deme or dyscerne,   *Ponder matters before you judge*
Lat right in causes holde the lantern,
Twene frende and foo stond evyn, and be egall,   *Between; foe*
And for no mede be nat parciall.   *reward (i.e., bribe)*

[*Secunda de Justicia.*   *The second is about Justice*

Furst in thy mesure loke ther be no lak,   *look; lack*
25   Of thy weyghtes hold justly the balaunce,
Be trew in rekenyng, set no som abak,   *Be honest in accounting; sum*
And in thy worde lat be no variaunce;
Of chere be sad, demure of governaunce,   *demeanor; serious*
Set folk at rest, and apese all trouble,   *appease*
30   Beware of flaterers and of tongys double.

[*Tercia de Temperancia.*   *The third is about Temperance*

By sapience tempre thou thy corage,   *desire*
Of hasty ire daunt the passion;
Dyfer vengeance tyll thy wrathe aswage,   *Defer; anger passes*
Reverence the good for theyr condicion;
35   Punyssh pacyently the transgression
Of men disrewlyd, redressyng errour,   *disobedient*
Mercy preferryng or thou do rygour.   *before you act harshly*

[*Quarta de Discrecione.*   *The fourth is about Discretion*

Discrecion, modyr and pryncesse,   *mother*
Of all vertues to governe hem and gye,   *them; guide*
40   And elumyneth with lyght of hygh noblesse   *illuminate*
Crownes of kynges, hold up theyr regaly,   *sovereignty*
Conserveth reames, by prudent polycy,   *realms*
Causeth provinces and every gret cyté
To contynew in long prosperyté.

[*Quinta de Racione.*   *The fifth is about Reason*

45   Thys emperesse, verrey celestiall,   *truly*
Most aungelyk of contenaunce and chere,   *manner*
To rewle man he be nat bestiall,
God gave hym reson, hys owne doughter dere,
Princesse of princesses, most sovereyn and entere,   *perfect*
50   To brydell in man the froward volunté   *bridle; willful desire*
That he not err by sensualyté.

[*Sexta de Placencia et Bona Voluntate.*[1]

Thys fayre lady, whyche callyd ys Plesaunce,
And eke Good Wyll, her owne doughter dere,

---

[1] *The sixth is about Happiness and Good Will*

	Beseke all folk, aftyr theyr suffysaunce,	*according to their ability*
55	With all theyr hert, to make ryght good chere,	
	With suche disport as they fynden here,	
	And that hem lyst benygnely advertyse,	*graciously show*
	Who that ys welcom hathe all that may suffyse.	

[*Septima de Fasetia et Nurturia.*   *The seventh is about Courtesy and Nurture*

	Thys goodly lady callyd Curtesy,	
60	And her sustyr, whos name ys Nurture,	*sister*
	By theyr offyce longyng to gentry	*belonging*
	Lowly requyryd to every creature,	
	As ferre as myght and power may endure,	*far*
	With hoole herte, body, wyll, and mynde,	
65	To be content with suche as they here fynde.	

[*Explicit.*

[*The fynders of the sevyn Sciences artificiall.*   *inventors*

	Jubal was fadyr and fynder of song,	*father; inventor*
	Of consonantes, and of armony,	*harmony*
	By noyse and strooke of hamors that were strong.	*hammers*
	Fro Jubal came furst the melody	
70	Of sugryd musyk, and of mynstralsy,	
	So procedyng down fro man to man	*from*
	Practyke of concorde, as I have told, began.	*Craft of harmony*

[*Saturne.*

	Saturne taught furst the tylthe of londe,	*cultivation*
	Hys doughter Ceres made men ere and sowe.	*plow*
75	The goldyn worde he compassyd with his honde,	*world (i.e., of the golden age)*
	Of sede and grayne the difference to knowe,	*seed*
	Of trees, herbes, growyng hygh and lowe;	
	Somer seson, there bawme above moste swote,	*balm; sweet*
	And in cold wynter ther vertu in the rote.	*root*

[*Mars.*

80	Though myghty Mars be callyd god of werres,	*wars*
	Prudent Pallas founde out furst armure,	*discovered; armor*
	Thys godde, thys goddes, syt among the sterres,	*stars*
	Tubalcaym of stele founde the temprure,	*steel; temper*
	Forgyd plates, longe to endure,	
85	And thus these thre, by marciall apparayll,	*martial*
	Be callyd in bokes patrones of batayll.	*battle*

[*Minerva.*

	Crafte of wolles and of cloth wevyng	*wool*
	Found Minerva, of spynnyng chief goddesse;	
	And Delbora of lynen clothe makyng	
90	The practyke sought, bokes bere wytnesse;	*method; books*
	In all suche craft was a chief masteresse;	
	But Semiranus, as bokes specyfy,	
	Fonde out furst breche, myn auctor lyst nat ly.	*breeches; my source doesn't lie*

[*Diana.*

	Lo, here Diana, princesse of venery,	*hunting*
95	In forest walkyng lyke an hunteresse,	
	Havyng her paleyce ferre above the sky,	*palace far*
	Callyd Lucina there shewyng her bryghtnes,	
	Of huntyng, hawkyng, fysshyng, chefe goddesse,	*chief*
	Every moneth her cours she dothe renew,	*month*
100	Now full, now wane, now bryght, now pale of hewe.	*hue*

[*Mercurius.*

	Mercury, callyd for mannys gret avayle	*man's great help*
	God of eloquence, and merchandyse;	
	Argon fond furst craft of shyp and sayle,	*discovered; sail*
	And Neptunus the saylyng gan devyse	*began to design*
105	To passe the see, in many sondry wyse,	*sea; different ways*
	Whyche to merchauntes ys full necessary,	
	Theyre stuff, theyr bales, fro londe to londe to cary.	*from*

[*Phebus.*

	Phebus fond furst craft of medicine,	
	By touche of pounce veyne, and inspeccions.	*artery (see note); examinations*
110	Esculapius taught the doctrine	
	To knowe the qualytees of foure compleccions,	
	Of letuaryes, drogges, and pocions;	*medicines*
	And among all there ys nothyng more mete	*fitting*
	To helthe of man then temperat diete.	*health*

[*Explicit.*

[*The sevyn sciences callyd lyberall.*

	Of sevyn sciences, callyd lyberall,	
115	Gramer techeth congruité and wrytyng,	*correctness*
	Philosophy in especiall	

Telleth natures of every maner thyng,
Ars metryk craft of proporcionyng,   *Arithmetic*
120 Musyk concord, rethoryk eloquence,
Astronomy by diurnall mevyng   *daily movement*
The world governeth, by hevenly influence.

[*Auctors of sevyn sciences.*

Auctor of gramer was whilom Precian,   *grammar*
Ewclyd excellyd in craft of geometry,   *Euclid*
125 Tully in rethoryk was a famous man,
Hermogines fadyr of phylosophy,
Boys wrote of musyk and of melody,   *Boethius*
Of methephysyk wrote Aristotyles,   *metaphysics*
Albimazar of astronomy,
130 Founders of sciences and vertuos encrese.   *beneficial knowledge*

[*Explicit.*

[*The Dysposicion of the sevyn planettes.*

Saturne disposeth a man to melancoly,
Jubiter reyseth man to gret nobles,   *raises; nobility*
And sturdy Mars to stryfe, were, and envy,   *war*
Phebus to wysdom and to hygh prowes,
135 Mercurius to be changeable and dowbylnes,   *deceitfulness*
The moone mutable, now glad, and now drypyng,   *misty (dripping)*
And gere Venus, full of new fangylnes,   *fickle; changeability*
Makyn men unstable here in her lyvyng.

[*Explicit.*

[*The dysposicion of the twelve sygnes.*   *signs [of the zodiac]*

Aries ys hoot, and also coleryk   *hot; quick-tempered*
140 And in the hede kepeth hys dominacion;
Taurus in the throte, be man hoole or seke,   *healthy or sick*
That part hath he in supportacion;
Geminus eke by revelucion   *revolution*
Hathe in armes hys influence and werkyng,
145 How shuld a man than be stedfast of lyvyng?

Cancer hathe the brest in hys demayne,   *domain*
Of the hert lordshyp hathe the Lyon,   *Lion (i.e., Leo)*
Virgo the governaunce hathe of twayne,
Of novell and wombe, and Libra lower downe.   *navel*
150 The membres of man governeth the Scorpioun,

By thys reson the philsofyrs seyng
Ys that man cannat be stedfast in lyvyng.

Of all the sygnes rekenyd here toforn,
The thyes of man governeth the Sagyttary   *thighs; Sagittarius*
155   And knees and legges hathe the Capricorn,
Eke the calfe downeward perteyneth to Aquary   *Aquarius*
And fro the feete, I wyll nat longer tary,
Piscis hath theym in hys kepyng;   *Pisces*
Howe shuld a man than be stedefast of lyvyng?

[*Explicit.*

[*The disposicion of the foure elementes.*

160   The world so wyde, the ayre so remevable,   *changeable*
The sely man so lytell of stature,   *virtuous*
The greve and the ground of clothyng so mutable,
The fyre so hote and subtyle of nature,
Watyr never in oon, what creature   *constant*
165   Made of these foure, whyche be so flyttyng   *changeable*
May stable be, here in hyr lyvyng?

Man of the erthe hathe slouthe and hevynes,   *sloth*
Flux and reflux by water made unstable,   *instability [of human nature]*
Kyndely of ayre he hath also swetnes,   *Thanks to air*
170   Be fyre made hasty, wode, and not tretable;   *fire; mad; reasonable*
To erthe agene, by processe comparable
Selde or never in oon poynt abydyng,   *Seldom*
Howe shuld he than be stable in lyvyng?   *then*

Fyre resolveth erthe to be watery,   *earth*
175   And watery thynges fyre turneth in eyre,   *fiery; air*
Maketh harde thynges nesshe, and fyre eke naturally   *soft*
Maketh nesshe thynges harde by his soden repeyr,   *sudden return*
Though harde he ys that shone bryght and feyre,
Whyche element hathe in man gret workyng,
180   How shuld he than be stable in lyvyng?

Ayre of kynde geveth inspiracion   *Air by nature gives breath*
To mannys hert thyng most temperatyf,   *man's heart; beneficent*
And kyndly hete geveth respiracion,   *natural heat*
Of subtyll, rare, and a gret medegatyf,   *palliative*
185   To tempre the spyrytes by vertew vegetatyf;   *by promoting vigor*
And syth that ayre in man ys thus mevyng,   *since; at work*
How shuld he than be stedfast of lyvyng?

Watyr somwhyle ys congeyled to crystall, *sometimes; ice*
Colde and moyst as of hys nature,
190 Now ebbeth, now floweth, whyche in speciall
The myght of the mone dothe her course recure, *moon; regain*
And syth thys element by recorde of scripture,
Ys oon of the foure compact of our makyng, *one; elements*
I wold enquere, what maner creature,
195 Made of these foure, were stedfast of lyvyng?

[*Explicit.*

[*The disposicion of the foure complexyons.*

The sanguyne man of blood hathe hardynes,
Wrought to be lovyng, large of dyspence, *generous in spending*
The fleumatyk man slow, oppressyd with dulnes, *phlegmatic*
Whyte of vysage, rude of elloquence,
200 And syth ther ys in man suche difference,
By complexions diversely workyng,
Answere herto, concludyng thys sentence,
How that man myght be stedfast of lyvyng.

The coleryk man, subtyle and dyssevable, *choleric; cunning; deceitful*
205 Sclender, lene, and cytryne of hys colour, *Slender, lean, and yellowish*
Wrothe sodenly, wood, and nat tretable, *Becomes angry*
And full of envy, malyce, and rancour,
Dry, thursty, and gret wastour, *spendthrift*
Dysposyd to many a sondry thyng,
210 With pompe and bost hasty to do rygour, *boast; act harshly*
Ben soche men stable here in theyr lyvyng? *such*

Melancolyk of hys complexioun,
Dysposyd of kynde for to be fraudulent, *Predisposed by nature*
Malicious, froward, and be decepcioun *unruly; by*
215 Forgyng discordes, double of hys entent; *deceitful in his intent*
Whyche thynges peysyd by good avysement, *considered thoughtfully*
I dar conclude, as to my felyng, *in my opinion*
By confirmacion as in sentement, *in effect*
Few men byn here stabyll in her lyvng. *their*

[*Explicit.*

[*The dysposicion of the foure tymes of the yere.*

220 Man hath in somer drynesse and hete, *heat*
In theyr bok as auctors lyst expresse, *as authors say*
And when Phebus entreth the Ariete *enters Aries (i.e., March to April)*

	Dygest humours upward done hem dresse,	*Digestive*
	Porys opyn that seson, of swetnesse	*Pores open*
225	And exaltacions, diverse wyrkyng,	*giving off of heat*
	How shuld man than be stable in lyvyng?	

	Autumpne to Veer foundyn ys contrary,	*Spring exists in opposition*
	As Galien seyth in all hys qualytees,	
	Disposyng a man that season to vary,	
230	To many uncouthe straunge infirmitees,	
	Of canyculer dayes takyng the propertees,	*dog days (July to September)*
	By revelacion of manyfold changyng,	
	How shuld man than be stable in lyvyng?	

	Man hathe in wynter in this present lyfe,	
235	By disposicion, colde and humylyté,	
	Whyche season ys to fleume nurtrytyfe,	*productive of phlegm*
	Spoyleth herbe and tre of ther fresshe beauté,	
	Closeth, constreyneth, the poores, men may se,	*pores*
	Causeth kyndly hete, inwarde to be wyrkyng,	*natural heat*
240	How shuld man then be stable in lyvyng?	

	By Veere man hathe hete and eke moystour,	*moisture*
	Atwene bothe a maner of temperaunce,	*Between; moderation*
	On whyche tweyne gret lust he doth recover,	
	Yef colde not put hym in dystemperaunce.	*out of balance*
245	Thus meynt with drede ys mannys governance,	*kept in uncertainty is man's*
	Ay in no certeyn, by recorde of wrytyng,	
	Howe shuld he than be stable in lyvyng?	

[*Explicit.*

[*The Dysposicion of the World.*

	The monthes vary, everyche hath his sygne	*[zodiacal] sign*
	And harde hit ys all wedyrs for to know,	*weather*
250	The tyme somewhyle ys gracious and benygne,	
	And uppon hilles and valeys that ben low	
	The foure wyndes contrariosly do blow	
	In every storme man ys here abydyng,	
	Som to release, and som to overthrow,	
255	How shuld man than be stedfast of lyvyng?	

	The worldly answer, fortune transmutable,	
	Trust of lordshyp a feynt sekernes,	*futile security*
	Every seson varyeth, frendshyp ys unstable,	
	Now myrthe, now sorow, now hele, now sekenes,	*health; sickness*
260	Now ebbe of povert, now flodys of ryches,	*poverty; floods*

All stont in chaunge, now losse, now wynnyng,   *stands*
Tempest in see and wyndes sturdynes
Maketh men unstable and ferefull of lyvyng.

Tytan somwhyle fresshly dothe appere,   *Titan (i.e., the sun)*
265 Then commeth a storme and doth hys lyght deface,
The soile of somer with floures glad of chere
Wynters rasure dothe all awey rase;   *erasure*
All erthely thynges sodenly do passe
Whyche may have here no seker abydyng,   *certain*
270 Eke all astates false fortune doth manase,   *menace*
How shuld a man than be stedfast of lyvyng?

Beholde and see the transmutacion,
Howe the seson of grene lusty age,
Force of Juventus, strong, hardy as a lyoun,   *(i.e., Youth), strong*
275 Tyme of manhode, wysdom, sad of corage,   *sober of heart*
And howe Decrepitus turnyth to dotage,
Cast all in a balance, and forgete nothyng,
And thow shalt fynd this lyfe a pylgremage,
In whyche ther ys no stedfast abydyng.

280 Then lyft up thyne ey unto the hevyn,
And pray thy Lord, whyche ys eternall,
That syt so ferr above the sterres sevyn,   *far*
In his palace most imperyall,
To graunt thee grace, here in thys lyfe mortall,
285 Contricion, shryft, and howsyll at thy departyng,   *good luck*
And, er thou passe hense, remyssion finall   *hence; forgiveness of sin*
Towarde the lyfe, where joy ys everlasting.

[*Amen.*

[*Explicit.*

A Procession of Corpus Christi

[*And now here folowethe an ordenaunce of a precessyoun of the feste of Corpus Cristi made in London by daun John Lydegate.*

This hye feste nowe for to magnefye,   *holy feast; celebrate*
Feste of festes moost hevenly and devyne,
In goostly gladnesse to governe us and guye,   *spiritual; guide*
By which al grace doothe uppon us shyne;
5 For now this day al derkenesse t'enlumyne,   *to illuminate*
In youre presence fette out of fygure,   *fashioned out of likenesses*

	Schal beo declared by many unkouthe signe	*strange signs*
	Gracyous misteryes grounded in scripture.	
	First, that this feste may more beo magnefyed,	
10	Seothe and considerthe in youre ymaginatyf	*mind's eye*
	For Adams synne how Cryst was crucefyed	
	Uppon a crosse, to stinten al oure stryf.	*to end*
	Fruyt celestyal hong on the tree of lyf,	
	The fruyt of fruytes, for shorte conclusyoun,	
15	Oure helpe, oure foode, and oure restoratyf	
	And cheef repaste of oure redempcioun.	
	Remembrethe eeke in youre inwarde entente	*thoughts*
	Melchysedec, that offred bred and wyne,	
	In fygure oonly of the sacrament,	
20	Steyned in Bosra, on Calvarye made red,	*Dyed*
	On Sherthorsday tofore er he was ded,	*Maundy Thursday*
	For memoryal mooste sovereyne and goode,	
	Gaf hees appostels, takethe hereof goode heed,	*take special note of this*
	His blessid body and his precyous bloode.	
25	Chosen of God this patryarch Abraham,	
	Example pleyne of hospitalytee,	
	Recorde I take, whan that the aungel came	*I make mention of*
	To his housholde, wheeche were in noumbre three,	
	In figure oonly of the Trynyté,	
30	Sette to hem brede with ful gladde chere,	
	Of gret counforte, a token who list see,	
	The sacrament that stondethe on the awter.	*altar*
	To Yssake God list His grace shewe	*chose to show His grace*
	Lyneally adowne frome that partye,	
35	In eorthes fatnesse, and in hevenly dewe	
	Frome the Olly Gooste descending to Marye;	*the Holy Ghost*
	That braunche of Gesse God list to glorefye,	*Jesse*
	This Roos of Jherico fresshest on lyve,	*Rose; alive*
	Blest among wymmen, Luc doothe specefye,	*[the apostle] Luke*
40	Whos name is fygurde here with lettres fyve.	
	Jacob saughe aungels goyng up and doune	*saw*
	Uppon a laddre, he sleeping certeyne	
	Lowe on a stoone for recreacyoun,	
	The whete glene crowned above the greyne,	
45	Forged of golde an Hoost thereinne eseyne;	*Host (i.e., eucharistic wafer); seen*
	This Crystes bred, delicyous unto kynges,	
	With goostly gladnesse, gracious and sovereyne,	*spiritual*
	Gayve forreyne damage of alle eorthely thinges.	*public compensation for*

	This noble duc, this prudent Moyses,	*Moses*
50	With goldin hornes lyche Phebus beemys bright,	*like Phebus' (i.e., the sun's) beams*
	His arche so ryche, his vyole for t'encresce,	*ark*
	With the manna to make oure hertes light;	*hearts*
	Figure and liknesse, who so looke aright,	
	This goostly manna being here present	
55	To us figurethe in oure inwarde sight	
	A symilitude of the sacrament.	*image*

	This chosen Aaron bering a liknesse,	*having the quality of*
	In hoolly writte as it is clerly founde,	
	Of trewe preesthode and goostly parfytnesse,	*spiritual perfection*
60	This innocent, this lambe with large wounde,	
	The feonde, oure enemy, outtraye and confounde,	*devil; vanquishes*
	Is token and signe of Crists passyoun,	*Christ's passion*
	Spirituel gladness and mooste fer to habounde,	
	This day mynisterd til oure reffeccion.	*spiritual refreshment*

65	Thou chose of God, David that sloughe Golye,	*chosen; killed*
	With slyng and stoone called the Chaumpyoun	
	Of al Isrel, as bookis specefye,	
	That sloughe the bere and venqwysshed the lyoun,	*bear; lion*
	Figure of Jhesu, that with his passyoun	
70	And verraye victorie of hees woundes fyve	*true; his*
	Brought Philisteys unto subjeccyoun,	*Philistines*
	Whan Longeus spere did thorgh his herte ryve.	

	Ecclesiaste, myrrour of sapience,	*wisdom*
	With cloose castel besyde a clowde reed,	*fortified; red cliff*
75	That same token by virgynal vydence	*manifestation*
	Sette in Marye flouring of maydenhede,	
	Which bare the fruyt, the celestial bred,	*bread*
	Of oure counfort and consolacyoun,	
	Into whos brest the Hoolly Gooste, tathe heede,	*take heed*
80	Sent to Nasareth gracyously came doune.	*Nazareth*

	Beholde this prophete called Jeremye,	
	B'avisyoun so hevenly devyne	*By prophetic dream*
	Tooke a chalyce and fast cane him hye	*quickly went to work*
	To presse owte lykoure of the rede vyne	
85	Greyne in the middes, which to make us dyne,	*dinner*
	Was beete and bulted floure to make of bred,	*beaten and sifted*
	A gracyous fygure that a pure virgyne	
	Should bere manna in which lay al our speede.	*good fortune*

	This Ysayes, in token of plentee,	
90	A braunche of vynes mooste gracious and meete	*fitting*

At a gret feest him thought that he did see,
And therewithal a gracyous glene of whete,   *sheaf of wheat*
Token of joye frome the hevenly seete,   *seat*
Whan God above list frome Jessyes lyne   *chosen from Jesse's lineage*
95   To make his grace as golde dewe doune to fleete,   *flow*
To stanche oure venymes wheeche were serpentyne.[1]

Holly Helyas, by grace that God him sent,   *Holy*
The noble prophete benigne and honurable,
Made strong in spirit fourty dayes wente
100   In his journey, the brede made him so stable,   *resolute*
Cristallyne water to him so comfortable,
Al his vyage boothe in brede and lenkethe,   *breadth and length*
A blessid fygure verray coumfortable,   *inspiring*
Of the sacrament komethe oure goostly strenkethe.   *spiritual strength*

105   Zacharye holding there the fayre sensier,   *censer*
With goostely fumys as any bawme so swoote,   *balm; sweet*
Beo meditacyouns and grete preyer   *By*
That uppe ascendithe frome the hertes roote,
Goostely tryacle and oure lyves boote,   *medicine; protection*
110   Ageynst the sorowes of worldely pestylence,
Alle infect ayres it puttethe under foote   *infectious airs*
Of hem that take this bred with reverence.

Blessed Baptyst, of clennesse locke and keye,   *purity*
Mooste devoutly gan marken and declare   *began to point out*
115   With his fingur, whan he seyde Agnus Dei,   *Lamb of God*
Shewing the lambe which caused oure welfare
On Good Frydaye was on the crosse made bare,
And offred up for oure redempcyoun
On Eestre morowe, to stinten al oure care,   *Easter morning to put an end to*
120   Ageynst seeknesse oure restauracyoun.   *sickness; restoration*

This holly man, th'evangelist Saint Jehan
Th'appocolips wrote, and eke dranke poysoun,   *The Apocalypse*
In Cristes feyth als stable as the stoone,   *as solid as a rock*
Aboode with Jhesu in his passyoun;   *Stayed with*
125   And for to make a declaracyoun,
O the chalyce patyn a chylde yong of age   *chalice cover*
Shewed after there the consecracyoun
This brede is he that dyed for oure outrage.   *sins*

---

[1] *To put an end to our sins, which were diabolical*

	This blessed Mark, resembling the lyoun,	
130	In his gospel parfyte, stable and goode,	*perfect*
	Of bred and wyn for confirmacion	
	On Sherthorsday remembrethe howe it stoode;	*Maundy Thursday*
	Seyde at his souper with a ful blessed moode	*spirit*
	To hees discyples, aforne er he arros:	*arose*
135	"This bred, my body, this wyne, it is my bloode	
	Which that for man dyed uppon the crosse."	

Hooly Mathewe this elate gospeller,   *exalted*
Stable, parfyte, and truwe in his entente,
He wrote and seyde, of holy herte and entiere,   *sincere*
140 Touching this blessed gloryous sacrament:
"This is the chalyce of nuwe testament   *new*
That shal beo shadde for many and not for oon,   *shed*
For Cryste Jhesu was frome his fader sent,
Excepcion noon, but dyen for ech oone."

145 Lucas confermethe of this hooly bloode,
T'avoyde aweye al ambeguytee: *To ward off all doubt*
"This is my bodye that schal for man beo ded,
Him to delyver frome infernal powstee;   *power*
To Jherusalem, th'emperyal citee,   *the imperial city*
150 Him to conduyte eternally t'abyde,   *safeguard; to abide*
Adam oure fader and his posteritee,
By Cryst that suffred a spere to perce his syde."   *spear; pierce*

Paulus doctor wrytethe in his scripture,   *St. Paul; writes*
The which affermethe and seythe us truly: *affirms; says*
155 "Yif there beo founden any creature
Which that this bred receyvethe unworthely,
He etethe his doome moste dampnabully,   *eats his fate; damnably*
For which I counseyle, and pleynly thus I mene,
Ech man beo ware to kepe him prudently,
160 Not to resceive it, but yif he beo clene."   *unless he is free of sin*

He that is cleped maystre of sentence,   *called master of doctrine*
Sette in a cloude holde here a fresshe ymage,
Remembrethe eeke by gret excellence,
In this mater avoyding al outrage,   *sin*
165 Given to man here in oure pilgrymage,
This sacrament after his doctryne
Is Crystis body, repaste of our passage,
By the Hooly Gooste take of a pure virgyne.   *taken from*

The noble clerc, the doctour ful famous,   *cleric*
170 Wrytethe and recordethe, remembring truly

  Geyns heretykes, hoolly Jeronimus,   *Against heretics*
  Howe that this hoost is hole in ech partye   *complete*
  Bothe God and man, Cryste Jhesus verraily,
  In eche partycle hoole and undevyded,
175 This oure byleve and creance feythfully,   *belief and doctrine*
  Oute of oure hertes alle errours circumcyded.   *purged*

  Moral Gregore, ful weele reherce he can   *recount*
  In his wryting and vertuous doctryne,
  This glorious doctour, this parfyte hooly man,
180 Touching this bred dothe thus determyne, *bread (i.e., the eucharistic wafer)*
  Howe it is flesshe toke of a pure virgyne.
  Geynst al seeknesse our cheef restoratyf, *Against; sickness; chief medicine*
  Oure helth, welfare, richchest medisyn,
  This sacrament this blessed bred of lyf.

185 Blessed Austyne rehersethe in sentence, *Augustine explains in [his] teaching*
  "Whan Cryste is ete or resceyved in substaunce,   *eaten*
  That lyf is eten of hevenly excellence,
  Oure force, oure might, our strenkethe, oure suffisaunce, *strength; livelihood*
  Qwykenyng oure herte with al goostly plesaunce,   *spiritual joy*
190 Repast ay lasting, restoratyf ternal,   *ever; eternal*
  And remedy geynst al oure olde grevaunce
  Brought ine by byting of an appul smale."   *apple*

  Ambrosius, with sugerd elloquence,   *sweet rhetoric*
  Wrytethe with his penne and langage laureate,
195 With Crystis worde substancial in sentence,   *weighty in meaning*
  "The sacrament is justely consecrate
  Oure daily foode, renuwyng oure estate,   *renewing; condition*
  Recounseylling us whan we trespas or erre,
  And mathe us mighty with Sathan to debate   *makes*
200 To wynne tryumphe in al his mortal werre."

  Maistre of storyes, this doctour ful notable,
  Holding a chalys here in a sonne clere,   *chalice; bright*
  An Ooste aloft gloryous and comendable, *Host (i.e., the eucharistic wafer)*
  A pytee pleyning with a ful hevy cheere, *A pietà (sorrow) lamenting; sad mien*
205 With face doune caste, shewing the manere
  Of hir compleynte with her pytous looke,
  Ellas, she bought hir sones dethe to deere,   *too dear*
  Whan he for man the raunsoun on him tooke.

  This hoolly Thomas, called of Algwyne,
210 By hie myracle that sawghe persones three,   *saw*
  An ooste ful rounde, a sunne about it shyne,
  Joyned in oon by parfyte unytee,   *one*

A gloryous liknesse of the Trynitee,
Gracyous and digne for to beo comended,   *worthy*
215   With feyth, with hope, with parfyte charitee,   *faith*
Al oure byleeve is thereinne comprehended.   *belief*

With theos figures shewed in youre presence,
By divers likenesses you to doo plesaunce,
Resceivethe hem with devoute reverence,
220   This bred of lyfe yee kepe in remembraunce
Oute of this Egipte of worldely grevaunce,
Youre restoratyf celestyal manna,
Of which God graunt eternal suffysaunce   *plenty*
Where aungels sing everlasting Osanna.

[*Shirley kouthe fynde no more of this copye.*   *could*

SOTELTES AT THE CORONATION BANQUET OF HENRY VI

[*This was the first cours at his coronacion, that is to say, first, furmentie,[1] with venyson. Viande Royal[2] plantid with losenges of golde. Borehedes in castelles of earmed with golde.[3] Beef. Moton. Signet (swan). Capon stued Heron. Grete pike. A redde lech with lions corven theryn of white.[4] Custade Rooial (a pastry) with a leparde of golde sittyng theryn. Fritour like a sonne with a flour de lice therynne. A soltelé, Seint Edward and Seint Lowes armed in cote armours (coats of arms) bryngyng yn bitwene hem the Kyng in his cote armour with this scripture suyng:*

Loo here twoo kynges righte perfit and right good,   *perfect*
Holy Seint Edwarde and Seint Lowes: *Louis*
And see the braunch borne of here blessid blode;   *their; blood*
Live, among Cristen, moost sovereigne of price,
5   Enheretour of the floure de lice!   *Inheritor; fleur-de-lys*
God graunte he may thurgh help of Crist Jhesu   *through*
This sixt Henry to reigne and be as wise   *sixth*
And hem resemble in knyghthod and vertue.   *him (i.e., Henry V)*

[*Here foloweth the second course: that is to wite: Viande blank, barrid of golde. Gely partid (particolored jelly) writen and notid Te Deum Laudamus. Pigge endored (roasted and glazed). Crane. Bitore (Bittern). Conyes. Chikyns endored. Partrich. Pecok enhakyll.[5] Greate*

---

[1] *frumenty, made of boiled grain with sweetened milk (or almond milk)*

[2] *a sweetened, jellied dish*

[3] *Boars heads in pastry castles decorated with gold*

[4] *a slice of red jelly with white lions carved into it*

[5] *roasted peacock served in its plumage*

*breame. Leches white[1] with an antelop of redde corven theryn, a crowne about his neck with
a cheyne of golde. Flampayne poudred with lepardis and floure de lices of golde.[2] Fritour
(fritter), a lepardis hedde with ii ostrich fethers. A sotelté, th'emperour and the kyng that ded
is, armed, and here mantelles of the garters;[3] and the kyng that nowe is, knelying bifore hem
with this reasoun:*

	Ageinst miscreauntes th'emperour Sigismound	*Against infidels the emperor*
10	Hath shewid his might which is imperial;	*shown*
	Sithen Henry the Fifth so noble a knight was founde	*Ever since*
	For Cristes cause in actis martial;	*military deeds*
	Cherisshying the Chirch, Lollardes had a falle,	
	To give exaumple to kynges that succede	
15	And to his braunche in especiall	*descendant (i.e., Henry VI) especially*
	While he dothe regne to love God and drede.	*dread*

*[The thrid course sueth (follows); that is to say: Blaunde Surrey[4] poudrid with quatrefoilis
gilt. Venyson rostid. Egrettes. Curlewe. Cokkes. Plover. Quailis. Snytes (Snipes). Grete birdes.
Larkes. Carpe. Crabbe. Lech of three colours. A colde bakemete (a cold meat pie) like a shelde
quarterly redde and white, set with losenges and gilt, and floures of borage. Fritour crispes.
A soltelté of Our Lady sittyng and hir Childe in hir lappe, and she holdying in hir hand a
crowne and Seint George knelyng on that oo (one) side and Seint Denyse on that other side,
presentyng the Kyng, knelyng, to Our Lady, with this reason folowyng:*

	O blessid Lady, Cristes moder dere,	*mother dear*
	And thou Seint George, that callid art hir knight;	*her*
	Holy Seint Denyse, O martir moost entier,	*Denis; perfect*
20	The sixt Henry here present in your sight,	
	Shewith of grace on hym your hevenly light,	*Show*
	His tendre yougth with vertue doth avaunce,	*increase*
	Bore by discent and by title of right	*Born; descent*
	Justly to reigne in England and in Fraunce.	

---

[1] *A jelly-like dish prepared from various ingredients — fruits, meats, and white sauce — and cut into thin slices*

[2] *Pork pie ornamented with leopards and gold fleur-de-lys*

[3] *their mantles of the Order of the Garter*

[4] *a dish of chopped eels or fish, here served white*

 **EXPLANATORY NOTES**

ABBREVIATIONS: *BD*: Chaucer, *Book of the Duchess*; **BL**: British Library; *CA*: Gower, *Confessio Amantis*; *CT*: Chaucer, *Canterbury Tales*; *FP*: Lydgate, *Fall of Princes*; **MED**: *Middle English Dictionary*; *MP*: *Minor Poems of John Lydgate*, ed. MacCracken; *OED*: *Oxford English Dictionary*; *PP*: Langland, *Piers Plowman*, B text; *PPC*: *Proceedings and Ordinances of the Privy Council*; **PRO**: Public Record Office; *RP*: *Rotuli Parliamentorum*; *TB*: Lydgate, *Troy Book*.

BYCORNE AND CHYCHEVACHE

Bycorne and Chychevache tells the satiric story of two legendary beasts, one of whom dines on patient men, the other on submissive women. Like the *Disguising at Hertford*, the poem is part of a misogynist tradition of complaints about unruly women and of advice on marital behavior, as is underscored by one manuscript of the poem, Trinity R.3.19, which also includes the conduct poems *How the Good Wife Taught Her Daughter* and *How the Wise Man Taught His Son*. *Bycorne* also echoes Chaucer's Wife of Bath's and Clerk's tales, with explicit references to patient Griselda and the question of sovereignty in marriage. While no direct source has been traced, Lydgate might have known French versions of the story, such as the *Dit de la Chincheface* (printed by Jubinal, 1:390). Pearsall notes that the story of *Bycorne and Chychevache*, already well known by Chaucer's time, became popular in murals and tapestries of the fifteenth century, the most famous example being the mural paintings in the castle of Villeneuve-Lembron in France, where the verses are written on scrolls between the pictures (*John Lydgate*, pp. 179–80). Lydgate's poem consists of nineteen stanzas written in rhyme royal: the first three stanzas are narrated by an *ymage in poete-wyse*, while the following stanzas consist of direct speech from Bycorne, a group of husbands, a woman who is being devoured by Chychevache, and, finally, Chychevache and an old man whose wife has been eaten. Prose headings between stanzas describe what is being portrayed by the verses. Like the identity of the worthy citizen of London for whom Shirley says it was written, the poem's date is unknown, although it may plausibly be dated to 1427–30, the period of Lydgate's other London poems (Pearsall, *Bio-Bibliography*, p. 31).

Shirley's headnote identifies *Bycorne and Chychevache* as "the devise of a peynted or desteyned clothe for an halle a parlour or a chaumbre," suggesting that the verses were meant for a wall-hanging or tapestry, although a note at the end of the version found in Trinity R.3.19 identifies the verses as having "been Compilyd by John Ludgate . . . to be paynted in a parlor" (fol. 159r), which may point to a wall-painting or mural (see Gerould, "Legends of St. Wulfhad and St. Ruffin," pp. 333–35). Kipling believes that Shirley uses the term "device" in the technical sense of written directions to guide an artisan, and that Lydgate is envisioning six painted cloth panels for which he gives iconographical descriptions in prose ("histories" or instructions to the painter) and verse scriptures ("reasons," which represent the words that are to be inscribed by the painter along with each image) ("Poet as Deviser," p. 82). Others have argued that the poem may have been intended for dramatic presentation, perhaps as a pantomimed mumming (see Schirmer, *John Lydgate*, pp. 98–100, and Wickham, *Early English Stages*, 1:191 and 1:205), a claim encouraged by the running titles in Trinity R.3.20, which identify the text as being in "the fourome of desguysinges . . . the maner of straunge desgysinges . . . the gyse of a mumynge," as well as by the direct speeches of the poetlike figure and characters in the poem. The impression that the text points to some sort of performance was shared by its first editor, Isaac Reed, who added the version found in BL MS Harley 2251 to his 1780 edition of Dodsley's *Select Collection of Old Plays*; it was also included on a list made c. 1820 of pre-1700 plays reputedly owned by John Warburton (1682–1759) that were destroyed by his cook (see Folger Library MS W.a.234 and the discussion in Freehafer, "John Warburton's Lost Plays").

The poem survives in three fifteenth-century manuscripts. The base text for this edition is Trinity R.3.20 (1450–75), pp. 10–15 (*MP*, 2:433–38), collated with Trinity R.3.19 and BL MS Harley 2251.

running titles: *the fourome of desguysinges / contreved by daun Johan Lidegate / the maner of / straunge desgysinges / the gyse of a mumynge*. The word *daun*, derived from the Latin *dominus*, was a title of respect used broadly for priests and monks as well as authors, classical gods, and historical figures.

headnote   *Loo* is an interjection, meaning "look" or "behold," often used to attract attention. The terms *devise* and *devised* had a range of late medieval meanings, including "plan" or "design" (*MED*, n. 3[a] and v. 4[a]). The phrase *werthy citeseyn* suggests an established resident of the city and a person of status.

rubric   *First there shal stonde . . . seying thees thre balades*. Kipling assumes that this and the following rubrics were part of Lydgate's original text and constituted his instructions to the painter ("Poet as Deviser," p. 82), but they may also have functioned as stage directions. A *balade* was a poem or stanza in rhyme royal (seven lines in iambic pentameter, rhyming ababbcc); as used here, it refers to the three following stanzas, which introduce the story. The use of *seying* here and of similar verbs in some of the subsequent rubrics may indicate that the verses were spoken aloud.

1   *takethe heed*. An injunction to the audience to pay attention, this phrase links the poem to a tradition of advice literature.

6   *derrain*. From *dereinen*, here meaning "to decide the outcome of (a battle)" (*MED*, v. 3[b]). Lydgate also uses this word in the *Disguising at Hertford* to describe the conflict between the wives and their husbands (lines 165–66).

7 ff. rubric   *purtrayed*. The Middle English verb *portraien* had a range of meanings, including to draw, to paint, to depict, or to create a mental image or verbal description. Pearsall thinks that the use of *purtrayed* (in contrast with the words *showeth*, *kometh*, and *demonstrando*, which Shirley uses in the rubrics to the mummings and disguisings) may point to painted images, although there is no way to be certain (*John Lydgate*, pp. 179–80 and 191n34).

8   *Chichevache . . . Bycorne*. From Old French *Chiche Vache* ("Lean Cow"; the Middle English word *chiche* or *chinche* had the meanings of "miserly," "stingy," or "greedy"), a monster in a French fable who is said to feed on virtuous women;

Chaucer's Clerk's Tale refers to Chychevache when wives are warned not to be "pacient and kynde" lest they be swallowed by Chychevache (*CT* IV[E]1188). According to the *MED*, *Bycorne* comes from the Latin *bicornis* and as used here means "fabulous (two horned) beast," and in his *Troy Book* Lydgate describes *Bycornys* as one of the gods of the forest (2.7702). For further discussion of the two names, see Hammond, *English Verse*, pp. 113–18; Denny-Brown, "Lydgate's Golden Cows," pp. 39–41; and Menner, "Bycorne-Bygorne."

32 *Theyre tunge clappethe*. In misogynist literature and conduct books, women were often castigated for talking excessively.

49 *Maken maystresses of theyre wyves*. The theme of men's ceding of mastery in marriage is a staple of medieval misogynist literature. Chaucer's Wife of Bath represents the most vigorous Middle English defense of the woman's right to mastery in marriage, but Lydgate here follows the more traditional line that men who allow their wives undue power will pay a penalty (in this case, by being devoured by Bycorne, an action that suggests that they have been cuckolded).

87 Griselda is the patient wife in Chaucer's Clerk's Tale and numerous other four-teenth-century sources who uncomplainingly endures her husband's torments.

92 *a dere yeere*. The envoy to the Clerk's Tale similarly laments the scarcity of submissive women (*CT* IV[E]1164–65). For discussion of the themes of appetite and avarice in *Bycorne* and of its connection to the Clerk's Tale, see Denny-Brown, "Lydgate's Golden Cows."

133 *Lynkeld in a double cheyne*. The final line sums up men's dilemma: if they submit to their wives, they will be eaten by Bycorne; if they stand up to their wives, they will live in fear. Compare Lydgate's description of the treatment of Diomede by Criseyde, who will "lynke hym in a cheyne" (*TB* 3.4859).

DISGUISING AT HERTFORD

Shirley says that the *Disguising at Hertford* was written at the request of the "Countré Roullour Brys slayne at Loviers"; John Brice, Henry VI's cofferer (not controller), was probably killed at the siege of Louviers in 1431 (see Renoir, "On the Date of John Lydgate's *Mumming at Hertford*," and Green, "Three Fifteenth-Century Notes"). If he is the Brice to whom Shirley refers, 1431 would be the end limit for the disguising, and, following Green's suggestion that it is unlikely to have been performed for a child younger than four, 1425 would be its earliest possible date. Since the Christmas season of 1429/30 is the likely date of the Windsor mumming, and since the king and queen spent the Christmasses of 1425/26 and 1428/29 at Eltham (see the explanatory notes for the *Mumming at Eltham*), with Henry in Rouen in 1430 and in Paris in 1431, then 1426/27 and 1427/28 would seem to be the possible dates for the Hertford disguising. Given that Henry VI was in Hertford during Easter in 1428, which suggests that he may have stayed on there after the Christmas season, and given that the accounts of Henry's treasurer, John Merston, show payments for transportation from Windsor to Eltham and on to Hertford during the Christmas season (October to January 12) of 1427/28 (*Foedera* 10.387), 1427/28 is perhaps the likeliest date for the disguising. Lydgate wrote another poem that was perhaps also intended for that holiday season: the balade "On a New Year's Gift of an Eagle" was composed, Shirley tells us, for presentation to Henry and his mother on New Year's day at Hertford Castle and may have accompanied the gift of "une Eyer d'Or," which Catherine gave to her son that year (*Foedera* 10.387). As cofferer, Brice was the chief deputy to the household controller and would have been in charge of the ordering of the hall and the meals and entertainments in it, including during the Christmas season of 1427/28.

While the details of the performance are unclear, critics have stressed the originality of the Hertford disguising, noting how Lydgate uses the Chaucerian themes of unruly wives and good governance to create a secular comedy that comes close to containing actual dialogue and that looks ahead to the Tudor masque (see Reyher, *Les masques Anglais*, p. 113; Wickham, *Early English Stages*, 1:221; and Withington, *English Pageantry*, 1:111). In organization, the disguising shows the influence of French *débats*, presenting first the complaint of the six peasant husbands about their wives' tyranny, then turning to the wives' response, and concluding with a noncommital decision by the king allowing the wives to continue dominating their husbands for another year while further investigation is undertaken. Apparently six actors impersonated the husbands, although they do not speak in their own voices; actors may also have played the six wives, who speak in the first person plural (with occasional slippage into the singular), perhaps through a presenter who "ventriloquizes" them, thus creating female impersonation of the sort found in the Bessy character of Plough Day festivities; Clopper believes that the contest between the men and the women "reflects a Hocktide game like that at Coventry, where the women capture and beat the men" (*Drama, Play, and Game*, p. 163) and Epstein notes that it is similar in some ways to vernacular plays, including the *Second Shepherds' Play* and the Towneley *Noah* ("Lydgate's Mummings," pp. 341–46). The king's response was also probably spoken by a presenter, or perhaps a herald as Wickham suggests (*Early English Stages*, 3:195). We do not know who acted the parts of the husbands and wives, although payments for services during the 1427/28 holidays were made to heralds, minstrels, Jakke Travaill and his London players (for performing "diverses Jeuues & Entreludes"), and players from Abingdon, who also performed interludes (*Foedera*, 10:387). It is possible, although unlikely, that the performers were local men (see the explanatory note to line 1) or members of the household: Crane notes that charivaris, aimed at the topic of unsuitable marriages or remarriages, could be found in courtly as well as rural contexts and cites evidence for participation by household members (*Performance of Self*, pp. 143–55).

Whether or not the anti-matrimonial sentiments of the Hertford mumming were a covert reference to Catherine of Valois' amorous liaison with Owen Tudor (Green, "Three Fifteenth-Century Notes," pp. 14–16, thinks they were, but Pearsall, *Bio-Bibliography*, p. 28, disagrees), the disguising would have been relevant for its sophisticated parody of royal supplication aimed at flattering and instructing young Henry by casting him in the role of arbiter. The disguising reshapes the problem of wifely disobedience as a problem of royal rule, thus setting up the king's response, which exhibits those virtues of deliberation, seeking of counsel, and following of reason that all present must have hoped Henry would eventually practice (see Watts, *Henry VI*, pp. 24–29, for these and other ideals of kingship).

Merston's accounts provide a short list of possible spectators who may have been present, including Humphrey, duke of Gloucester (who gave Henry a gift on January 1, 1428); William Pope, esquire (who presented Henry with a gift from Catherine); various noblemen as well as "Varlettz, Garcions, and Pages"; Alice Boutiller (Henry's governess); and others (*Foedera* 10.387–88). The same accounts indicate that Shirley himself received a gold livery collar that year raising the interesting possibility that Shirley was at Hertford with the earl of Warwick during the Christmas season, in which case he may have seen the disguising. (For other possible spectators, based on known members of Henry's household in the late 1420s, see Forbes, *Lydgate's Disguising at Hertford Castle*, pp. 49–51).

The *Disguising at Hertford* survives in Trinity R.3.20 (1450–75), pp. 40–48, as well as in Stow's copy of it, now Additional MS 29729. Trinity R.3.20 is the base text for this edition (*MP*, 2:675–82), collated with Additional 29729.

running titles: *A desgysinge to fore the kynge / At cristmisse in the castel of hertforde / A desguysinge to fore the kyng / In cristemasse in the castell of hertford / the desgysinge for the kynge / At cristemasse at hertford / A desguysinge to fore the kynge / And qwene.* Not noted in *MP*.

headnote   Shirley seems to be using the term "bille" in the sense of a formal written petition to the king or parliament (see *MED* n. 3[a]). Hertford castle was twenty miles north of London on the river Lea; it was given to Catherine of Valois by Henry V on their marriage and was one of her principal residences in the 1420s. Shirley mistakenly identifies Brice as the Controller of the Royal Household, but between 1422 and 1452 that office was held by John Feriby and Thomas Stanley; Privy Council minutes for March 16, 1431 mention a John Brice who as the king's Cofferer was the Controller's deputy and most likely the man Shirley has in mind (*PPC*, 4:79). Louviers was near Rouen on the route to Paris; after being seized by the Dauphin in 1430 it was recaptured by the English in 1431, during which siege Brice was apparently killed. The last four words of the headnote are in slightly darker ink (although Hammond, "Lydgate's Mumming at Hertford," p. 365, mistakenly describes them as paler), perhaps suggesting Shirley added those words after he learned of Brice's death. In his verse preface, copied by Stow into Additional 29729, Shirley echoes the phrase "the rude upplandisshe people," this time applying it to himself ("my rude vplandishe wise") while asking his readers to pardon any flaws in his copying efforts (see Connolly's transcription, *John Shirley*, p. 209, line 14).

1   *with support of your Grace.* These words stress that the disguisers are invited guests, not unwelcome intruders, and along with lines 6–7 (*Certeyne sweynes . . . comen*) may possibly suggest performance by local men, although there is no other evidence for that conjecture.

5   *the vigyle of this nuwe yeere.* If taken literally, this phrase suggests that the disguising was performed on 31 December.

25 ff.   Latin marginalia: *i. demonstrando vi. rusticos* [six rustics for the showing]. This apparent stage direction seems to indicate the entrance of the men impersonating the husbands. The mark before *demonstrando* is printed as an *i* by MacCracken (*MP*, 2:676), but Forbes (*Lydgate's Disguising at Hertford Castle*, p. 36, note to line 25) notes that it could also be a mark like a tilde (~), which sometimes appears in later manuscripts after stage directions in the right margin.

28   *Karycantowe.* The *MED* cites this as the only example of *karicantoue* (n.), which it defines as a nonce word for "the dance of hen-pecked husbands." Forbes imagines that Karycantowe is one of the rustics (*Lydgate's Disguising at Hertford Castle*, p. 47), but the text does not readily support that interpretation.

30　　　　*Obbe the Reeve*. A reeve was a manorial officer or bailiff, charged with overseeing the lord's demesne farm. Hobbe is later called Robyn (line 44).

39　　　　*jowsy*. Lydgate seems to have been the only writer to use this adjective; see *MED*, *iousi*, adj.

40　　　　*pouped*. Apparently adopted from Chaucer: the only other instances of this word noted by the *MED* are in the Nun's Priest's Tale (*CT* VII[B²]3399) and the Manciple's Prologue (*CT* IX[H]90).

52　　　　*distaff*. A tool used in spinning, traditionally associated with women.

55　　　　*Colyn Cobeller*. Compare the French farce of a cobbler who quarrels with his wife over who should shut the door (the *Farce nouvelle très bonne des drois de la Porte Bodès et de Fermer l'huis*, in *Recueil de farces françaises*, pp. 159–64, discussed by Enders, *Rhetoric*, pp. 210–16).

55 ff.　　Latin marginalia: *demonstrando pictaciarium*. A second apparent stage direction, pointing to the entrance of the cobbler.

65　　　　*qwytt*. Another Chaucerian echo (e.g., *CT* I[A]4324: "Thus have I quyt the Millere in my tale").

70　　　　Cicely's actions are doubly reprehensible: not only does she drink away her husband's pay but she does it on a Sunday.

72–73　　The reference to "game" and "play" here and in line 161 echoes the Merchant's Tale: "it is no childes pley / To take a wyf withouten avysement" (*CT* IV[E] 1530–31); see Nolan, *John Lydgate*, pp. 166–67, for a discussion of Lydgate's response to the Chaucerian dichotomy of "earnest" and "game."

87　　　　Compare the Merchant's Tale, in which Justinus warns January about wifely "purgatorie" (*CT* IV[E]1670).

91 ff.　　Latin marginalia: *demonstrando carnificem* [a butcher for the showing].

93　　　　*Berthilmewe*. St. Bartholomew was martyred by flaying and thus came to be associated with butchers; compare *Berthylmew the Bochere* in the N-Town "Trial of Joseph and Mary," line 16.

95　　　　*holde chaumpartye*. To engage in a dispute or contest with (*MED*, *champartie*, n. 2[b]); Lydgate uses the phrase in a number of his other works, including *TB* 2.5681 and *FP* 1.6334.

101　　　*Pernelle*. A name often given to a proud woman; a prostitute or concubine (*MED*). Compare *PP*, passus 5, line 26.

106　　　*Bid him goo pleye him a twenty devel wey*. See note to line 161 below and compare Chaucer's Miller's Tale, *CT* I(A)3713.

111　　　*no taylle, but qwytt him*. Compare the Shipman's Tale, in which the wife punningly tells her husband to "score it upon my taille" (*CT* VII[B²]416).

115　　　*Thome Tynker*. Compare *PP*, passus 5, line 310.

115 ff.　Latin marginalia: *demonstrando the Tynker* [a tinker for the showing]

116   *wyres of Banebury*. Forbes (*Lydgate's Disguising at Hertford Castle*, pp. 13–14) thinks this means "wire-work" from Banbury, but *wyres* is probably a variant spelling of *wares*.

118   *Bare up his arme*. A gesture of self-defense to ward off blows.

126   *Phelyce*. Compare *PP*, passus 5, line 29.

140   *sauf-conduyt*. The husbands are seeking a safe-conduct from the king and ask to be granted franchise and liberty (line 138) as well as the king's protection (line 142).

146   *The Olde Testament for to modefye*. The husbands ask the king to use his power to amend the "old law" of matriarchal custom claimed by wives as a "right" of women ruling over men. Also see lines 213–14, where the wives ask the king to uphold the *statuyt of olde antiquytee*.

156 ff.   *i. distaves*. [The distaffs, i.e., the wives.]

161   *It is no game with wyves for to pleye*. A pun on *ple* (meaning complaint or lawsuit) and *pleie* (play). For the meanings of *pleie* in relation to drama, see Clopper, *Drama, Play, and Game*, pp. 12–17, and Coldewey, "Plays and 'Play,'"). Also see the note to lines 72–73 above.

164   Twycross and Carpenter note that despite the appearance of direct speech, the wives' answer "is also a 'bill' by way of *replicatio*, which could be delivered by a representative" (*Masks and Masking*, p. 160n44). Nolan argues that Lydgate lets the wives speak to show that like Chaucer's Wife of Bath "they are by nature *compelled* to speak" (*John Lydgate*, p. 65); the dramatic innovation of direct speech arises from the gender dynamics of the piece, when men are unable to voice the women's subjective claims. Crane (*Performance of Self*, p. 141) notes that Charles d'Orléans on one occasion writes in the voice of a company of women and may have read the poem himself to accompany women's mumming (see ballad 88, in his *Poésies*, 1:128–29).

168   *the worthy Wyf of Bathe*. A reference to Chaucer's Wife of Bath.

170   *make hir housbandes wynne heven*. Compare Justinus' observation in the Merchant's Tale that such wives of Bath may be "Goddes whippe; / Than youre soule up to hevene skippe / Swifter than dooth an arwe out of a bowe" (*CT* IV[E]1671–73).

176   *Gresyldes story*. A reference to Chaucer's Clerk's Tale.

186–87   These lines echo the Wife of Bath's Prologue (*CT* III[D]217–18) and refer to the custom at Dunmow, Essex, of awarding a side of bacon to spouses who lived a year and a day without quarreling.

203   *prescripcyoun*. Title or right acquired by virtue of uninterrupted possession or use.

rubric   Clopper (*Drama, Play, and Game*, p. 163) sees the king's decision to postpone judgment for a year (line 239) as a parody of Chaucer's Lady Tercelet, but slowness to judge is part of the serious advice given to kings and is recommended to Henry VI in Lydgate's *Ballade to King Henry VI on His Coronation* (*MP*,

2:624–30, line 133). Parry ("On the Continuity of English Civic Pageantry," p. 225) notes that the device of flattering a monarch by making him or her the arbiter in a dispute was used in Elizabethan entertainments, including in Elizabeth's visit to the manor house of the earl of Leicester in 1578, where in the earl's garden someone dressed like "an honeste mans wyf of the Countrie" appeared and asked the queen's advice as to which of two suitors would be the better match for her daughter.

251   *I.* The shift from description of the king's judgment to the first-person pronoun is not explained in the text. Note the similar slip from *we* to *I* in line 186 of the wives' reply. One often finds this appropriation of voice in Chaucer, particularly with the Wife of Bath.

254   *with asure or with golde.* Azure and gold were the colors of the French royal arms, and the image of a marital prison painted in those colors may refer to Queen Catherine's affair with Owen Tudor and the 1427–28 parliamentary act, presumably inspired by her earlier liaison with Edmund Beaufort, imposing strictures on her remarriage (see Green, "Three Fifteenth-Century Notes," p. 16, although Pearsall, *Bio-Bibliography*, p. 28, argues that since Catherine was a member of the king's household until 1430 Lydgate would have been unlikely to make "sly digs at her").

DISGUISING AT LONDON

Shirley describes the *Disguising at London* as being made "for the gret estates of this lande, thanne being at London," which has led to the supposition that Lydgate wrote it for a gathering of Parliament, possibly the one that opened at Westminster on October 13, 1427 (see Schirmer, *John Lydgate*, p. 186). Parliament also met at Westminster from September 22, 1429, to February 23, 1430, although Pearsall aptly comments that a disguising for that session would probably have mentioned the coronation of Henry VI on November 6, 1429 (*Bio-Bibliography*, p. 47n65). The disguising need not, however, have been associated with this or any other Parliament (see A. Lancashire, *London Civic Theatre*, pp. 122–23n33), and the reference to Henry V (at lines 267–76) coupled with no mention of Henry VI may argue for an earlier date. Whatever the precise date or occasion, the text makes clear that the disguising was designed for household performance (lines 335 and 337) during the long Christmas season (line 280) that ran from October through early January; the hope expressed in line 334 that the virtues bestowed by the disguising will last "al this yeer" may possibly allow us to locate the performance more precisely on the last day of December or sometime in early January.

The disguising opens with the appearance of Dame Fortune, whose dangerous mutability sets the stage for the introduction of four protectors — Dames Prudence, Righteousness, Fortitude, and Temperance — who promise to defend any who serve them. The disguising's 342 lines of rhyming couplets consist of lengthy descriptions of each of the Virtues; it ends with a song by the Four Virtues and the banishing of Fortune. A central concern of the disguising is good governance, which is seen as a remedy for Fortune's dangerous instability; the gift-giving associated with mumming here takes the abstract form of gifts of virtue, which will reside "in this housholde" (line 335) for the year. As Benson notes, although the disguising was apparently intended for a national, not a municipal, occasion its values "are practical and bourgeois": the tone is optimistic, emphasizing "the sort of pragmatic, decent, and well-regulated communal behavior advocated by medieval London citizens" ("Civic Lydgate," p. 160). Nolan argues that the disguising aims "to develop a notion of virtue fit for the public realm of politics, a secularized (though hardly secular) code of behavior particularly suited to the governing classes" (*John Lydgate*, p. 143).

There are several clues to performance in this "script-like" text (Kipling, "Poet as Deviser," pp. 97–98). Entrances are marked by brief stage directions, the narrator interacts with the audience and the actors (by drawing attention to the arrival of each new character, banishing Fortune, and commanding the Four Virtues to sing), and the text specifies some props (Prudence's mirror, Righteousness' balance, Fortitude's sword). The lack of dialogue suggests that a presenter probably read the text aloud, as Fortune and the Four Virtues made their appearances. Although there is no indication of any actions they might have performed, Twycross and Carpenter think the Virtues may have presented the "gift" of their attributes to the presiding dignitaries (*Masks and Masking*, p. 158n39). The final lines of the disguising command the four protectors to sing "Some nuwe songe aboute the fuyre" (lines 338–40), which hints that the disguising ended with music.

The *Disguising at London* survives in Trinity R.3.20 (1450–75), pp. 55–65, as well as in Stow's copy of it, now Additional MS 29729. Trinity R.3.20 is the base text for this edition (*MP*, 2:682–91), collated with Additional 29729.

running titles: *A desguysing made by Lydgate / of the foure cardynale virtues / the foure / cardynale vertues / the foure / cardinale virtues / the foure cardinale / virtues / of the foure cardinale / virtues.* Not noted in *MP*.

headnote   Kipling argues that Shirley's use of *devyse* here refers to a device (or plan) covering the entire performance that other artisans — costumers, actors, prop makers — used to shape their own contributions ("Poet as Deviser," p. 98). The stage direction in the last sentence (*Loo, firste komethe in Dame Fortune*) and elsewhere may be Shirley's additions rather than part of Lydgate's text, but the text itself indicates the entries of the various characters too (e.g., *Loo here this lady that yee may see*, line 1).

1–13   Lydgate's lines closely follow the *Roman de la Rose* (which is explicitly mentioned in line 9), in which Fortune's dwelling is described as being on a rock in the sea, where the weather is changeable; Lydgate's description of the "instability" of her house, which is ugly on one side and beautiful on the other (lines 40–51), echoes her own nature. Lydgate's fullest examination of the theme of Fortune is in his *Fall of Princes*.

20–35   Compare *BD*, lines 287 ff., where the birds make heavenly melody, some high, some low, while Zephyrus and Flora temper the air.

48   *Ay in poynt to falle adoun.* Compare *BD*, line 13.

64   Alexander the Great (356–323 B.C.), king of Macedonia, was well known in the Middle Ages from both romances and histories (see Cary, *Medieval Alexander*). His story also appears in Chaucer's Monk's Tale (*CT* VII[B²]2631–70) and in several places in Gower's *Confessio Amantis*.

67–70   Marginalia: *Sesar a bakars seon.* [Caesar was a baker's son.] Julius Caesar (c. 100–44 B.C.) became emperor of Rome before being slain at the Capitol. Following the

    Chessbook of Jacob de Cessolis, Hoccleve's *Regiment of Princes*, lines 3513–21, identifies Julius Caesar as a baker's son. Caesar also appears in Chaucer's Monk's Tale (*CT* VII[B²]2671–2726).

73   *Maugrey the Senaat and al theyre might.* Nolan (*John Lydgate*, p. 138) notes that Lydgate adds this line, which is not found in Chaucer's Monk's Tale.

96   According to the legend first mentioned by Plato in the *Republic* (2.359a–2.360d), Gyges of Lydia was a shepherd, who stole a golden ring from a corpse he found in a cave. Using the power of invisibility given him by the ring, Gyges seduced the queen and murdered the king of Lydia.

102 Croesus, Gyges' descendant, was the last king of Lydia, reigning c. 560–546 B.C. The story of Croesus' dream is found in the *Roman de la Rose*, lines 6489–6630, and is the concluding story of Chaucer's Monk's Tale (*CT* VII[B²]2727–60), which Lydgate follows in detail, except that in Chaucer, the king's daughter is called "Phanye." Lydgate changes her name to *Leryopee*, which comes from Ovid's *Metamorphoses*, book 3 line 342, where "Liriope" is the name of Narcissus' mother. Nolan speculates that Lydgate may have made the change to stress the theme of prophecy (*John Lydgate*, p. 177n48).

108 Marginalia: *Ecclesiaticus xxvi °cap°.* [Chapter 26 of Ecclesiasticus deals with good and bad women.]

    Juvo is Juno. The name is spelled this way in Harley 2251, fol. 249b, as well.

109 Jupiter (or Jove) was chief of the Roman gods.

111 Phoebus Apollo, the classical god and mythological figure, who was associated with the sun, thus his drying power.

115 *Leryopee.* See note to line 102.

123–27 For Lydgate's view of tragedy and comedy, see *TB*, 2.850 ff.; also see Nolan (*John Lydgate*, pp. 124–31).

138 *hir double face.* Fortune was often described as having two faces; see Patch, *Goddess Fortuna*, pp. 42–43.

140 ff. Prudence was traditionally depicted with three eyes for viewing past, present, and future; see *TB*, 2.2308, and Chaucer, *Troilus and Criseyde*, 5.743–45. She is also the central protagonist of the Tale of Melibee. Lydgate cites Seneca as his source, but the idea of the cardinal virtues derives from Cicero's *De Inventione* and Macrobius' *Somnium Scipionis*, and appeared in the work of many medieval authors (see Tuve, *Allegorical Imagery*, pp. 57–88). The king's bedroom at Westminster contained a painting of the virtues battling the vices and the rebuilt London Guildhall, 1411–30, included statues of Fortitude, Justice, Temperance, and Discipline (see Binski, *Painted Chamber*, pp. 41–43, and Barron, *Medieval Guildhall of London*, p. 27 and plates 9a, 9b, and 10). When Henry VII entered Bristol in 1486, he was greeted by Prudence and Justice (Parry, "On the Continuity of English Civic Pageantry," pp. 226–27). Watts notes that the four cardinal virtues were urged on the late medieval king and took precedence over

the "theological" virtues of Faith, Hope, and Charity, since they were seen as more socially useful (*Henry VI*, p. 23).

165   Latin marginalia: *i. providencia* [providence]

173 ff.   The scales of balance of Righteousness signify her unbiased deliberativeness that can't be bought; she had neither hand (so as not to receive gifts) nor eyes (so as to treat all equally).

193 ff.   For a similar exemplum of an incorruptible judge, see *St. Erkenwald*.

222 ff.   See Tuve (pp. 57–60) for the identification of Fortitude with the quality of magnificence, as in Skelton's *Magnyfycence*. Edwards (*TB*, p. 428) notes that as Aristotle explains in the *Nicomachean Ethics* (4.2), "magnificence is a moral virtue akin to generosity but differing from generosity by being on a larger scale and directed toward public display." She carries a sword to maintain the common good.

247   Presumably a reference to Diogenes of Sinope (c. 404–323 B.C.), the best known of the cynic philosophers.

248   I.e., the Greek philosophers Plato (c. 427–348 B.C.) and Socrates (c. 469–399 B.C.).

249   I.e., Scipio Africanus (c. 236–183 B.C.). This line seems to suggest that Scipio was from Carthage, when in fact he was a Roman who defeated the Carthaginians in battle during the Punic Wars. Compare *Henry VI's Triumphal Entry*, line 520, where Lydgate correctly identifies Scipio as the conqueror of Carthage.

251   Latin marginalia: *i. republica.* [Republic]. Middleton ("Idea of Public Poetry," p. 96) notes that "common profit" is the usual Middle English translation of *res publica*; see Nolan (*John Lydgate*, p. 146) for the emphasis on common profit in this disguising.

255   In Greek mythology, Hector is the Trojan prince who valiantly fought for Troy before being killed by Achilles.

264   The Nine Worthies comprised three groups of chivalric heroes: Hector, Julius Caesar, and Alexander the Great (Gentiles); Joshua, David, and Judas Maccabeus (Jews); and Arthur, Charlemagne, and Godfrey of Bouillon (Christians). In the "Envoy" to *TB*, Lydgate praises Henry V as equal to the Nine Worthies (line 4).

267 ff.   The reference to Henry V (king of England from 1413–22) in the past tense provides an earliest possible date for the disguising. Nolan argues that mention of Henry V introduces a note of historical contingency and instability as did Chaucer's use of four modern examples in Monk's Tale (*John Lydgate*, pp. 151–53).

279   *to more and lasse*. Suggests a socially mixed audience for the disguising.

280   *this Cristmasse*. Suggests the disguising was performed during the holiday season, which stretched from October to early January.

283 ff.   Lydgate's longest discussion of Temperance comes in *Mesure Is Tresour*, which argues for the value of temperance or moderation — the "roote of al good policye" (line 9) — for all social classes.

315–27   Twycross and Carpenter (*Masks and Masking*, p. 158n39) think this is the moment in the performance when the virtues might have presented their attributes to the dignitaries at what they take to have been a feast.

334   *abyde here al this yeer*. Perhaps suggests a performance date of December 31 or shortly thereafter; Wickham (*Early English Stages*, 3:50) thinks the *Disguising at London* was prepared for January 1, given its concern with Dame Fortune.

335   *In this housholde*. Suggests indoor performance.

338   *yee all foure*. I.e., the Four Virtues.

340   *nuwe songe aboute the fuyre*. For the use of music in medieval performances, see Rastall, *Music in Early English Religious Drama*.

HENRY VI'S TRIUMPHAL ENTRY INTO LONDON

After two years in France where he had been crowned king, Henry VI landed at Dover and made his way to Blackheath where on February 21, 1432 he was met by the mayor, aldermen, and other Londoners, and led past seven pageants that had been set up at various locations in the city. The pageants included a giant at London Bridge, who was flanked by two antelopes bearing the arms of England and France, with an inscription declaring that the giant would protect the king from foreign enemies; a tower erected in the middle of the bridge, featuring Nature, Grace, and Fortune along with seven maidens representing the seven gifts of the Holy Spirit, who sang a roundel of welcome to the king; a tabernacle at Cornhill, with Dame Sapience and the seven sciences; at the conduit a child-king on a throne surrounded by Mercy, Truth, and Clemency; at the conduit in Cheapside, a well at which Mercy, Grace, and Pity offered wine and a paradise of fruit trees near which stood Enoch and Elias; a castle of jasper, with a pedigree showing Henry's lineage and a Jesse tree; and at the conduit in St. Paul's, an image of the Trinity with angels. When Henry reached St. Paul's, he dismounted and entered the church, where he was greeted by the archbishop and other clerics, then continued on to Westminster, where the abbot and monks met him with the scepter of Saint Edward. On the following Saturday, the mayor and aldermen solidified their welcome to the king by offering him a golden hamper filled with a thousand pounds of gold. As Henry VI processed through London, he was enveloped in the qualities of the ideal king on a kind of pilgrimage that ended at the celestial city at St. Paul's. The pageantry conveyed the hopes of Londoners for their king, advice to him about the qualities needed for good rule, and an attempt to demonstrate London's prestige and importance.

Lydgate's poem is a versified account in English of the entry, which appears to have been based on an informal Latin letter from John Carpenter, who as the town clerk of London probably organized the event and entered his letter in the city's letter book (see Barron, *London*, p. 21). Although some scholars have suggested that Lydgate helped plan the pageants (see Ebin, *John Lydgate*, p. 83, and Schirmer, *John Lydgate*, pp. 139–43), it seems unlikely that he devised any of the pageants. Lydgate probably witnessed the entry, however, since he offers information not given in Carpenter's letter, such as the presence of the figures of Mercy, Grace, and Pity, as well as an explanation for the allegorization of the mayor's name in one of the displays, among others. Carpenter's letter (a copy of which survives in Guildhall Letter Book K, fols. 103b–104b, printed by Riley in *Munimenta Gildhallae Londoniensis*, 3:457–64), is addressed to a "reverende frater et amice praestantissime," presumably Lydgate, suggesting that the letter was designed to assist Lydgate in crafting an official commemoration (see MacCracken, "King Henry's Triumphal Entry," p. 11, and Kipling, "Poet as Deviser," pp. 87–89). Another Latin account, which differs somewhat from Carpenter's, can be found in Lambeth Palace Library, Lambeth MS 12 (see Osberg, "Lambeth Palace," for a discussion of its political differences from both Carpenter and Lydgate). Pearsall has aptly described Lydgate's poem as a kind of souvenir program (*Bio-Bibliography*, p. 170), and Nolan (*John Lydgate*, p. 235) notes that Lydgate's verses, with their introduction of poetic set pieces, offer a reinterpretation of the public event of the entry that transformed the spectacle into poetry. The praise for London in the final stanzas of the poem underscores the attempt to craft an enduring poetic representation of the event.

   Henry VI's Triumphal Entry survives in six manuscripts and in three prose paraphrases, which might be independent accounts, in one case possibly by an eyewitness (see McLaren, *London Chronicles*, pp. 53–54, and Osberg, "Lambeth Palace") and a 1516 printing by Pynson; the base text for this edition is BL MS Cotton Julius B.ii, fols. 89r–100v (*MP*, 2:630–48), collated with BL MS Cleopatra C.iv, fols. 38r–48r and BL MS Harley 565, fols. 114v–124r.

2–4	The astrological conceit in these lines, not present in Carpenter's letter, is typical of the flourishes Lydgate adds to his fairly straightforward source. For a stanza-by-stanza comparison of Lydate's poem to the Latin letter, see MacCracken, "King Henry's Triumphal Entry."
10–14	Henry VI lived from 1421 to 1471, reigning from 1422 to 1461, and again in 1470–71. His coronation as king of England took place on November 6, 1429, at Westminster, and as king of France on December 16, 1431, at Paris. See Bryant, "Configurations of the Community," for a discussion of the political context of the 1432 entry.
22–28	See Kipling (*Enter the King*, pp. 15–16 and pp. 143–44) for the significance of the comparison of Henry to the biblical King David and of London to Jerusalem. Andrew Horn, city chamberlain of London, described London as the "new Jerusalem" in writing of the reception of Edward II and Isabella in 1308 (*Annales Londinienses*, p. 152). Ganim notes that in medieval literature, the city "was always being filtered through the ways in which the city of God was visualized" ("Experience of Modernity," pp. 86–87).
30	The mayor of London in 1432 was John Welles, grocer and alderman of Langbourn Ward, five times member of parliament for the city between 1417 and 1433, sheriff in 1420–21, and mayor in 1431–32 (*Chronicles of London*, p. 303, note to p. 109, line 15).
42	The Londoners wore white, with guilds adding their own distinctive insignia (*devyses*).
43–46	The list of "aliens" present at the entry is Lydgate's substitution for the minstrels and servants mentioned by Carpenter. MacCracken suggests that Lydgate may have made the change to suit the mayor, but adds that Lydgate's "own interest

	accounts well enough" for the substitution ("King Henry's Triumphal Entry," p. 79).
50	Blackheath was the customary place at which the mayor and citizens welcomed royalty entering London: Henry V was greeted there in 1415, Emperor Sigismund in 1416, Catherine of Valois in 1421, and Margaret of Anjou in 1445.
54–55	The *moste princypall* among the Londoners (e.g., the aldermen) wore red.
After 63	The mayor's speech is recorded in English by Carpenter, with slightly different wording; MacCracken ("King Henry's Triumphal Entry," pp. 80–81) suggests that Lydgate's changes, which improve the speech, were made with the help of the mayor.
64 ff.	Lydgate omits a paragraph in which Carpenter describes 120 clergy assembled at Deptford to sing praises to the king, going straight to description of the pageants arranged by the city. The *Noble devyses* and *dyvers ordenaunces* refer to those pageants while the phrase *Conveyed by scripture* refers to the biblical quotations that accompanied the pageants as written mottoes.
71 ff.	The first of the pageants Henry encountered was at the entrance to London Bridge, where a giant stood with raised sword; on either side was a scripture (which Carpenter gives in Latin and Lydgate renders in English) explaining that he is the king's protector. A giant, a champion of the city, seems to have been standard for pageants at this location; in 1415, a giant held an axe in one hand and the keys to the city in the other, and was accompanied by a giantess, the two in Kingsford's view representing "the medieval ancestors of Gog and Magog" (*Chronicles of London*, p. 302, note to p. 100, line 4). The 1432 giant was flanked by two antelopes, one of the heraldic devices associated with the Lancastrians (an antelope atop a pillar and wearing a shield of the royal arms around its neck was one of the figures on London Bridge in the entry of Henry V in 1415; see *Gesta Henrici Quinti*, pp. 60–67).
76	*gan manace.* Lydgate's description suggests that the giant was rigged for movement, as apparently were the giants who bowed in the pageants for Catherine of Valois in 1421 (see Redman, *Vita Henrici Quinti*, pp. 297–98).
85 ff.	Latin marginalia: *Inimicos eius induam confusione.* [His enemies I will clothe with confusion (Psalm 131:18).] MacCracken notes that there is no evidence that Lydgate's "scriptures," such as this one written near the giant, are anything other than translations of the Latin Vulgate Bible mottoes supplied by Carpenter ("King Henry's Triumphal Entry," p. 98). The 1392 show for Richard II included a *custos* or expositor who traveled with the king and made formal speeches explaining each pageant, while the actors who were costumed as angels and saints sang songs and delivered gifts for the king to the *custos* (see Kipling, "London Pageants for Margaret of Anjou," p. 25n8), but there is no mention of a similar translator for Henry in 1432 and Lydgate assumes in lines 265–68 that at least some of the mottoes were meant to be readily legible by the king and other spectators.

99 ff.   The second pageant, located in the middle of the bridge, featured a tower out of which came three empresses — Nature, Grace, and Fortune — who gave the king gifts of various strengths and virtues, intended to ensure his long reign. They were accompanied, on the right, by seven angelic maidens dressed in white, who presented the king with seven gifts of the Holy Ghost in the guise of seven white doves (which Carpenter's letter makes clear were actually released [*per emissionem septem albarum columbarum*]) and a scripture, which Lydgate has them saying, and, on the left, by seven virgins, who also presented symbolic gifts to the king and sang a roundel of welcome. The 1431 Paris entry included the gift of three hearts to the king, which opened to release birds and flowers (see Wolffe, *Henry VI*, p. 60). The account of the 1432 entry found in Trinity MS 0.9.1 says Henry was given actual objects by Nature, Grace, and Fortune: a crown of glory, scepter of meekness and piety, sword of might and victory, mantle of prudence, shield of faith, helm of health, and girdle of love and perfect peace (see *The Brut*) which as McLaren (*London Chronicles*, p. 54) notes, resembles metaphorical dressing of a knight in Caxton's *Boke of the Ordre of Chyualry* and the garbing of the king in coronation. Although MacCracken ("King Henry's Triumphal Entry," p. 100n1) asserts that the whole entry is more "monkish than civic," Benson notes that the second pageant had a domestic message that emphasized bourgeois values of comfort and prosperity ("Civic Lydgate," p. 156).

113   Marginalia: *Nature*.

119   Marginalia: *Grace*.

129   Marginalia: *Fortune*.

133   *crounes tweyne*. A reference to the dual monarchy.

134   Marginalia: *Nature, Grace, and Fortune*.

135   The *goostly giftes* presented by Nature, Grace, and Fortune are consistent with the pageantry's emphasis on portraying the king, as Straker puts it, "in a state of potentiality and as an object of instruction" ("Propaganda, Intentionality, and the Lancastrian Lydgate," p. 119).

143 ff.   Latin marginalia: *Intende, prospere [procede] et regna.* [Set out, proceed prosperously, and reign (Psalm 44:5).]

181–86   Lydgate changes Carpenter's account by describing actors who seem to speak in English to the crowds, while Carpenter's hold placards in Latin; although Carpenter records the English speech of the mayor when he greeted the king and the song of the seven virgins offering gifts to the king, he usually emphasizes that the verses were written, using *rescribere* and *subscribere*, since he also uses *recitata*.

183 ff.   Latin marginalia: *Impleat te Deus spiritu sapiencie et intellectus, spiritui consilij et fortitudinis et sciencie et pietatis et spiritui timoris Domini.* [God send you the spirit of wisdom, and of understanding, the spirit of counsel, and of fortitude, the spirit of knowledge, and of godliness (Isaiah 11:2).]

197 ff. Latin marginalia: *Induat te Dominus corona glorie, gladio iusticie, septro clemencie, palio prudencie, scuto fidei, galea salutis et vinculo pacis.* [The Lord clothe you with the crown of glory, the sword of justice, the scepter of mercy, the mantle of prudence, the shield of faith, the helmet of health, and the girdle of peace.] McLaren (*London Chronicles*, p. 54 and p. 54n10) reads these gifts as a "manifestation of the metaphorical dressing of a knight in Caxton's *Boke of the Ordre of Chyualry* and of the king in coronation."

211–22   The roundel of the seven virgins is written in English in Carpenter's letter, and, in MacCracken's view, is both a good example of a fifteenth-century lyric and the one that was actually sung, while Lydgate's version offers "an artistic revision" of the roundel ("King Henry's Triumphal Entry," p. 98). We do not know who played the roles of the seven virgins and sang this roundel, but the boys of St. Magnus the Martyr, located at London Bridge, sang for the entry of Elizabeth Woodville some forty years later (I. Lancashire, *Dramatic Texts and Records* no. 942 [wrongly dating the entry to 1464]).

223 ff. At Cornhill, the king encountered the third pageant, a tabernacle built for Dame Sapience and the seven liberal sciences and their classical practitioners. Benson ("Civic Lydgate," p. 156) notes that the third and fourth pageants, both of which are in Cornhill, emphasize the law and justice in a part of the city in which commercial abuses were punished by the pillory. Saygin argues that Gloucester asked for the Sapience pageant as part of his educative plans for Henry VI ("Humphrey," p. 57).

233   Latin marginalia: *Septem sciencie liberales.* [Seven liberal sciences.] The *trivium* (grammar, dialectic [logic], and rhetoric) and the *quadrivium* (arithmetic, music, geometry, and astronomy) formed the core curriculum of medieval universities.

239   *Precian.* Priscian (fl. 500 A.D.) was a Latin grammarian whose *Institutiones grammaticae* was the standard text for the study of Latin in the Middle Ages.

243   *Tulyus.* The Roman statesman Marcus Tullius Cicero (106–43 B.C.) was known for his oratorical skill.

245   *Boece.* Boethius' *De institutione musica* was from the ninth century on considered to be the chief authority for music.

256   *Albunisar.* Albumazar (Abu-Mashar Jafar ibn Muhammed) was an influential ninth-century Persian astronomer, whose works were translated into Latin in the twelfth century.

258–71   Latin marginalia: *Per me reges regnant et gloriam sapiencie possidebunt.* [Through me kings reign and possess the glory of wisdom (Proverbs 8:15).] Sapience has a scripture before her, which she reads aloud (signaled by use of the word *quod*, a word that indicates direct quotations (see *MED*, s.v. *quthen*) and then presents another scripture in English, one that can be read *with-oute a spectakle* (in large enough letters for viewers to see them without artificial assistance). Nolan argues that by having Sapience read aloud, Lydgate transforms Carpenter's Latin mottoes, which would have been legible to only a few, into direct address to the English people (*John Lydgate*, p. 238). Kipling ("London Pageants for Margaret of Anjou," p. 6) argues that Lydgate's manner of referring to the scriptures suggested the use of actual speeches to the designers of the 1445 entry into London for Queen Margaret.

265 ff. Latin marginalia: *Et nunc reges intelligite et erudimini qui iudicatis terram.* [And now, kings, understand and receive instruction, you who judge the earth (Psalm 2:10).]

272 MacCracken notes that Lydgate uses phrases like "the matere doth devyse" when following a source ("King Henry's Triumphal Entry," p. 88).

274 ff. The fourth pageant was at the conduit in Cornhill and featured a child on a throne, dressed like a king, accompanied by Mercy, Truth, and Clemency, as well as two judges and eight sergeants-at-arms with a scripture emphasizing equity and justice. MacCracken notes that the phrase *the matere doth devyse* with which Lydgate begins the description of this pageant is one he uses when following a source ("King Henry's Triumphal Entry," p. 88). The child-king pageant was clearly designed with an eye to Henry as its chief spectator, a tactic adopted in other royal entries, including Henry's Paris entry of the previous year (*Parisian Journal*, p. 270).

274 *the Conduyte made in cercle wyse.* Kingsford (*Chronicles of London*, p. 303, note to p. 106, line 28) notes that the castellated conduit in Cornhill was built in 1282 as a prison for nightwalkers and in the fifteenth century still featured a timber cage used for that purpose, with stocks and a pillory for fraudulent bakers. The conduit was called the Tun (since it resembled a tun standing on one end) and in 1401 was made into a cistern for water carried by lead pipes from Tybourn. Wickham discusses the importance of conduits as locations for stages (*Early English Stages*, 1:55–58).

279 Latin marginalia: *Domina misericordia a dexteris et Domina veritatis a senistris cum clemencia roborabitur thronus eius.* [Lady Mercy to the right and Lady Truth to the left, with Clemency his throne shall be strengthened (see Proverbs 20:28).]

289 Latin marginalia: *Misericordia et veritas custodiunt regem.* [Mercy and Truth preserve the king (Proverbs 20:28).]

293 Latin marginalia: *Iudicium et Iusticiam* [Judgment and justice (compare Psalm 88:15)]. Osberg ("Lambeth Palace," pp. 258–59) believes that this gloss points to a "scripture" for the fourth pageant that is missing in Carpenter and Lydgate.

296 Latin marginalia: *Honor Regis Iudicium diligit* [The king's honor loves judgment (Psalm 98:4)].

300 Latin marginalia: *Deus iudicium tuum Regi da et iusticiam tuam filio Regis* [Give to the king thy judgment, O God, and to the king's son thy justice (Psalm 71:2)].

307 ff. The fifth pageant was in Cheapside, at its conduit, where a Wells of Paradise scene depicted the water from the fountains being miraculously turned into wine. For lines 314–63, Lydgate's account is independent of Carpenter's letter: he adds a description of three virgins who draw up the wine (Mercy, Grace, and Pity) and points out the pun linking the name of the mayor (John Welles) to the

fountains (*thes welles*) while describing the elaborate fruit trees that had been arranged there. MacCracken argues that Lydgate added these details at Welles' instigation to underscore the mayor's efforts in arranging the pageants ("King Henry's Triumphal Entry," pp. 90–91). Kipling, however, argues that Lydgate may have seen the Wells of Paradise pageant himself ("Poet as Deviser," pp. 87–89, and *Enter the King*, pp. 142–69). But Welles punned on his own name on other occasions; see *Chronicles of London*, p. 303, note to p. 109, line 15. Kipling argues that the fifth pageant enacts Henry VI's capacity to "transform the city into a holy place" (*Enter the King*, p. 163), but Benson observes that it is a distinctly earthly paradise in which the commerical heart of London becomes a place of pleasure and abundance ("Civic Lydgate," pp. 156–57); see also DeVries, "And Away Go Troubles," for the urban problem of clean water.

308   *a place of alle delycys.* Cheapside was a busy section in the middle of London, known for its market, Goldsmiths' Row, and the Mercers' shops; as the widest street in medieval London, it was a prime location for processions, civic ceremonies, and even tournaments (see A. Lancashire, *London Civic Theatre*, p. 28). The Great Conduit stood at the intersection of Poultry and Cheapside; Stow (*Survey of London*, 1:17 and 1:264) says it was built around 1285.

312   *Archedeclyne.* The master of the feast at Cana (John 2:1–10), used both as a common noun and a proper name. See *MED arch(i)triclin* (n.), which cites this line, along with the Towneley Plays and five other instances from the mid-thirteenth century on.

313   Latin marginalia: *Verba translatoris.* [The translator's words.] The same phrase appears at the opening of Lydgate's *Dance of Death*.

       turned into wyne. The first reference to the practice of having the conduit in Cheap flow with wine for all to drink comes in descriptions of the coronation of Edward I in 1274 (Barron, *London*, p. 19).

314   Latin marginalia: *Thetes est dea aquarum.* [Thetis is the goddess of the sea.]

319   Latin marginalia: *Bachus vere est deus vini.* [Bacchus is really the god of wine.]

328 ff. Kipling thinks that Mercy, Grace, and Pity were introduced by the pageant maker to solve the problem of a disorderly scrambling for the wine, while also adding allegorical significance and ceremony to the dispensing of wine to the king when he approached this pageant ("Poet as Deviser," p. 87); Carpenter's letter doesn't include them, because he is working from the original device for the entry, which didn't envision that problem or solution.

345   Latin marginalia: *Nomen Maioris Iohannes Welles.* [The name of the mayor is John Welles.]

349–62 Lydgate translates Carpenter's reference to "stallatum floribus et arboribus fructiforis" into two full stanzas, which Nolan (*John Lydgate*, p. 137) describes as a "poetic set piece" that takes the reader out of the world of the pageant into the world of poetic composition that substitutes for historical reality. For Lydgate's use of the orchard, see Wickham, *Early English Stages*, 1:91.

354–59   For the meanings of the names of these fruits, see the *MED*: *Blaunderells* were a kind of especially prized apples; *quenings* and *costards* were kinds of apple (*costards* were described in the nineteenth century as having five prominent ridges); *wardouns* were a variety of pear; *pomewaters* and *ricardouns* were varieties of apple.

366–67   Enoch and Elijah were known as the guardians of Paradise. In the Hebrew Bible, they are also lawgivers, suggesting that an earthly paradise requires law and order.

370   Latin marginalia: *Nichil proficiat Inimicus in eo. Et filius iniquitatis non apponat nocere ei.* [The enemy shall have no advantage over him: nor the son of iniquity have power to hurt him (Psalm 88:23).]

379   Latin marginalia: *Dominus conseruet eum et uiviticet eum et beatum faciet eum.* [The Lord preserve him and give him life, and make him blessed (Psalm 40:3).]

386   Latin marginalia: *Haurietis aquas in gaudio de fontibus Salvatoris.* [Thou shall draw waters with joy out of the savior's fountains (Isaiah 12:3).]

391 ff.   The sixth pageant featured a castle made of jasper (at the Cross in Cheapside, according to Carpenter, though Lydgate omits the location), with, in Lydgate's but not Carpenter's account, a pedigree showing Henry VI's descent from two trees springing from Saint Edward and Saint Louis (patron saints of England and France, respectively). On the other side of the castle is a Tree of Jesse, showing David's descent from Jesus. See Osberg ("Jesse Tree") for a discussion of the Jesse tree in this entry.

419–25   MacCracken ("King Henry's Triumphal Entry," p. 93) argues that Lydgate's defense of the Jesse-tree pageant at the Cross in Cheap, which is absent from Carpenter's letter, may be evidence that he devised the pageant himself or that it may have been added because the mayor had been criticized for its inclusion.

426 ff.   The final pageant, at the Little Conduit in Paul's, showed a likeness of the Trinity on a throne surrounded by angels, and had a precept in scripture written at the front of "the hyhe stage" (suggesting that the pageant was elevated on a stage). In lines 440–46, Lydgate adds a second set of verses not found in Carpenter, which he describes as being written on the front of the pageant, and concludes with an additional stanza offering wishes of good will to the king as well as to the mayor and the city.

435 ff.   Latin marginalia: *Angelus eius mandavit de te.* [For he hath given his angels charge over thee (Psalm 90:11).]

449   *nyne sperys*. In the Ptolemaic system, the planets and stars revolve around the earth in nine concentric spheres.

454 ff.   In Carpenter's letter the description of the proceedings at St. Paul's is brief and there is no account of events inside the church at Westminster, perhaps because he did not see them firsthand or had no source for them. MacCracken believes that Lydgate witnessed the two church processions and elaborates on them from memory ("King Henry's Triumphal Entry," p. 95).

457   I.e., Henry Chichele, archbishop of Canterbury from 1414 to 1443, and Chancellor John Kemp, a supporter of Henry Beaufort, who as a concession to Gloucester was forced to resign the chancellorship on February 28, 1432.

458–61   I.e., the bishops of Lincoln (William Gray), Bath (John Stafford), Salisbury (Robert Neville), Norwich (William Alnwick), and Ely (Philip Morgan). The bishop of Rochester in 1432 was John Langdon.

478   The scepter of St. Edward was a relic of Edward the Confessor; it was housed in Westminster and used for coronation ceremonies until it was destroyed in 1649 along with other royal regalia.

484   *Te Deum*. The *Te Deum laudamus (We praise Thee, Lord)* is one of the most familiar hymns of praise, sung at the end of matins when the Gloria has been said, and on special occasions such as the election of a pope, consecration of a bishop, or canonization of a saint. The friar in Chaucer's Summoner's Tale claims that he and his confreres sang one to accompany heavenward the soul of the son of Thomas and his pretty wife; the child had died a couple of weeks earlier (*CT* III[D]1866). The hymn is often sung in the cycle plays.

487   Latin marginalia: *Ex duabus arboribus Sancti Edwardi et Sancti Lodowici.* [From two trees, Saint Edward and Saint Louis.]

490   *Unto his paleys*. I.e., Westminster palace.

496 ff.   Carpenter describes the Saturday gift-giving and quotes the mayor's speech in English; Lydgate's version follows it closely. The hamper filled with gold brought by the mayor, aldermen, and sheriffs of London to the king was a *lytyll gifte*, as the mayor modestly says in his speech, designed to make the king look favorably on the city and remind him of his obligations toward it. Kingsford notes that in 1415 Londoners presented Henry V with 1000 pounds in gold in two gold baskets (*Chronicles of London*, p. 303, note to p. 114, line 21).

510 ff.   Lydgate here adds three stanzas of praise to London, not found in Carpenter's letter. In BL MS Cotton Cleopatra C.iv and BL MS Harley 565, these stanzas are prefaced by the Latin marginalia *Verba translatoris*.

512   *Newe Troye*. According to the legendary history of England recounted by Geoffrey of Monmouth in his *Historia Regum Britannorum*, Brutus, a descendant of Aeneas, with other exiles from the Trojan war came to the island of Albion and built a capital city called Trojanova or Troynovant (New Troy). The notion of *translatio imperii*, that Troy was the original of later cities, was a medieval commonplace.

517–23   Lydgate's *Serpent of Division*, probably written in the crisis of rule just after the death of Henry V, retells the life of Caesar as a lesson in the consequences of political and social divisiveness, and presents Caesar as a virtuous pagan. Nolan (*John Lydgate*, pp. 186 and 233) argues that the comparison of Henry VI's entry to Caesar's triumph is the first explicit forging of a connection between medieval royal entries and Roman practices and reveals Lydgate's ambivalence about Lancastrian propaganda.

530   *The Kyngis Chambre.* The notion that London is the king's chamber recognizes the city's special relationship with the king and suggests that London is his dwelling place (see McLaren, *London Chronicles*, p. 55n13).

531–37   The envoy contains a conventional humility *topos* addressed to the mayor, asking forgiveness for the poet's efforts (his *symple makyng*, line 535); for a discussion of the fifteenth-century uses of this *topos*, see Lawton, "Dullness and the Fifteenth Century," p. 762. The last line offers the only explicit evidence that the poem was written at the mayor's request. Lydgate was presumably paid by Londoners for his efforts, as in all likelihood was Richard Maidstone for his Latin poem describing the four pageants in the reconciliation ceremonies between London and Richard II; see Barron, *London*, p. 20.

532   Nolan (*John Lydgate*, p. 239) notes that Lydgate's real and imaginary audience has expanded from the "wyse governours" of the 1422 *Serpent of Division* to "alle that duelle in this citee" (an illusory expansion, of course, since there is no documented increase in the number of Lydgate's readers).

THE LEGEND OF ST. GEORGE

Shirley describes *The Legend of St. George* as "the devyse of a steyned halle" made by Lydgate for the armorers of London and seems to suggest that Lydgate came up with ("ymagyned") both the pictorial scheme and the verses. Although Stow's note, written at the top of page 315 in Trinity R.3.21 ("The lyfe of saynt gorge compyled by John lidgate monke of bery at the request of the armerers of london to peynt about ther haulle") implies that the verses were for a mural, the term *steyned halle* more likely refers to a painted wall-hanging (see Floyd, "St. George," pp. 145–48). A. Lancashire (*London Civic Theatre*, p. 124) notes that there might also have been an accompanying mimed performance, perhaps one similar to that recorded in 1585 at an election feast of the armorers and brasiers where an armed boy representing St. George and a lady leading a lamb accompanied by drum and flute marched around the hall and gave a speech. Textual evidence may support the possibility that Lydgate's verses were read aloud as the armorers and their guests looked at the images (or watched possible mimed action) (see lines 1–3 and 32).

The verses, which draw on material from the *Legenda Aurea* (see Schirmer, *John Lydgate*, p. 157n1), tell two stories: St. George's rescue of a king's daughter from a dragon and the subsequent conversion of her city, and his encounter with the tyrant Dacian, who tortures the saint for his beliefs (George escapes all harm, destroys the pagan temple, and converts Dacian's wife, before finally being beheaded, after which Dacian is stricken and dies). Pearsall makes the point that "as befits the occasion and the audience," the poem "is remarkably straightforward and free of the amplification that Lydgate generally introduced in purely literary treatments of saints' lives" (*John Lydgate*, p. 181). Its thirty-five rhyme-royal stanzas are lively, full of action, and move smoothly to the saint's final prayer.

St. George's chivalrous protection of women, his piety, his generosity to the poor, and his military prowess — all attributes noted by Lydgate — made him popular among the knightly classes and in the 1340s, Edward III dedicated his Order of the Garter to St. George (as the second stanza of Lydgate's poem mentions). By the end of the fourteenth century St. George had become the patron saint of England, and in 1415, after the English victory at Agincourt, where troops had carried the banner of St. George (see *Chronicle of*

London, p. 228), Archbishop Chichele raised St. George's day (April 23) to the status of a Great Feast and ordered it to be celebrated on a par with Christmas. St. George was the armorers' patron saint and Lydgate's verses may have been commissioned for one of their feasts in his honor, perhaps the one that coincided with completion of construction on a new hall for their guild, in other words, April 23, 1430 (see Floyd, "St. George," p. 144).

   The Legend of St. George survives in four fifteenth-century manuscripts; the base text for this edition is Trinity MS R.3.20 (1450–75), pp. 74–81 (*MP*, 1:145–54), collated by MacCracken with Trinity College Cambridge MS R.3.21 and Bodleian Library MS 2527 (Bodley 686).

running titles: *A story made of Saint / George by Lidegate / A story of Saint / George / A story of / Saint George / A storye of / Saint George.*

headnote   *ymagyned*. The most pertinent meaning of the the verb *imaginen* given by *MED* is "3.(a) To plan (sth.), intend, plot; devise (a scheme)."

            th'armorieres. The armorers of London made and repaired armor and weapons. For discussion of the activities, status, and patronage of St. George, see Floyd, "St. George," pp. 144–45.

rubric   *The poete first declarethe*. This phrase may refer to a painted representation similar to the *ymage in poete-wyse* of *Bycorne and Chychevache*, or may imply that the verses were read aloud, as Pearsall suggests (*John Lydgate*, p. 181). Schirmer, *John Lydgate*, p. 157, believes Lydgate himself recited them.

1   *O yee folk that heer present be*. This opening line may hint at recitation to a group of people assembled in the armorers' hall or may address viewers of the wall hanging.

2–3   *inspeccion . . . beholde and see*. These lines imply that the representation included one or more visual images or mimetic representations which the audience could *inspect* (contemplate) and *beholde* (discern) *and see* while hearing or reading Lydgate's verses.

8–14   Edward III founded the Order of the Garter c. 1349. Membership was limited to twenty-five plus the king, although a sorority of women, the Ladies of the Fraternity of Saint George and the Society of the Garter, was also established (see Gillespie, "Ladies of the Fraternity"). The feast day of Saint George (*his day*) was April 23.

18   Here and in lines 23, 26, 148, 211, and 218, Lydgate invokes his sources for the life of St. George, chiefly the *Legenda Aurea*.

32   *whoso list to looke*. Possibly a reference to the painted images in the hall, but more likely a nod towards Lydgate's sources.

72   *no meede*. Literally, "no reward" (i.e., nothing could spare the princess from her doom).

85   *Oure Ladyes owen knight*. I.e., the Virgin Mary's knight.

96   *Chaumpyoun*. Someone who engages in battle for another's sake (*MED* n. 2[a]). The term was also used to refer to judicial duels or trials by battle, in which under

English law representatives (champions) of the two parties would fight to deter-
mine the case, with divine intervention assigning victory to the rightful side. Its use
here is consistent with Lydgate's depiction of St. George as a model of chivalry.

162 ff.   Pearsall (*John Lydgate*, pp. 277–78) notes that Lydgate's treatment of George's
          martyrdom contrasts with the colloquialism and violence of the version in the
          South English Legendary: the torture scene in this and the next stanzas avoids the
          physical detail and appeal to emotions of the *Legendary* and "deflects the edge
          of suffering" through the use of conventional literary phrasing, such as the
          absolute constructions of lines 174–75, which make the actions seem pre-
          ordained not humanly planned.

169 ff.   Wylie and Waugh (*Reign of Henry the Fifth*, 2:117) note that these lines shed light
          on contemporary methods of hanging men.

187–96   George's poisoner is converted, then martyred; compare the conversion of St.
          Cecilia's jailor in Chaucer's Second Nun's Tale (*CT* VIII[G]400–05).

232–38   The saint's prayer on behalf of those who venerate him is a conventional motif;
          Pearsall (*John Lydgate*, p. 278) observes that Lydgate's "abstraction and generality"
          in this stanza contrast with the "homely practicality" of the *South English Legendary*.

240   *A voyce was herd doune frome the hye heven.* Compare The Man of Law's Tale (*CT*
          II[B¹]673–76).

MESURE IS TRESOUR

These verses elaborate on the proverbial saying that "measure is treasure" and argue
that moderation should be the guiding principle for all estates, both high and low. *Mesure*
is seen as the "roote of al good policye" (line 9) that should shape the actions of every social
group from popes and prelates to emperors, kings, and knights, and on to judges, mayors,
merchants, ploughmen, and other commoners that are "alle set here in portrature" (line
108). Examples from ancient myth and history (Alexander, Cambises, Hercules) underscore
the dangers of overreaching. The poem expresses a number of Lydgate's typical concerns:
defense of the Church against heretics, the dangers of division, and the virtues of hierarchy
for common profit (see Schirmer's discussion of *Mesure* alongside Lydgate's other moral and
didactic poems, *John Lydgate*, pp. 198–205). The last two stanzas are explicitly in the voice
of a shepherd, who is compared to the biblical examples of Isaac and Jacob and is described
as being "set here to stondyn at dyfence" (line 138) to "kepe in sekirnesse / This hows in
sewyrté" (lines 149–50), that is, to guard the household.

Lines 108, 134, and 142 indicate that the various estates described in the poem were
present in some visual form; Pearsall (*John Lydgate*, p. 181) believes that the verses were
intended to be read aloud alongside a painting. The use of the first-person pronoun by the
shepherd in the last two stanzas may possibly have provided an opportunity for mimicry or
impersonation, although that is by no means certain. In any event, the shepherd appears
as some sort of visual representation.

The unique copy of the poem is in MS Harley 2255 (1448?–49?), the base text for this
edition; Harley 2255 is an anthology of some forty-five lyrics, most or all of which appear
to be by Lydgate. The manuscript belonged to Lydgate's abbot at Bury, William Curteys (see
Pearsall, *Bio-Bibliography*, p. 82) and was perhaps assembled at Bury St. Edmunds, possibly

under the supervision of Lydgate himself. The poem has been edited by Halliwell and by MacCracken, in *MP*, 2:776–80.

1	*mesour is tresour*. A proverbial saying; see Whiting, *Proverbs*, M461 and Duschl, *Sprichwort*, p. 20, on its classification. Compare Lydgate's "Song of Just Mesure" (*MP* 2:772–75).
33–40	The story of the victory of Alexander the Great (356–323 B.C.) over Porrus and his search for the Earthly Paradise were well known from various French and Middle English Alexander romances (see Bunt, *Alexander the Great*).
43–44	The Roman Scipio defeated the Carthaginian force led by Hannibal in a decisive battle during the Second Punic War in 202 B.C.
52	*comoun profight*. See note to *Disguising at London*, line 251.
67	The story of Cambises, king of Persia (529–522 B.C.), derives from Herodotus. He was commonly taken as an example of an unjust tyrant and an admonitory figure against anger and pride, whose death in a hunting accident was seen as fitting punishment for his crimes. Compare Chaucer's Summoner's Tale (*CT* III[D]2043–78).
81	*Among yoursilf suffre noon extorcioun*. Compare the envoy to Chaucer's "Lak of Stedfastnesse," where Richard himself is exhorted to "hate extorcioun" (line 23).
110 ff.	Compare *Mumming at Bishopswood*, lines 50 ff.
118–21	The plowman was a traditional symbol of the ideal Christian (see Barney, "Plowshare of the Tongue").
131–32	The biblical patriarchs Isaac and Jacob were shepherds (see Genesis 22:27 and 24:28).

MUMMING AT BISHOPSWOOD

Shirley describes the *Mumming at Bishopswood* as a balade made by Lydgate for a May Day dinner of London's sheriffs and their *bretherne* being held at Bishop's Wood, a place owned by the bishop of London outside London in what is now Stepney (see I. Lancashire, *Dramatic Texts and Records*, no. 1414). MacCracken calls *Bishopswood* a mumming (*MP*, 2:1668), but Shirley does not, and, unlike most other fourteenth- and fifteenth-century mummings, it did not take place during the Christmas season, although it does feature the visit of outsiders bearing gifts (in this case, seemingly just abstract ones, but see Norton-Smith, *John Lydgate: Poems*, p. 123) that is characteristic of the genre. No presenter is identified, but the messenger (*poursyvant*) who brought the balade may have read it aloud while silent characters impersonated Ver (Spring) and possibly Flora (although the text implies that she is not present), as well as May (if May is a figure distinct from Ver); there may also have been a musical interlude by figures from classical mythology (Venus, Cupid, and Orpheus, at lines 99–105), although these lines are probably meant merely as a poetic description. If *Bishopswood* had four performers (a presenter and three silent actors) it would match the size of the usual London performing company of the period (A. Lancashire, *London Civic Theatre*, pp. 120 and 262n27).

Bishopswood is undated, but Pearsall (*Bio-Bibliography*, p. 51) places it in May of 1429, arguing that it might have accompanied the mummings for the Mercers and Goldsmiths earlier that year in honor of William Estfeld; if Pearsall is correct, the actual date would have to be May of 1430, since as Anne Lancashire has pointed out Estfeld was mayor from October 29, 1429, to October 29, 1430. Noting that the coronation of Henry VI in London on November 6, 1429, might have raised ordinary festivities to a higher level in the next six months, Lancashire (*London Civic Theatre*, pp. 121–22) posits May Day of 1430 as a likely date for a special commission from Lydgate for the sheriffs' dinner, especially since he had provided entertainments for the coronation ceremonies and had written the mummings for the mercers and goldsmiths for performance in early 1430 as well. A wider range of dates for the mumming cannot be ruled out, however, since the sole extant copy is in Bodley Ashmole 59, which Shirley compiled in 1447–49 while resident in the close of St. Bartholomew's Hospital in London (see Connolly, "John Shirley," p. 152); Shirley's inclusion of *Bishopswood* while he did not recopy any of the mummings from Trinity R.3.20, which he used as a partial exemplar for Ashmole 59, perhaps suggests that he did not have a copy of the mumming when he made Trinity R.3.20 in the early 1430s. Stow included the first two stanzas, derived from Ashmole 59 which passed through his hands, in his *Survey of London* (1598), as an example of the "great Mayings and maygames made by the gouernors and Maisters of this Citie" (p. 99), although the earliest recorded May game in London dates to 1458 (in the parish of Saint Nicholas Shambles) (see Clopper, *Drama, Play, and Game*, p. 160n57).

The poem consists of sixteen rhyme-royal stanzas that offer political and social commentary embedded within praise of the coming of spring, in the guise of Flora's daughter Ver, who bids flowers to bloom and birds to sing, as signs that winter has fled. Ver also ushers in prosperity, peace, and unity after the adversity and troubles of winter, and the nature imagery soon develops into a social and political commentary that imagines all estates united, with each fulfilling its proper duties so that righteousness destroys the "darkness" of extortion and leads to a joyful summer (see Wickham, *Early English Stages* 3:50, and Ebin, *John Lydgate*, p. 87). While much of this commentary deals with conventional themes of the proper roles of the various estates, it may also address real contemporary concerns, especially in its references to discord and dissension. Like many of Lydgate's other poems for Londoners, *Bishopswood* speaks to the concerns and aspirations of the city's elites, particularly for order and prosperity. The poem ends with a four-stanza envoy addressed to all the estates who are present, proclaiming that May has now come to bring them "joye and fresshnesse." By adding an elevating classical note in the description of Parnassus and the muses, the envoy also seems designed to make clear to the audience the values of the poetic conceits to which they have listened.

Critical opinion on the aesthetic qualities of *Bishopswood* has been mixed. While Pearsall admires the learned philosophical and scientific description of spring, he finds the verses to be "cumbersome and awkward" (*John Lydgate*, p. 186). Norton-Smith (*John Lydgate: Poems*, pp. 123–24) points out, however, that while the poem may seem diffuse and repetitive there is a progression from Ver (who presides over March and April) to May (whom he takes to be a separate figure), with verbal repetition of words such as *lusty*, *swote*, *ermonye*, and *lustynes*, which builds to the core of the poem in stanza fifteen where earthly harmony and unity are related to heavenly Parnassus. And Schirmer (*John Lydgate*, p. 104) argues for its innovative blending of pantomime-type pageants such as those found in royal entries and didactic scholastic drama such as the *Pageant of Knowledge*.

The base text for this edition is Ashmole 59, fols. 62r–64r (*MP*, 2:668–71). In Ashmole 59, Shirley does not separate the verses into stanzas but does include a mark (which resembles an "m" or an "n" with a front tail) to the left of the first line of each stanza. See the discussion of this mark in the Introduction; I have followed MacCracken in creating stanza divisions.

running titles: *Lydegates balade sente / to the Shirrefe dyner / At the Shirreve dyner / Lidegates balade*; not noted by *MP*.

headnote   A *poursyvant* was a messenger, an attendant on a herald, or a junior heraldic officer attached to a royal or noble household. Besides administering tournaments, heralds also made announcements and proclamations, carried letters, and served as masters-of-ceremonies; in wardrobe accounts they are often grouped with minstrels and other performers, underscoring the confusion between heralds and minstrels. According to Shirley, the *Mumming for the Mercers* was also brought by a pursuivant "in wyse of mommers desguysed" while the *Mumming for the Goldsmiths* was "brought and presented" by a herald called Fortune. Schirmer (*John Lydgate*, p. 103) thinks the occasion was a kind of picnic, and that the balade was "presented by a page who steps out of the wood into the clearing" and then reads the poem or hands it to a narrator to read while Ver dances and panto-mimes, but the dinner was almost certainly indoors (see Pearsall, *John Lydgate*, p. 186). Stow identifies Bishopswood as being in the parish of Stebunheath [Stepney], further elaborating: "Bishops wood / Bishops hall / by Blethenhall greene" [Bethnal Green] (*Survey of London*, 1:99). Barron notes that Londoners claimed their principal hunting rights on the lands of the bishop of London in Stepney (*London*, p. 192). On May Day in 1430 the two sheriffs were a goldsmith and a merchant taylor (A. Lancashire, *London Civic Theatre*, p. 276n32).

1   Flora was the Roman goddess of flowering plants and fertility. The syntax of the first stanza is confusing and apparently led Shirley to make a mistake in copying the verb in line 2 (see Textual Notes) and caused MacCracken (*MP*, 2:668) and Ebin (*John Lydgate*, p. 87) to think that Flora is a character in the mumming (sent by her mother Ver, Ebin says); but the correct reading, corroborated by repeated mentions of Ver later in the verses, seems to be that Flora has sent her daughter Ver to the sheriffs' feast.

5   *entent*. I.e., [*hir*] (Flora's) intention.

6   *th'estates wheoche that nowe sitte here*. A reference to the occasion and to the assembled audience. Here and in other lines, Lydgate presents an inclusive, if hierarchical, view of society, one in which all estates are supposed to perform their roles properly and to treat even the lowliest as "truwe comunes" (line 55).

7   *Veere*. Ver, or springtime personified. Although Norton-Smith (*John Lydgate: Poems*, p. 124) claims that Ver is an uncommon personification in Middle English verse, with only one reference to her in Gower (*CA*, 7.1014, where Ver is not gendered female) and in Chaucer (*Troilus and Criseyde*, 1.157), the *MED* cites a number of other examples. In *FP*, Lydgate imagines Ver as male (5.1509).

9   *vertue vegytable*. Animating, or life-giving, force (see *MED*, *vegetable*, adj. a.). Norton-Smith (*John Lydgate: Poems*, p. 125) notes that Lydgate often shows "a scientific interest" in botanical processes, as in this stanza; compare *TB*, 2.3915 ff. and *Reson and Sensuallyte*, line 2747.

15   *swaged*. Norton-Smith (*John Lydgate: Poems*, p. 125) notes that this is a term used to describe frost, as in *TB* 2.5067 ff.

17–18 For the notion that birds choose their mates in the springtime, see Chaucer's *Parliament of Fowles*.

27   *proygne*. "Preen"; usually used of birds, as here, but occasionally applied to humans (*MED*, *proinen* v.).

29–35 This stanza introduces the idea that Ver offers an escape from the adversity and troubles of winter by bringing not only springtime but also prosperity, peace, and stability.

35   *youre hye renoun*. A form of honorific address, similar to those in lines 80 and 111. It is unclear in these three instances precisely who is being addressed. Although the phrase could be directed to the two sheriffs, it may be that the mayor, or another high-ranking person, was present; see A. Lancashire, *London Civic Theatre*, p. 71, for prominent guests, including royalty, at company feasts and compare the *Mumming for the Goldsmiths*, in which the mayor is addressed as "youre Hyeghnesse" (line 75).

42   The dangers of discord and division are explored at length in Lydgate's *Serpent of Division*. Compare with lines 47 ("for to exyle duplicytee"), 63 ("That noone oppression beo done to the pourayle"), 70 ("Represse . . . al extorcyoune"), and 72 ("Troubles exylinge").

51   *the hede*. Oblique reference to the notion of the body politic; see *FP* 2.827–903 for a fuller version of the same conceit.

55   *truwe comunes*. Compare the language of commonalty found in the *Disguising at London* and *Mesure Is Tresour*.

75   *mynistre of lustynesse*. Ver was often viewed as the season of youth, regeneration, mating, and procreation; see *MED*, n. 1(c).

76–77 These lines possibly refer to the presence of someone actually impersonating Ver, but they are too vague to let us say for sure.

80   *May*. The introduction of May, who has not been mentioned up to this point, is somewhat confusing. Norton-Smith (*John Lydgate: Poems*, p. 124) argues that there is a progression from Ver (who presides over March and April) to May, who presides over the day and the following season, but it seems odd that Lydgate would devote eleven stanzas to Ver and just one to May before turning to the envoy (in which May, but not Ver, is mentioned); May is possibly a synonym for Ver, rather than another character. Perhaps Shirley's age at the time of copying the mumming (he would have been over eighty) explains this and other confusion that crops up elsewhere in Ashmole 59 (see Connolly, "John Shirley," p. 152).

80   *youre Hye Excellence.* See note to line 35.

84 ff.   *L'envoye to alle th'estates present.* This rubric may perhaps have been misplaced by
            Shirley, as it makes better sense following line 105.

85   *This Princesse.* A reference to May; see also line 78. The *MED* notes that the word
            princes(se) (n. [d]) is often used with personifications of fortune, nature, wisdom,
            and so forth, particularly by Lydgate.

92   *motleys.* From the noun *motle,* meaning "variegated cloth," here used in the sense
            of a multicolored blanket of flowers covering the hills; see *FP,* 6.183.

95   *Tytane.* Titan, a name for the sun.

99   The muses were the nine daughters of Zeus and Mnemosyne. Lydgate's descrip-
            tion of Parnassus here and in the *Mumming for the Mercers* echoes Chaucer's in
            Anelida and Arcite, lines 15 ff., and derives from Servius' commentary on Virgil
            and Isidore's *Etymologiae,* 14.8, lines 11–12 (see Norton-Smith, *John Lydgate:*
            Poems, p. 126). While this stanza introduces new imagery to the poem (Schirmer,
            John Lydgate, p. 103, describes it as "a touch of humanistic fantasy"), its linking
            of earthly harmony and unity with heavenly Parnassus is typical of Lydgate's
            tactics of elevation that both flatter and instruct his audiences.

100   *Citherra.* An alternate name for Venus, derived from the name of the island of
            Cythera.

102   *wellis.* As Norton-Smith (*John Lydgate: Poems,* p. 126) notes, this is a reference to
            the rivers Helicon and Hippocrene, sacred to the Muses.

103   *hem.* Refers to Venus and her son, Cupid.

104   Norton-Smith (*John Lydgate: Poems,* p. 126) observes that Lydgate here combines
            two passages from Chaucer on Orpheus' music, from *Hous of Fame,* 1201 ff., and
            the translation of Boethius' *De Consolatione,* III.M.2.21 ff.

108   *tofore yow.* Perhaps a reference to the presence of someone who is impersonating
            May; compare with lines 76–77.

111   *youre Hyenesse.* See note to line 35.

MUMMING AT ELTHAM

Shirley calls this a balade made by Lydgate for a Christmas mumming at Eltham for the
king and queen, presumably Henry VI and his mother, Catherine of Valois. It consists of
twelve rhyme-royal stanzas that describe the meaning of the gifts Bacchus, Juno, and Ceres
send to the king and queen — via merchants that are present (line 5) — gifts of wine, oil,
and wheat betokening peace, plenty, and gladness. While the mumming touches on the
legitimacy of the dual monarchy, its chief concern, emphasized in the final line of each
stanza, is to offer reassurances that troubles and discord will be banished and that mother
and son will enjoy peace, prosperity, and happiness.

Various dates between 1424 and 1429 have been proposed for the mumming, but
contemporary sources place Henry VI at Eltham for Christmas in only two of those years:
1425/26 and 1428/29. Privy Council records mention a ring that was given to Henry VI by

the duke of Bedford "a Noel tenu a Eltham l'an de votre graciouse regne quarte," i.e., during the Christmas season of 1425/26 (*PPC*, 3:284–86) and London companies were at Eltham then (PRO, E404/44/334; Griffiths, *Reign of King Henry VI*, p. 64n17). Amundesham (*Annales monasterii S. Albani*, 1:32) claims that Henry was at Eltham for the Christmas season of 1428/29, a date Pearsall argues fits best with Lydgate's career (*Bio-Bibliography*, p. 29). As for the other possible dates, 1424/25 cannot be ruled out and is the date given by I. Lancashire (*Dramatic Texts and Records*, no. 636, citing no source) and Schirmer (*John Lydgate*, p. 101n1, based on an unnamed citation in Kingsford that I have been unable to locate). The holiday season of 1426/27 may also be a possibility, but 1427/28 is probably not: I. Lancashire (*Dramatic Texts and Records*, nos. 637 and 638) follows Wolffe (*Henry VI*, p. 37) in claiming that Jack Travaill's players and four boys of Thomas Beaufort, duke of Exeter, were at Eltham at Christmas in 1426 and that Travaill was back at Eltham for Christmas of 1427 along with players from Abingdon, but Wolffe's dates seem to be based on a misinterpretation of the accounts of Henry VI's chamber treasurer, John Merston (PRO E404/42/306; E404/44/334; printed in *Foedera* 10:387–88): Merston's entries were recorded in February of 1428 for the 1427/28 holiday season, which seems to have been spent at Hertford (see the Explanatory Notes for the *Disguising at Hertford*).

Shirley's phrasing seems to suggest that Lydgate was at Eltham when he made the balade, which perhaps encouraged Schirmer (*John Lydgate*, p. 101) to imagine that the verses might have been read aloud by Lydgate himself, especially since there is no mention of a herald or presenter. Lydgate's text may have been an explanatory speech that introduced the mummers who then performed the gift-giving (see Welsford, *Court Masque*, p. 54) or may have accompanied their mimed action. Pearsall (*John Lydgate*, p. 184) thinks there may have been two groups of actors — the three deities in a tableau and the merchants who presented the actual gifts. A. Lancashire (*London Civic Theatre*, pp. 102–03) notes that judging by records of payments acting troupes in the fifteenth century usually consisted of four adults, which means that Travaill's players (or Exeter's four boys or the Abingdon company) could have played the parts of the speaker and three deities. Kipling suggests that after being read aloud, Lydgate's verses might have been presented in commemoration of the event, thus heightening the ceremony of gift-giving ("Poet as Deviser," p. 93).

Surviving records tell us of earlier mummings at Eltham. The first was on January 6, 1393 when citizens of London entertained Richard II with music, dancing, and costumes (the Londoners came with "glorioso apparatu"), and brought gifts (a dromedary and a great bird; see Strohm, *Hochon's Arrow*, pp. 106–07); fines owed by the city to the king were negotiated then, too (see *Westminster Chronicle*, pp. 510–11; discussed by Barron, "Quarrel of Richard II with London"). The second was in 1400–01 when Londoners dressed as twelve aldermen and their sons performed a mumming for the visiting emperor of Constantinople, Manuel II (see A. Lancashire, *London Civic Theatre*, p. 42). A third, less friendly one was planned for Twelfth Night in 1414 by Lollards who "hadde caste to have made a mommynge at Eltham, and undyr coloure of the mommynge to have destryte the kyng and Hooly Chirche," but the plot was discovered before the mumming could be undertaken (*Historical Collections of a Citizen of London*, p. 108).

Who commissioned the *Mumming at Eltham*? Although we can only speculate, the reference to "marchandes that here be" may indicate some collaboration between Londoners (Eltham lies just outside the city) and Henry VI's controller or his staff (who would normally be responsible for overseeing household entertainments) in asking Lydgate to write verses to accompany the presentation of the merchants' gifts. It is possible to see traces of what Benson has called a "civic voice" ("Civic Lydgate," pp. 148–49) in the mumming, particularly in the emphasis on the bourgeois values of stability and prosperity. But if there is a civic voice in this mumming, it shares space with courtly concerns of peace, unity, and control of rebels and infidels, as well as what seems to be genuine solicitousness for Catherine's happiness in the four stanzas addressed to her (see Pearsall, *Bio-Bibliography*, p. 30, for other poems to Catherine that might date to the same period, in which Lydgate had "comparatively close contact with the court").

The *Mumming at Eltham* survives in Trinity R.3.20 (1450–75), pp. 37–40, as well as in Stow's copy of it, now Additional MS 29729. Trinity R.3.20 is the base text for this edition (*MP*, 2:672–74), collated with Additional 29729.

running titles: R.3.20 contains running titles that identify the verses as *the maner of a momynge / to fore the kynge at Elthame / A desgysinge to fore the kynge / At cristmesse in the castel of eltham*; not noted in *MP*.

headnote   *Eltham in Cristmasse*. The palace at Eltham, located two miles southeast of Greenwich, was fortress-like, with ditches, battlements, an inner courtyard, and forty-six large rooms, as well as a banqueting hall in which parliament occasionally met and which was well suited to dramatic performances (Schirmer, *John Lydgate*, p. 101; descriptions of Eltham palace and the plan of the great hall can be found in Hasted, *History and Topographical Survey of the County of Kent*, 1:463–68). A. Lancashire (*London Civic Theatre*, p. 276n31) points out that the Christmas season at court ran at least through the twelve days of Christmas, from December 26 to January 6 (Twelfth Night), but the reference to *This hyeghe feest* in line 80 suggests that the mumming dates to Christmas day.

1–2   Bacchus was the Roman god of wine and fertililty; Juno, sister and wife of Jupiter, was the Roman goddess of marriage, the home, and childbirth; Ceres was the Roman goddess of grain.

4   *theyre giftes*. Parry ("On the Continuity of English Civic Pageantry," pp. 224–25) notes that Queen Elizabeth's visit to Kenilworth in 1575, like the Eltham mumming, featured deities, including Ceres and Bacchus (in this case apparently not impersonated), who presented gifts of produce on seven posts spanning a bridge, while a poet pointed to each post and described the gifts. The choice of wine, wheat, and oil — all of which were imported goods — suggests that the merchants in question were probably from London and may indicate that they were mercers (who traded in such goods), but Shirley's lack of a specific trade name may point to a more diverse group of merchant gift-givers on this occasion. It may have been that the merchants gave Henry and Catherine token gifts of wine, wheat, and oil in containers of precious metal, thus increasing the monetary value of the gifts, or the gifts may have been in sufficient quantity to be provender for the feast (see Merston's accounts for payments for kids and pheasants during the Christmas season of 1427–28, in *Foedera* 10:387).

5   *marchandes that here be*. Nolan (*John Lydgate*, p. 85) thinks that the appearance of merchants is "perhaps a gesture toward the civic origin" of mummings, but that the real issue is the dual monarchy; the text, however, shows little concern with that issue.

15   *Ysaak.* For Isaac's three gifts to Jacob, see Genesis 27:28; here, as elsewhere in his writings, Lydgate blends classical and biblical imagery, turning to two examples of biblical tripartite gifts to amplify the significance of the gifts brought by the three pagan deities. An effigy of Isaac was among the pageants that Londoners designed to greet the duke of Bedford and his duchess on London Bridge when he entered London in 1426 on his return from France (A. Lancashire, *London Civic Theatre*, pp. 136–37 and 285n54; I. Lancashire, *Dramatic Texts and Records*, no. 929, misdated to 1427).

24   *rebelles.* Brotanek (*Englischen Maskenspiele*, p. 305) claims that the *rebelles* are the French, and Nolan (*John Lydgate*, p. 85) agrees, suggesting that the reference links the mumming to 1428, when the Dauphin and the French army had threatened the English to such an extent that the stability of the *two reaumes* (line 27) was in doubt; as Jacob (*Fifteenth Century*, pp. 243–47) shows, however, the entire strife-filled period from the battle of Verneuil (August 1424) to the siege of Orléans (1428) could form a possible context for the strife and disobedience mentioned in this stanza.

25   *cruwel werre.* Schirmer (*John Lydgate*, p. 101) thinks that Mars may have also been represented in the mumming and then driven away by the uniting of Henry's two realms, although it seems more likely that Lydgate refers to Mars merely to introduce the topic of the *cruwel werre* and that only Bacchus, Juno, and Ceres were impersonated (see line 80).

39   *mescreantes in actes marcyal.* Brotanek (*Englischen Maskenspiele*, pp. 305–06) believes this is a reference to Henry Beaufort's attempt at a Hussite crusade.

45   *Provydence, hir sustre.* Schirmer's argument about Mars (see line 25) could also apply to Providence, although once again Lydgate is probably simply describing her attributes.

52   Latin marginalia: *Ad reginam Katerinam mother to Henrie the VI.* [To Queen Catherine, mother to Henry VI.]

       borne of Saint Lowys blood. Catherine was the daughter of Charles VI of France, and thus descended from St. Louis.

53   The banishing of *sorowe* and *hevynesse* here and in line 65 may refer to Catherine's inconclusive affair with Edmund Beaufort, which seems to have begun in 1425 or 1426, and which may have been a source of the crisis of 1425–26 and the quarrel between Gloucester and Henry Beaufort, Edmund's uncle, although that can only remain conjectural (see Harriss, *Cardinal Beaufort*, pp. 143–44).

59–61   The topic of Fortune's *varyaunce* is one Lydgate takes up in a number of his poems; see Lerer (*Chaucer and His Readers*, p. 13) for the pervasive Boethianism Lydgate shares with other fifteenth-century writers, which Lerer views as a response to the upheavals of the period that defined the writer's social role as being "to offer counsel in a fickle world."

80   *This hyeghe feest.* I.e., the feast of Christmas.

81, 84   In these two lines the envoy repeats the refrain of the two parts of the mumming, thus bringing together its hopes for Henry and Catherine.

MUMMING AT WINDSOR

The *Mumming at Windsor* tells the story of the conversion of Clovis by St. Clothilde and the miraculous appearance of the fleur-de-lys and the golden ampoule from which French kings were traditionally anointed at Rheims. Since the mumming mentions that the sacred oil kept at Rheims will soon be used to anoint Henry VI, it presumably dates to the Christmas season of 1429/30, after Henry's coronation on November 6 at Westminster in 1429 and before his departure for France early in 1430; this date gains some slight additional support from Schirmer's claim that Windsor was Henry's permanent winter residence from 1428 onward (*John Lydgate*, p. 106). The mumming, which is addressed to Henry, adroitly combines instruction, entertainment, and propaganda, using French history to shore up Henry's claims to the dual monarchy (see Wickham, *Early English Stages*, 3:50, who notes its educative aspect but thinks it "exists simply to pass time agreeably;" Nolan [*John Lydgate*, pp. 86–87], who discusses the mumming's topical instrumentality; and Green [*Poets and Princepleasers*, p. 189], who describes this as one of Lydgate's "apologist" poems for the Lancastrian dynasty). The mumming is concerned with lineage and hereditary rights, the ever-present worries of Henry's minority, but the mumming also contains a strong subcurrent of praise for women (Clothilde is called the "floure of wommanhede," constant in word and deed), which draws a bantering marginal comment from Shirley and reminds us that Henry's mother Catherine, who is directly addressed in Lydgate's two other royal mummings and who was Henry's most visible link to the French crown, was probably present.

Shirley's description of the poem as "the devyse of a momyng" has led to a number of hypotheses about the nature of the performance to which the text relates, with most scholars agreeing that Lydgate's verses served as a kind of preface for "the story" of the fleur-de-lys that was subsequently "shewed" before the king and were recited by a presenter ("almost certainly Lydgate himself," according to Pearsall [*John Lydgate*, pp. 185–86], a view seconded by Westfall [*Patrons and Performance*, pp. 35–37], who notes that Shirley doesn't mention a herald or pursuivant). There is no consensus as to the precise nature of the ensuing show. Kipling follows Wickham (*Early English Stages*, 1:205) in thinking that Shirley's description of Windsor as a mumming is a mistake given the lack of a visit by strangers and the absence of gift-giving and argues that *Windsor* resembles a disguising, not a mumming ("Poet as Deviser," p. 97).

To enact the events described in Lydgate's verses would seem to call for mechanical effects to make the angel and the dove descend from heaven, a font for the baptism scene, and height for heavenly characters; Westfall suggests that the costuming would have been extravagant, special effects of a flash of light would have accompanied Clovis' conversion (as in the Digby *Conversion of St. Paul*), and harmonic singing would have been used to imply heaven. Westfall also argues that chapel members participated in Lydgate's three mummings for the royal household, noting that as a monk, Lydgate would have been familiar with the capabilities of choristers and thus in a position to employ them in his mummings; *Windsor*, in particular, seems to have required the participation of the chapel, Westfall believes, given its staging demands (*Patrons and Performance*, pp. 35–37).

The *Mumming at Windsor* survives in Trinity R.3.20 (1450–75), pp. 71–74, as well as in Stow's copy of it, Additional MS 29729. Trinity R.3.20 is the base text for this edition (*MP*, 2:691–94), collated with Additional 29729.

running titles: *Howe th'ampoule and the floure delyce came to the kynges of fraunce / of the Ampoull / And the flour delyce*. Not noted in *MP*.

headnote	Windsor Castle was originally built by William the Conqueror as a fortress and was expanded under later kings into a royal residence. In the 1360s, Edward III built the St. George Chapel at Windsor for the use of the Knights of the Order of the Garter. The hall was repaired and rebuilt by Richard II, under the supervision of Chaucer, then clerk of the king's works.
12	*Cloudovee*. Clovis I (c. 466–511) was king of the Franks, who, according to a legend that arose in the ninth century, in a battle against the Alamans vowed that he would convert to Christianity if he were victorious. On the day of Clovis' baptism, the crowds were said to have prevented the priest with the chrism from reaching the baptistry and so a white dove appeared holding in its beak an ampoule with the chrism for completing the ceremony. Thus the first Christian king of the Franks was anointed through a divine miracle (see Oppenheimer, *Legend of the Ste. Ampoule*, pp. 23–24 and 173–77). At Christmas in 1430, Henry VI received a book of hours with a miniature depicting St. Clothilde bestowing the fleur-de-lys on Clovis, given to him by Anne of Bohemia, wife of the duke of Bedford; the book had been commissioned by Bedford in 1423 as a gift for Anne (see McKenna, "Henry VI of England and the Dual Monarchy," p. 155 and plate 28a).
21	*Cloote*. Clothilde (475–545) was the Burgundian Christian wife of Clovis.
34–35	The royal arms of France since 1376 consisted of an azure shield with three fleur-de-lys of gold.
49	Marginalia: *A daun Johan, est y vray?* Brotanek (*Englischen Maskenspiele*, p. 318) translates what is apparently Shirley's question as "Lieber Freund Johan, ist das auch wahr?" [Dear friend John, is that really true?] but Brusendorff (*Chaucer Tradition*, pp. 460–61 and 466) claims that *yvray* is the Old French synonym for *ivrogne* and translates the line as "Oh, Dan John must have been in his cups when he wrote that!" claiming that bantering remarks such as this indicate a close relationship between Lydgate and Shirley. For similar scribal outbursts against clerical misogyny, see Hammond, "Reproof."
66	*three crepaudes*. Clovis' heraldic device had included three black toads, which he abandoned on his conversion, replacing them with the fleur-de-lys.
69	*Reynes*. From the Carolingian period on, Rheims was the traditional place for the anointing of French kings and queens (see Oppenheimer, *Legend of the Ste. Ampoule*, p. 245 ff.).
70	*Saint Remigius*. St. Remi (c. 437–533), a Gallo-Roman of noble birth, was bishop of Rheims; he converted Clovis to Christianity (see Oppenheimer, *Legend of the Ste. Ampoule*, p. 155).
71	*Th'aumpolle*. Ampoules were small glass phials used since Roman times for oils and ointments; the Ste. Ampoule was described in the seventeenth century as being the size and shape of a fig (Oppenheimer, *Legend of the Ste. Ampoule*, pp. 149–51).

82   *T'annoynte.* During the anointing, a small particle of the sediment in the Ste.
            Ampoule was extracted by the archbishop and mixed with chrism. Using his
            right thumb, the archbishop anointed the king in seven places (head, chest,
            between the shoulders, on both shoulders, and the jointures of both arms) and
            in later years, on the palms (Oppenheimer, *Legend of the Ste. Ampoule*, p. 268).

85 ff.   Charles VII had been crowned at Rheims on July 17, 1429, and it was initially
            the plan to crown Henry there as well, but the English were not able to secure
            the area and the coronation was moved to Paris instead (see Jacob, *Fifteenth
            Century*, pp. 248–50).

91   *By tytle of right.* A reference to Henry's right to the French crown; compare
            Lydgate's *Title and Pedigree of Henry VI*, translated at the command of the earl of
            Warwick, according to Shirley (*MP*, 2:613–22).

92   *Saint Lowys.* Louis IX (1226–70), king of France, also known as Saint Louis. The
            point here is to link Henry VI (through his mother, Catherine of Valois) to the
            lineage of St. Louis.

94–98   These lines imply that the miracle of the fleur-de-lys will now be presented
            (*shewed*), suggesting that the preceding verses served as a kind of prelude to the
            performance.

MUMMING FOR THE GOLDSMITHS OF LONDON

According to Shirley, the *Mumming for the Goldsmiths of London* was performed on
Candlemas for Mayor Estfeld; Estfeld was mayor in 1429–30 and again in 1437, but it must
be the earlier date that is meant here because the manuscript in which the mumming is
copied was completed well before 1437. Since Estfeld was elected on October 13, 1429, the
mumming would have been performed on February 2, 1430. Although there is no reference
to this mumming in their records, the goldsmiths had a tradition of entertainments on their
annual St. Dunstan's Day feast and in mayoral processions; they owned musical instruments
as well as a "summer-castle" that (equipped with "virgins" throwing silver leaves) was used
in the entry of Richard II in 1377 and again in 1382, and on occasion they hired minstrels
and choristers from St. Paul's (see A. Lancashire, *London Civic Theatre*, pp. 45–46; Robertson
and Gordon, "Calendar of Dramatic Records," p. 139; and Osberg, "Goldsmiths'
'Chastell'"). The goldsmiths' pageantry was well enough known for Henry VI to refer to it
in a letter of 1444–45, in which he requested a lavish display for Queen Margaret's entry
(see *Wardens' Accounts*, pp. 178, 196, and 532–34).

We do not know how the goldsmiths came to commission these verses from Lydgate, but
the goldsmiths' prestige would have brought at least some of them into orbit with Lydgate's
circle. London goldsmiths, who in 1404 numbered 102 men in the livery company (the elite
group) plus another eighty out of livery, were substantial citizens, involved in London's
government and with an international reputation as skilled craftsmen (see Reddaway and
Walker, *Early History of the Goldsmiths' Company*, pp. 79 and 139). As makers of luxury goods,
goldsmiths had contacts with the wealthy and powerful: John Orewell, for example, who was
the king's engraver, made a silver-gilt crozier for the abbot of Bury St. Edmunds in 1430
(Barron, *London*, p. 72), and in 1379–80 Edward III's daughter Isabella, the mayor, Lord
Latimer, the Master of St John of Clerkenwell and others were invited to one of the
goldsmiths' feasts (*Wardens' Accounts*, pp. 186–91).

Like the verses Lydgate wrote for the mercers, the *Mumming for the Goldsmiths* takes the form of a letter in the style of a balade that a herald named Fortune presents to the mayor. No speaker is identified, but Fortune probably read the fourteen rhyme-royal stanzas aloud to introduce the mummers, who are costumed as David and the twelve tribes of Israel and who bring an ark, which in a twist on the biblical Ark of the Covenant contains a writ instructing the mayor in the performance of his duties. The mumming is striking for its mixing of the chivalric (e.g., the herald; "royal gyftes" [line 6] for the mayor), the biblical (with an emphasis on lineage via the Jesse tree, Mary, and Christ, and Samuel's anointing of David), and the mercantile (stressing good governance). It also deftly combines flattery of the mayor with an assertion for the need for humble and responsible governance, thus demonstrating Lydgate's ability to craft entertainments for London's wealthy and politically influential establishment that celebrate London and its values, while also subtly voicing concerns about civic government and urban power (see Benson, "Civic Lydgate," p. 164, and Sponsler, "Alien Nation").

The *Mumming for the Goldsmiths* survives in Trinity R.3.20 (1450–75), pp. 175–78, as well as in Stow's copy of it, Additional MS 29729. Trinity R.3.20 is the base text for this edition (*MP*, 2:698–701), collated with Additional 29729.

running titles: *A desguysing to the mayre by the Goldsmithes / A desgysing to the meyre / By the Goldsmythes*. Not noted in *MP*.

headnote   Candlemas was the Feast of the Purification of Mary, and the occasion perhaps suggested to Lydgate the Marian themes of the Ark and lineage that appear in the mumming. The *Mumming for the Goldsmiths* may have been performed either in the goldsmiths' hall or in the mayor's. *Welych* (line 3) comes from the adjective "welch," meaning "Welsh," and by extension "strange," "foreign," or "alien" (see *MED welch*, adj 2a).

2   The Jesse tree was associated with the lineages of Christ and Mary and makes sense for the Feast of Purification.

4   The image of Samuel anointing David comes from 2 Samuel 16. Nolan (*John Lydgate*, p. 88) notes that the reference to Samuel raises the problem of succession, which in the mumming leads to emphasis on the need for humility on the mayor's part.

23   *of humble wille*. David was traditionally taken to represent humility and patience (see Isidore of Seville, *De ortu*, chap. 33 and Augustine, *De civitate Dei*, 17.20), and was viewed as a shepherd of the people of God (1 Chronicles 11–29), both of which Lydgate makes relevant to Mayor Estfeld.

24   The Ark was associated with both Mary, as a vessel carrying precious cargo, and Christ, whom David prefigures; Kipling thinks that the ark brought by the "Levites" was probably a chest or coffer richly made by the Goldsmiths ("Poet as Deviser," pp. 95–96n30).

29   According to 1 Paralipomenon (1 Chronicles) 16:4, Levites were appointed to minister before the Ark.

34   *Syngethe*. The instruction to the Levites to sing suggests that music accompanied the mumming, but presumably only after the whole letter had been read aloud.

36   Marginalia: *Palladyone was a relyk and an ymage sent by the goddes into the cytee of Troye the which kept hem in longe prosperité ageynst alle hir enemys.* Shirley's gloss explaining this reference perhaps reveals his concern with making sure readers understand Lydgate's references.

37   *Ebdomadon.* While transporting the Ark to Zion, David temporarily left the Ark in the house of Obededom the Gittite (2 Samuel 6:1–11; 1 Chronicles 13:1–13), whose house was blessed by its presence.

39   *Palladyone of Troye.* The Palladium was a sacred image kept in the temple of Athena at Troy and was believed to confer protection on the city so long as it remained there. Shirley's gloss explaining this reference perhaps reveals his concern with making sure readers understand Lydgate's allusions.

53   For David's dance before the Ark, see 2 Samuel 6. This passage was taken as a defense of festivity on holidays and feast days (see *A Treatise of Miraclis Pleyinge*, lines 724–25) and the connection of David's dancing with performance goes back at least to Bernard of Clairvaux. Nolan (*John Lydgate*, pp. 91–94) notes that while the dance compliments the mayor it also invites interpretation by any reader who notices the absence in Lydgate's version of the part of the story in which Saul's daughter Michal scornfully rebukes David.

55   *ephod.* For his dance, David girded himself with a linen ephod, a ritual garment worn by the Jewish high priest (2 Samuel 6:14; 1 Chronicles 15:27).

64 ff.   Latin marginalia: *Surge domine in requiem tuam, tu et archa santificacionis tue.* [Arise, O Lord, into thy resting place: thou and the ark, which thou hast sanctified (Psalm 131:8).] This psalm often appeared in primers and books of hours and was linked to Marian devotion.

69   *Nuwe Troye.* According to legend, Brutus called his capital Trojanova (New Troy), later Trinovantus and eventually London.

78–84   Nolan argues that in this stanza the ark trumps the mayor's authority and "places him in his proper relation both to God and to the Goldsmiths" thus stressing the need for humility during his term of office (*John Lydgate*, p. 97).

81   As Clopper notes, the gifts of "konnyng, grace, and might" conveyed by the ark are the attributes of the Trinity, which are here linked to the ideals of proper civic governance: wisdom, peace, and right (*Drama, Play, and Game*, p. 162).

85   *wrytt.* The written document is a kind of Ten Commandments, relating who shall be punished and who rewarded. Nolan notes that the gift of a writ is more complex than simple gifts of wine or wheat, and demands "an active and engaged response" (*John Lydgate*, p. 89).

98   *Duryng youre tyme.* A reference to Estfeld's first term as mayor, which ran from October 29, 1429, to October 29, 1430; see A. Lancashire, *London Civic Theatre*, p. 121.

MUMMING FOR THE MERCERS OF LONDON

Shirley claims that the *Mumming for the Mercers of London* was presented to Mayor Estfeld on Twelfth Night, the Feast of the Epiphany, that is, on January 6, 1430 (for the year, see the Explanatory Notes to the *Mumming for the Goldsmiths*). The verses, which appear to have been devised by Lydgate to assist the mercers in entertaining the mayor, consist of a long introductory speech that was probably spoken by a presenter (a *poursuyaunt*) and seems designed to usher into the hall three ships, possibly with mummers disguised as merchants from the Far East aboard them. As Wickham notes, Lydgate "allegorizes" this visual spectacle by combining the idea of the Magi with the miraculous draught of fishes to enhance the presentation of gifts to Estfeld (*Early English Stages*, 3:49). The text is a kind of geographic, mythological, and literary grand tour that describes how Jupiter's messenger travels from the Euphrates to the Thames, passing various mythic sites, including those important for the origins of poetry, and encountering along the way three ships with slogans on their sides. The messenger finally reaches London, coming ashore where the mercers have gathered to honor the mayor. The actual performance, which probably followed the reading of the letter and which the running titles refer to as a disguising, seems to have been as elaborate as Shirley's comment that it was "ordeyned ryallych" (i.e., royally arranged) suggests: the verses imply that three pageant ships, disguised Orientals, music, dancing, action in which the first ship casts its nets and draws nothing while the third draws a full harvest, and gift-giving were part of the entertainment.

As first in precedence among London's companies, with many members becoming mayor or sheriff, the mercers certainly possessed the means for an elaborate mumming like this one. By the fifteenth century, the mercers had a hall, a chapel, and at least one other room (as well as a chest for keeping records) in the church of St. Thomas of Acre in Cheapside, near the birthplace of Thomas à Becket in an area once occupied by prosperous Jews (Keene, intro. to Imray, *Mercers' Hall*, pp. 1–13); while their hall would have been suitable for feasts and entertainments, this mumming was probably performed in the mayor's hall, as line 102 suggests. Estfeld was an especially illustrious mercer, serving as alderman, sheriff, mayor, and member of Parliament for the city. He built the conduits at Aldermanbury and at the Standard in Fleet and was a benefactor of St. Mary Aldermanbury, where he was buried (*Chronicles of London*, p. 312, note to p. 146, line 13). He appears to have been knighted in the 1430s (Barron, *London*, p. 144). Unfortunately, although the Mercers' accounts show payments toward royal mummings in the 1390s and in 1400/01 (see A. Lancashire, *London Civic Theatre*, p. 42), and although the mercers seem to have had an interest in the short-lived London puy, as records from a case in 1304 show (see Keene, intro. to Imray, *Mercers' Hall*, pp. 12 and 438n29), there is no record of this performance.

The mumming may make reference to contemporary events, perhaps commercial transactions involving Mayor Estfeld, as Welsford has suggested (*Court Masque*, p. 55), but its larger function appears to have been to enhance the cultural capital of Londoners by envisioning the city as a cosmopolitan trading hub capable of assimilating exotic visitors and its elites as sophisticated consumers of aristocratic culture (see Nolan, *John Lydgate*, pp. 101–03). We cannot say whether or not the mercers and Mayor Estfeld grasped all of that cultural material, but Shirley seems to have assumed that readers in the Beauchamp household would need help and supplied extensive glosses to explain Lydgate's references.

The *Mumming for the Mercers* survives in Trinity R.3.20 (1450–75), pp. 171–75, as well as in Stow's copy of it, Additional MS 29729. Trinity R.3.20 is the base text for this edition (*MP*, 2:695–98), collated with Additional 29729.

running titles: *Desgysing made to Estfelde thane / mayre of London made by Lidgate / desgysinge to the mayre.*

headnote   See McLaren (*London Chronicles*, pp. 57–58), for the use of the term *ryallych* in London chronicles to emphasize majesty and to appropriate royal privilege. Clopper notes that the sudden appearance of the pursuivant at the feast "recalls the romance conventions of other courtly revels" and that the journey is through "an allegorical romance landscape" (*Drama, Play, and Game*, p. 161).

1   Latin marginalia: *Iubiter i. omnia iubens.* [Jupiter is the ruler of everything.] Jupiter was the supreme deity in Roman mythology.

3   Latin marginalia: *Phebus i. sol.* [Phebus is the sun.]

5   Marginalia: *Eufrates is oon of the foure floodes of Paradys.* Here and in lines 43–49 Lydgate introduces biblical topography into a landscape of classical mythology and European poetry; Nolan suggests that the "biblical geography [serves] as a kind of gateway to Europe" (*John Lydgate*, p. 104), although the Christian references seem overwhelmed by the other geographies (see Sponsler, "Alien Nation").

8   Marginalia: *Mars is god of batayle.*

8–14   Lydgate's sources for the description of Parnassus were Virgil and Isidore of Seville's *Etymologiae*; see Norton-Smith, *John Lydgate: Poems*, p. 126.

10   Marginalia: *Venus is called the goddesse of love. She is called Cytherea after Cytheron, the hill wher she is worshiped.*

12   Marginalia: *Perseus is a knight which that rood upon an hors that was called Pegase.*

15   Marginalia: *The nyen Muses dwelle bysyde Ellycon, the welle; wheeche beon the nyen sustres of Musyk and of Eloquences and Calyope is oone of hem.* Shirley's gloss makes the same mistake as Chaucer (*House of Fame*, line 522) and other medieval writers in identifying Helicon as a well; see Norton-Smith, *John Lydgate: Poems*, p. 126. Helicon was actually one of the ridges of Parnassus. Nolan claims that Lydgate's is a literary, rather than a "real," geography, and his interest is in linking the landscape with the origins of poetry (*John Lydgate*, pp. 101–02).

22   Marginal gloss: *Bacus is cleped god of wyne and Thagus is a ryver of which the gravelles and the sandes beon of golde.* In Ovid's *Metamorphoses* (11.84 ff.), Bacchus gave Midas the golden touch, and it was removed by the river Thagus.

27   While it is tempting to imagine that use of the first-person pronoun in this line hints that Lydgate himself may have read the verses aloud, as Schirmer suggested (*John Lydgate*, p. 108), there is no other evidence to support that assumption; see the notes to lines 43 and 96 for the pursuivant's role.

29   Marginalia: *Tulius a poete and a rethorisyen of Rome.*

29–35   Lerer views the lists of "poets laureate" as examples of Lydgate's tendency to construct historical space between great writers of old and his own age (*Chaucer and His Readers*, p. 36). Nolan argues that the omission of Chaucer from this list stresses an unmediated relation to a European poetic tradition and Lydgate's "own centrality to the didactic project of the text and performance" (*John Lydgate*, p. 103).

30   Marginalia: *Macrobye an olde philosofre.*

31   Marginalia: *Ovyde and Virgilius were olde poetes, that oon of Rome, that other of Naples afore the tyme of Cryst.*

32   Marginalia: *Fraunces Petrark was a poete of Florence. So were Bochas and Dante withinne this hundrethe yeere; and they were called laureate for they were coroned with laurer in token that they excelled other in poetrye.*

34–35   *aureate.* Lydgate's coinage, probably from the late Latin *aureatus*, to refer to eloquence. Here Lydgate associates the spoken sound of eloquent language with botanical "baum" (i.e., "fragrance"); see the discussion of Lydgate's aureate diction in Norton-Smith, *John Lydgate: Poems*, pp. 192–95. Lerer notes that "laureate" and "aureate" tend in Lydgate's poetry to rely on sound rather than sense for their force and to serve as general terms of praise, often being used, as here, in rhyming pairs, devoid of specific meaning (*Chaucer and His Readers*, p. 45).

39   Marginalia: *Poetes feynen that the gret god Jupiter came doune from heven for to ravisshe a kynges doughter cleped Europa, after whame alle the cuntreys of Europ berethe the name.*

43–49   See note to line 5. The reference to Jupiter's pursuivant in line 43 (and again in line 96) perhaps suggests that the pursuivant was a participant in the mumming and that someone else read the verses aloud.

46   *valeye of the Drye Tree.* Latin marginalia: *In baculo isto transivi Jordanem istum* [On his staff he passed over the Jordan].

51   Marginalia: *Phebus in Aquario is als miche to seyne as thanne the sonne is in that signe.*

55   Marginalia: *Cyrsees is a goddesse of the see, which turnethe men into liknesse of bestis, and nymphes ben goddesses of smale ryvers.*

62–63   *Grande travayle . . . Nulle avayle.* [Much labor, no result.] The mottoes or "reasons" on the ships echo the practice of providing "scriptures" on pageants or subtilties to explain their meaning. Wickham thinks that the lines describing the ships refer to three pageant ships in which the mercers, disguised as Orientals, enter the hall (*Early English Stages*, 1:201–02), but Kipling ("Poet as Deviser," pp. 94–95) doubts that ships were there, since Lydgate doesn't use the rhetorical "Loo here . . . that yee may see" strategy that he uses elsewhere for introducing characters. While it is unclear whether or not ships were depicted in the mumming, other entertainments in halls used such devices (compare Chaucer's Franklin's Tale: "For ofte at feestes have I wel herd seye / That tregetours withinne an halle large / Haue maad come in a water and a barge / And in the halle rowen up and doun" [*CT* V[F]1142–45]).

71   *sakk.* A geographical formation thought to be in the shape of a sack; see *MED*, *sak*, n. 3(b). The Isle of Portland lies in the English Channel just south of Weymouth and was an important harbor in Lydgate's day.

72   The French town of Calais, located at the narrowest part of the Channel, was for English merchants an important gateway to the Continent, especially for trade in such staples as tin, lead, cloth, and wool. It was assigned to English rule in 1360 by the Treaty of Brétigny and remained an outpost of England until the middle of the sixteenth century.

73   The Godwin (Goodwin) Sands, a series of sand banks in the English Channel near Dover, were the frequent site of shipwrecks.

76   Although he is not mentioned in any classical texts and is presumably not a historical figure, according to legend Brutus of Troy, a descendant of Aeneas, was known in medieval England as founder and first king of Britain; see Geoffrey of Monmouth's *Historia Regum Britanniae*.

87   Marginalia: *Neptunus is also a goddesse of the see*.

90–91   *grande peyne . . . grande gayne*. [Great effort, great gain.]

101   A reference to the mercers.

102–05   The phrasing implies that the mercers/mummers have come to visit the mayor and deferentially hope that they will be admitted.

OF THE SODEIN FAL OF PRINCES IN OURE DAYES

Although Shirley's headnote describes *Of the Sodein Fal of Princes* as "seven balades made by Daun Iohn Lydgate" and does not mention any performance context, internal evidence ("Beholde . . . Se howe . . . Se nowe . . . Lo here") suggests that the verses were designed to accompany a visual display, possibly a tapestry or wall-painting (Hammond, "Two Tapestry Poems," p. 11, and Gerould, "Legends of St. Wulfhad and St. Ruffin," p. 323), a processional (Pearsall, *John Lydgate*, p. 180), or a mumming (Robbins, *Secular Lyrics*, p. 110, and *Historical Poems*, p. 342). Pearsall (*John Lydgate*, pp. 180–81) notes that the medieval technique of isolating figures in a series of "stills" that pass before the reader or viewer — common in glass- and panel-painting — was readily transferable to verbal narrative and can be found in various of Lydgate's compositions including the mural-poem, *The Dance of Death* (in which Death addresses in turn thirty-five representatives of secular and religious society from pope to child), the *Fall of Princes*, and even parts of the *Troy Book*. Parry observes that genealogical pageants of this sort are common in Tudor and Stuart pageantry, as in the pageantry featuring six kings named Henry who welcomed Henry VII at York in 1486 or in the pageant alluded to in the "shew of eight Kings, and Banquo," which greets Macbeth in *Macbeth* ("On the Continuity of English Civic Pageantry," pp. 231–32).

The seven stanzas of *Sodein Fal* are an offshoot of Boccaccio's *De casibus virorum illustrium* and represent a condensed updating of Lydgate's *Fall of Princes*, extending that poem's wheel-of-Fortune theme to contemporary English history, perhaps in imitation of Chaucer's Monk's Tale. While there is no descriptive headnote indicating provenance, the snapshot portraits of Edward II, Richard II, Charles VI of France, the duke of Orléans, Edward III's son Thomas of Gloucester, John of Burgundy, and the duke of Ireland, who are brought low because of evil counsel, sickness possibly brought on by sorcery, lechery, murder, the failure of kin and allliances to offer protection, and divorce, would have had relevance for the young Henry VI (whom the council in 1428 had instructed the earl of Warwick to teach with historical exempla [*PPC*, 3:299]) or his uncle Humphrey, duke of Gloucester, who had commissioned the *Fall of Princes*, divorced his first wife, and long been at odds with his brother and uncle over the governance of England. Schirmer (*John Lydgate*, p. 226) sees *Sodein Fal* as a kind of epilogue to the *Fall of Princes*, but notes that Lydgate's adoption of a pro-Burgundian, anti-Armagnac attitude combined with a "comparatively immature" approach make it likely that *Sodein Fal* was written before the *Fall of Princes*. Mention of the death of Charles VI of France, who died in 1422, provides a *terminus a quo* for dating the poem.

Of the Sodein Fal of Princes survives in Trinity College Cambridge R.3.20, folios 359r–361r; Harley 2251, folio 254r–v; and Stow's copy of R.3.20, Additional 29729, folios 169v–170r; R.3.20 is the base text for this edition (*MP*, 2:660–61), collated with the other two manuscripts. The poem has also been edited by Robbins, *Historical Poems*, pp. 174–75.

running titles: *the fale of prynces / of the fal of prynces / the fal of prynces.*

headnote   *Here folowen seven balades made by Daun John Lydegate of the sodeine fal of certain Princes of Fraunce and Englande nowe late in oure dayes.*

1   Marginalia: *Kyng Edwarde of Carnarvan.* Edward II (1284–1327), king of England from 1307–27, was known as Edward of Carnarvon for his birthpace in Wales. Edward's reliance on first Piers Gaveston and later the Despensers angered the barons, and in 1326–27 Edward's queen, Isabella, forced the execution of the Despensers and Edward's abdication. He was imprisoned in Berkeley Castle, where he was probably murdered — according to some accounts by having a hot soldering iron thrust up his rectum so as to leave no trace of wounds and thus allowing his murderers to escape being charged with treason (see Stow, *Annales*, p. 227). Unlike the *FP*, which contains no modern examples of victims of Fortune's wheel, *Sodein Fal* features seven contemporary men who were brought low. Lydgate's great men fall because they bring it upon themselves, a vision of agency and morality that differs from Chaucer's complex narrative of the role of personal responsibility in the downfalls described in the Monk's Tale.

8   Marginalia: *Kyng Richard the Seconde.* Richard II (1367–1400) came to the throne in 1377 at the age of ten and ruled for twenty-two years before being deposed. While notable for its encouragement of a flourishing literary and artistic culture, Richard's reign was marked by serious political difficulties, including the uprising known as the Peasants' Revolt of 1381 and various conflicts with the barons, which (after Richard confiscated the Lancastrian estates on the death of his uncle John of Gaunt in 1399) culminated in a military invasion led by the previously exiled duke of Hereford (Henry IV), who forced Richard's abdication and imprisoned him in Pontefract Castle, where he died in 1400, probably from murder.

15   Marginalia: *Kyng Charlles.* Charles VI (1368–1422) was king of France from 1380 to 1422. He suffered from bouts of insanity that earned him the nickname "Charles the Mad" and left him unable to govern effectively. In 1420, he was forced to accept the Treaty of Troyes, which designated Henry V of England as his successor.

22   Marginalia: *the Duc of Orlyence.* Louis, duc d'Orléans (1372–1407), was the brother of Charles VI. After 1392, when Charles' attacks of insanity began, Louis became involved in a struggle for influence with his uncle, Philip the Bold of Burgundy, and with his cousin, John the Fearless; he was killed by John's

supporters in 1407. Louis was rumored to have had sexual relations with several noble women, including his sister-in-law, Isabella of Bavaria, wife of Charles VI (see Robbins, *Historical Poems*, p. 343, note to line 26).

27   Marginalia: *i. Duc of Burgoigne John*. See note to line 36 below.

29   Marginalia: *Thomas Duc of Gloucestre*. Thomas of Woodstock, duke of Gloucester and son of Edward III, was arrested for treason against Richard II in 1397, after being betrayed by the earl of Derby, and was sent under arrest to Calais. He could not be produced by his keeper, the earl of Nottingham, the next year, when his case was considered by Parliament, suggesting that he had been quietly murdered. Thomas falls in spite of his *trouthe* (line 32) and devotion to *comune profit* (line 35) because of Fortune's unexpected blows.

36   Marginalia: *John Duc of Bourgoyne*. John the Fearless (1371–1419) was duke of Burgundy from 1404–19. He undertook a series of popular governmental reforms but his rivalry with supporters of Louis, duc d'Orléans, whom he had assassinated, led by 1411 to civil war between his side (the Burgundians) and the Armagnacs. While negotiating with the English invaders under Henry V and with the Dauphin (leader of the Armagnacs and later King Charles VII), John was assassinated.

37   *douspiers*. The twelve great peers of France consisted of six spiritual lords (the archbishop of Rheims and the bishops of Laon, Langres, Beauvais, Chalons, and Noyon) and six temporal lords (the dukes of Normandy, Burgundy, and Aquitaine, and the counts of Toulouse, Flanders, and Champagne). In romances the twelve peers were often taken as representing the bravest of knights; compare the tapestry cited in an inventory in 1423 (2 Henry VI) of goods owned by Henry V (*RP*, 4:214–41), described as "ung pece d'Aras, de xii duszeperes, saunz ore, qui comence en l'estorie 'Diue vous doit'" (*RP*, 4:229).

43   Marginalia: *The Duc of Yrland*. Robert de Vere, earl of Oxford (1362–92), was one of Richard II's favorites and was made duke of Ireland in 1386. In the Merciless Parliament of 1388, he was among the supporters of Richard who were accused of treason by the five Lords Appellant. Sentenced to death in 1388, he fled to Louvain and was killed by a boar in 1392 while hunting. De Vere was married to Philippa de Coucy, the king's cousin, and had an affair with one of the queen's ladies in waiting, Agnes de Launcekrona (see next note).

46   Marginalia: *i. laumerrane*. This marginal gloss (in BL MS Additional 29729: *loomcerean*) is an error for *Launcecrona*, which is described by Walsingham, *Historia anglicana*, 2:160, as a vulgar term: "et aliam duceret, quae cum Regina Anna venerat de Boemia, ut fertur, cujusdam sellarii filiam, ignobilem prorsus atque foedam; ob quam causam magna surrepsit occasion scandalorum: — cujus nomen erat, in vulgari idiomate 'Launcecrona'" ["and took another woman, who had come with Queen Anne of Bohemia and who was said to be a saddler's daughter, low-ranking and ugly; for which reason there was great occasion for scandal to spread: her name in the common idiom was 'Launcecrona'"]. See Robbins, *Historical Poems*, pp. 343–44, note to line 46.

PAGEANT OF KNOWLEDGE

The *Pageant of Knowledge* does not survive in a manuscript copied by Shirley and lacks headnotes or other information about possible performance. It does, however, contain the Latin rubric "Septem Pagine sequntur sapiencie" ("Here follow seven pageants on wisdom"), which suggests that at least part of it was meant to be performed. MacCracken (*MP*, 2:724–34) prints the *Pageant of Knowledge* as one complete 287-line text, but in Trinity R.3.21 on which his edition is based, the verses are punctuated by "explicits" that divide the text into ten parts, or perhaps indicate ten separate texts, some of which appear individually in other manuscripts. The *Pageant* starts with a description of the seven estates plus the "ryche," all of whom are in the next stanza given a line each that may have been spoken; the pageant then moves to description — which was perhaps recited by a presenter — of various allegorical and mythological figures and signs of the zodiac, finally becoming what seems to be a nondramatic didactic poem. As its layout suggests, the *Pageant* may be a compilation of poems, of which only one or two were meant for performance; a thread of continuity is provided, however, by variants of the tag line "How shuld a man than be stedfast of lyvyng," which unites stanzas 20 through 38, with stanza 39's advice to aim for heavenly stability serving as the answer to that repeated question. Although Trinity R.3.21 does not specify an author, Stow's annotations in that manuscript attribute five of the ten groupings to Lydgate, and MacCracken ascribes the entire 287 lines to Lydgate based on "the uniform style of the entire piece" (*MP*, 1:xxiii, no. 90); Bühler has also noted that some of the poem's stanzas are repeated in Lydgate's other works ("Lydgate's *Horse, Sheep and Goose*," p. 563).

MacCracken takes his title from the use of the word *pagine* (pageant) in the heading to one of the groups of stanzas, which he believes points to performance of the whole as a school play, like Ausonius' *Ludus septem sapientum*, which MacCracken thinks is its model (*MP*, 1:xxiii, no. 90; see Ausonius, *Works*, pp. 184–92 for the Latin text of the *Ludus*, which features seven wise men who give brief expositions of their apothegms); Ausonius was not widely known in the Middle Ages until the fourteenth century and beyond, when copies showed up in the hands of Petrarch, Boccacio, and Salutati, among others (Ausonius, *Works*, p. 597). Schirmer likewise believes that the pageant was a scholastic drama in which performance would have enlivened the dry instructional material (*John Lydgate*, p. 104), while Pearsall views the first part of the text (through the signs of the zodiac) as a tableau-presentation, with some parts of this performance section being "obviously more panto-mimic than others" and with one stanza (the tableau-group of the seven estates plus *Rycheman*) even including "speech-prefixes as in a play" before each character's line (*John Lydgate*, p. 183). The word "pageant" had various meanings, not all of them pointing to mimesis: it could refer to a representation or device carried in display or even something as simple as a banner or tapestry (*OED*, s.v. *Pageant sb.*, no. 3; also 1. [d] "A scene represented on tapestry; or the like"). In the contents list on fol. 2r of Ashmole 59, the *Pageant* is described as "A comedye of the fyndinge of success." Part of the *Pageant* also survives in a fifteenth-century commonplace book that includes the Brome *Abraham and Isaac* (*The Book of Brome*).

The date and auspices of the *Pageant* are unknown. A. Lancashire (*London Civic Theatre*, p. 125) considers it briefly in her discussion of London drama, but notes that without fuller information it is difficult to say whether or not it had civic associations. Trinity R.3.21 was written sometime during or after the reign of Edward IV, by scribes who had access to Shirley manuscripts (see Hammond, "Two British Museum Manuscripts," p. 27), which provides a last possible date for the composition of the *Pageant*. Its appearance in a London manuscript, owned at one point by the well-to-do London mercer Roger Thorney (c.

1450–1515) and later by the Londoner Stow (see *Manuscript Trinity R.3.19*, p. xxx), perhaps argues for a London context for the *Pageant*.

The *Pageant of Knowledge* survives in complete form in just one manuscript, Trinity R.3.21 (1461–83), fols. 287a–289b, although parts of the poem were copied in various other manuscripts. Trinity R.3.21 is the base text for this edition (*MP*, 2:724–34). The whole of the undertaking bears similarities to Gower's *Confessio Amantis* book 7 and portions of books 4 and 5, with their pageant-like lists of inventors, Greek and Roman gods, the humors, and the seven liberal arts, especially astronomy.

1–8	The notion of a social order composed of seven estates was an expansion of the old idea of the three orders of society: those who fought, those who prayed, and those who labored. In contrast with the notion of orders, the estates model emphasized ranks rather than functions and allowed for a broader categorization of social groups.
5	"Common profit" is the usual translation of *res publica*; for its importance as a social and poetic ideal, see Middleton, "Idea of Public Poetry."
9	This assertion of the right of princes to govern priests may have had special force in the wake of Henry V's attempts to reform the monastic orders and of ongoing struggles between the crown and monasteries, including Bury St. Edmunds.
rubric	*sapiencie*. In scholasticism, *sapientia* (heart thinking) was distinguished from *scientia* (head thinking).
17–37	Compare the descriptions of Prudence, Rightwysnesse (Justice), and Temperance in the *Disguising at London*.
25	*Of thy weyghtes*. An allusion to Justice's scales, with a plea that judges make sure that their reckoning is fair.
59	There was an extensive body of courtesy literature in Latin (the *facetia* tradition) and in English, devoted to advice about bodily comportment and behavior. Compare Lydgate's *Stans Puer ad Mensam* and *Dietary*.
64	*herte, body, wyll, and mynde*. Compare *BD*, lines 116 and 767.
66	Jubal, a descendant of Cain and the ancestor of all who play the lyre and pipe; see Genesis 4:21 and Chaucer: "Tubal, / That found out first the art of songe; / For as hys brothres hamers ronge / Upon hys anvelt up and doun, / Therof he took the firste soun" (*BD* 1162–66). See also *CA*, 4.2416–18. Medieval writers often confused his name with that of his brother Tubal, who was the first to work the forge for iron and steel crafts. See lines 83–86.
73	The Roman god Saturn (from *satus*, "sowing") was credited with inventing agriculture. See *CA* 5.1221–31.
74	Ceres is the goddess of grain, also known for inventing the craft of tilling. Lydgate follows tradition in identifying her as Saturn's daughter, but she is described as his wife in the *Third Vatican Mythographer*, book 2. See *CA* 5.1231–44.
80	Mars was the Roman god of war.

81   In the *Iliad*, 5.733–37, Homer describes how Athena removed the robe she had made for herself and armed herself. She was known as a patron of the crafts and as a goddess of war, who created armor.

83–86   Tubalcain, brother of Jubal, was identified as the maker of steel and was associated with artificers who used brass and iron (see Genesis 4:22). See note 66, above.

88   The Roman goddess Minerva was associated with weaving (see Trevisa, *Polychronicon* 2, cap. 11, p. 297 and *CA* 3.2435).

89   Lydgate follows Gower (*CA* 2.2437) in assigning the discovery of linen to Delbora. Gower's source is uncertain, but Peck notes that the invention of linen, supposedly the purest of cloth, may have become linked to her through the purity of Seth's line in the ancestry of Christ; see *CA*, notes to 2.2437.

92   Semiramis, the legendary Assyrian queen, was often depicted wearing men's breeches; see Samuel.

93   *myn auctor*. Lydgate's sources in the *Pageant* have been identified as Isidore of Seville, Vincent of Beauvais, Chaucer (see Gattinger, *Lyrik Lydgates*, pp. 17, 39, 41, and 66), and Gower.

94   Diana, the Roman goddess of the wood and hunting, was identified with the moon and thus also known as Lucina (as in line 97). Compare *TB*, Prol.132, and *CT* V[F]1045 ff.

101–03   Compare Lydgate's description of Mercury in *TB*, 2.2486 ff., and Edwards' note (*TB*, p. 373).

104   Neptune was the Roman god of the sea; see Chaucer's Franklin's Tale for his rule over the sea (*CT* V[F]1047).

108   Phoebus Apollo, the classical god, was linked to medicine; see Godfrey of Viterbo, 6, col. 157: "Apollo etiam citharam condidit et artem medicinalem invenit" (*Pantheon*, 2.508) [Apollo invented the harp and the art of medicine].

109   *pounce veyne*. An artery where the pulse can be felt. See *MED pous(e)* (n.).

110   Aesculapius, the Greco-Roman god of healing, was the legendary founder of medicine. See *CA* 5.1059–82. Also see Chaucer's description of the Physician (*CT* I[A]429) as knowing the standard medical authorities, including Aesculapius.

114 ff.   After the explicit, the word *Lidgatt* appears in Stow's hand.

115 ff.   The basic curriculum of undergraduate education was the Trivium (grammar, rhetoric, logic), which could be supplemented by the Quadrivium (arithmetic, geometry, astronomy, music), whose study led to the master of arts.

123   Priscian (fifth–sixth centuries) was the most important of the late Latin grammarians, author of the *Institutiones*, a summary of Greco-Roman grammatical theory and practice.

124   Euclid, the Greek mathematician (fl. 300 B.C.), was known as the author of the *Elements*, the standard textbook of elementary mathematics in medieval Europe.

125   Marcus Tullius Cicero (106–43 B.C.) was known for his oratorical skills; he was the author of the *De inventione*, a treatise on rhetorical argument.

126   Hermogenes of Tarusus (second century) wrote a set of textbooks on rhetoric.

127   Boethius' treatise *De musica* was standard reading in medieval universities and formed the basis for medieval musical theory; compare *CT* VII(B^2)3293–94, where the fox compares Chauntecleer's skill at singing to Boethius.

128   The *Metaphysics* of Aristotle, the Greek philosopher (384–322 B.C.), strongly influenced the development of medieval philosophy.

129   Abu-Mashar Jafar ibn Muhammad (787–886) was the leading astrologer of the Arab world. See *CA* 7.1237–70, on Albumazar and the founding of astronomy.

131–38   It was a convention of medieval cosmology that the planets (Saturn, Jupiter, Mars, the sun, Venus, and Mercury) controlled the human body and human behavior. See John of Salisbury, *Policraticus*, 2.18–19, and the Wife of Bath's description of herself in terms of planetary influence (*CT* III[D]609–19).

139 ff.   The signs of the zodiac were thought to correspond to and govern parts of the body. See *CA* 7.955–1270 on the signs of the zodiac, and 7.1291–1438 on the fifteen stars and their relationship to the seven planets and various herbs. See also Chaucer's "Treatise on the Astrolabe" 1.21.70–73, which links each sign to a part of the body as does the drawing of the anatomical man in Jean duc du Berry's *Trés Riches Heures* plate 14 (New York: George Braziller, 1969), one of the greatest of the books of hours which is in and of itself a kind of pageant.

160 ff.   After the explicit, the words *John Lidgat* are written in Stow's hand.

160–66   This stanza appears alone in somewhat different form in seven manuscripts (see *Manual of the Writings in Middle English* XVI, p. 2142) and in *Debate of the Horse, Goose, and Sheep*. Medieval Europe inherited from the Greeks a model of the physical world in which the four elements — earth, fire, air, and water — joined with the four qualities — moistness, aridity, heat, and cold — as the building blocks of life. The elements and qualities were assumed to correspond to the four bodily humors — melancholy, choler, blood, and phlegm. These correspondences were set out in a number of written texts, such as *CA* 7.393–462, and the widely-read pseudo-Aristotelian *Secreta secretorum*, and in pictorial images as well.

195 ff.   After the explicit, the words *John Lidgatt* are written in Stow's hand. Complexions, or temperaments, were thought to derive from the humors and thus physiological traits were assumed to have a physical basis. The sanguine person, for example, is dominated by the blood and is cheerful and outgoing; compare Chaucer's description of the Franklin as sanguine (*CT* I[A]333) and the jolly Wife of Bath with her "reed of hewe" face (*CT* I[A]458).

219 ff.   Written in Stow's hand after the explicit: *John Lydgatt*.

247 ff.   Written in Stow's hand after the explicit: *By Lydgatt*.

282   *sterres sevyn*. A reference to the seven regularly visible stars of the Pleiades, the seven Ptolemaic planets, or the seven stars of Ursa Minor.

287 ff.   Written in Stow's hand after the *Amen*: *John Lydgat*.

A PROCESSION OF CORPUS CHRISTI

The *Procession of Corpus Christi* is described by Shirley as "an ordenaunce of a precessyoun of the feste of corpus cristi made in london by daun John Lydegate." Although Shirley's headnote does not make clear whether it was the procession that took place in London or the writing of the poem, the verses are usually taken to refer to a procession in that city (but see Gibson, "Bury St. Edmunds, Lydgate, and the *N-Town Cycle*," pp. 60–61, who notes that late medieval Bury had both an *interludium* and a procession of Corpus Christi, and Clopper, *Drama, Play, and Game*, p. 164, who thinks the verses are "a sermon, or 'process,' centered on imagined *figurae* or pictures of them" not a description of a procession).

The first stanza, which functions as a kind of introduction, announces that "Gracyous misteryes grounded in scripture" shall be "In youre presence fette out of fygure" and "declared by many unkouthe signe," and the final stanza repeats that "theos figures" were "shewed in youre presence," suggesting that the verses describe or usher in a series of tableaux of mostly biblical figures and Fathers of the Church. The remaining stanzas take up one figure each, giving a brief description and exhorting listeners to reflect on the meaning of each figure ("considerthe in youre ymaginatyf," line 10) the better to appreciate the significance of the feast day. Some of the stanzas contain what may be instructions for or descriptions of the figures and their tableaux (e.g., Ecclesiastes with his castle enclosed by a red cloud; Zacharia holding a censer), but it is difficult to say much about what the procession, if indeed that is what it was, looked like. The verses end with a note stating, "Shirley kouthe fynde no more of this copye," but whatever is lacking was probably brief, since the verses seem complete as is.

If the verses were linked to a London procession, the most likely candidate is the annual Corpus Christi procession of the Skinners' Company, which is referred to in Skinners' 1392 Company Charter and continued into the sixteenth century (A. Lancashire, *London Civic Theatre*, p. 277n43). Stow claimed that the procession passed through the main streets of the cities and included the skinners carrying wax torches, with more than 200 clerks and priests singing, followed by sheriffs, the mayor, aldermen, and others, accompanied by minstrels outfitted with wings (*Survey of London*, 1:230–31). A. Lancashire (*London Civic Theatre*, pp. 59–60) suggests that Stow may have been right in his assertion that the Skinners were connected with the Clerkenwell/Skinners' Well biblical play referred to in late fourteenth- and early fifteenth-century records, and that their involvement turned at some point in the 1390s into their annual Corpus Christi procession. While Schirmer thought that the *Procession* was probably commissioned by Lydgate's monastery (*John Lydgate*, p. 175), A. Lancashire (*London Civic Theatre*, p. 126) raises the stronger possibility that the Skinners at some point asked Lydgate to record their procession, a possibility that gains additional weight from the fact that the Skinners' fraternity of Corpus Christi had links to royalty and nobility, including Lydgate's patrons Henry V, Henry VI, and Humphrey, duke of Gloucester (see Lambert, *Records of the Skinners*, p. 54). If the Skinners did make such a commission, it must have been before 1430, the completion date of Trinity R.3.20 in which the *Procession* appears.

A *Procession of Corpus Christi* survives in Trinity R.3.20 (1456?), pp. 349–56; Harley 2251, fols. 224b–227b (a manuscript based in part on R.3.20); and Stow's copy of R.3.20, Additional 29729, fols. 166r–168r; R.3.20 is the base text for this edition (*MP*, 1:35–43), collated with Harley 2251.

running titles: *A procession of corpus christi by Lidegate / A procession of corpus / cristi / procession of corpus / christi feste by Ledegate / processione of corpus / cristi feste*; not noted in *MP*.

headnote *MED*, n. 10(a) defines *ordenaunce* as preparations or arrangements, but the meaning seems closer to "device" or even pageant; compare *Henry VI's Entry*, which Shirley describes as *ordenaunces* and Lydgate's reference to the pageantry of the 1432 entry as including *Noble devyses, dyvers ordenaunces / Conveyed by scripture* . . . (lines 66–67).

1 *feste*. I.e., the Feast of Corpus Christi, established by the Church in the early fourteenth century. The feast commemorates the institution of the Holy Eucharist and falls on the first Thursday following Trinity Sunday (anywhere from late May to late June). Corpus Christi was an important force in the development in the fourteenth-century of English cycle plays; see Mervyn James, "Ritual, Drama and Social Body."

3 *to governe us*. While addressing his audience with the familiar and informal "you" and "youre," Lydgate also liberally uses "us" and "oure" to imagine a religious community into which he inserts himself as a member.

6 *In youre presence fette out of fygure*. The meaning of this phrase is open to interpretation; it may refer to images or likenesses (*fygure*) brought forth (*fette out*; see *MED, fetten* v. 3) or, as Clopper believes, figures in the technical sense of *figurae* "demonstrated" for the audience (*Drama, Play, and Game*, p. 164n67). The references to *Figure and liknesse* (line 53) and *divers likenesses* (line 218) along with the insistence that these "figures" will be explained and shown *in youre presence* (lines 6 and 217) would seem to point to actual representations of some sort.

10 *Seothe and considerthe in youre ymaginatyf*. A commonplace of meditational instruction; Clopper (*Drama, Play, and Game*, p. 164n67) notes that Lydgate stresses the role of memory in this meditation. Compare lines 17 (*in youre inwarde entente*), and 55 (*oure inwarde sight*).

11 Marginalia: *Adam*.

18 Marginalia: *Melchisedech*. Melchizedek, who in Hebrews 7:3 is called is a king "without father or mother or genealogy," was seen as a type of Christ. In Genesis 14, he brings bread and wine to Abraham when Abraham returns from his battle with the four kings who besieged Sodom and Gomorrah; see the painting of the "Meeting of Abraham and Melchizedek" (1464–67) by Dieric Bouts the Elder.

20 *Steyned in Bosra*. Literally, "dyed red in Bosra," a reference to Isaiah 63:1–7, where God returns from battle in a blood-stained robe; the passage was often interpreted as applying to the crucified Jesus.

25 Marginalia: *Abraham*.

29   Latin marginalia: *ponam bucellam panis / Genesis xliii^e*. [And I will set a morsel of bread / Genesis 18(:5).]

33   Marginalia: *Isaake*.

35   Latin marginalia: *In pinguedinis terre et rore celi*. "In the fatness of the earth and the dew of heaven" (Genesis 27:28).

38–40 These lines refer to the Virgin Mary. The Rose of Jericho marked the spot where the Holy Family stopped to rest during their flight; in the Middle Ages, roses became associated with the Virgin, whose name (Maria) has five letters.

41   Marginalia: *Jacob*.

42   Latin marginalia: *pinguis est panis Christi / Genesis xl. ix^e*. [The bread of Christ shall be fat / Genesis 49(:20).]

49   Marginalia: *Moyses*.

50   *With goldin hornes*. The Latin Vulgate's mistranslation of the Herbrew word *qaran* in Exodus 34:29 as "horns" rather than "rays" led to the Christian represen-tation of Moses with a ram's horns.

51   *arche*. When Moses received the Ten Commandments, he also received instruc-tions to build an ark in which to carry them; it was covered with gold and two cherubim were placed on top.

57   Marginalia: *Aaron*.

65   Marginalia: *David*.

73   Marginalia: *Ecclesiaste*.

73–74 *Ecclesiaste . . . / With cloose castel besyde a clowde reed*. These lines seem to be instructions for or a description of the image of Ecclesiastes.

81   Marginalia: *Jeremye*. On the significance of depicting Jeremiah as carrying a chalice with "Greyne in the middes," see Aston, who notes that Christ was sometimes linked to grain, milling, grinding, flour and bread, especially in Corpus Christi rituals ("Corpus Christi and Corpus Regni," p. 28).

89   Marginalia: *Ysayes*.

97   Marginalia: *Helyas*.

105   Marginalia: *Zacharye*. As in the case of the image of Ecclesiastes, this line seems to be an instruction for or a description of the representation of Zacharia.

113   Marginalia: *Baptist*.

121   Marginalia: *John Evangelist*.

128   Latin marginalia: *is est Jesus*. [He is Jesus.]

129   Latin marginalia: *Marcus*.

135   Latin marginalia: *hoc est corpus meum*. [This is my body.]

137	Latin marginalia: *Matheus*.
145	Latin marginalia: *Lucas*.

156–60   These lines refer to stipulations regulating who may receive the communion Host (i.e., only the pure). See 1 Corinthians 11: 27–29.

153   Latin marginalia: *Paulus doctor gencium et apostolus* [Paul was a teacher of men and an apostle.]

161–62   Latin marginalia: *Magister historiarum* [*Magister historiarum* ("master of stories") usually refers to Peter Comestor, who appears later in the procession (see note to line 201 below); the gloss here should read *Magister sententiarum*, i.e., Peter Lombard (c. 1100–60), the scholastic theologian and author of four books known as the "Sentences."]

169   Latin marginalia: *Jeronimus*. I.e., St. Jerome, the translator of the Vulgate.

172–76   Here and in lines 210–16, Lydgate stresses the orthodox doctrine of transubstantiation (the belief that the substance of the bread and of the wine changes into the body and blood of Christ in the celebration of the Eucharist).

177   Latin marginalia: *Gregorius*.

185   Latin marginalia: *Augustinus*.

186–92   *Whan Cryste is ete . . . / remedy geynst al oure olde grevaunce / Brought ine by . . . an appul smale*. I have been unable to locate the precise passage in Augustine, though the idea is akin to *On Forgiveness of Sins and Baptism*, where we are told that newborn infants bear the sins of Adam and "will not have life if they eat not the flesh of the Son of Man" (ch. 27); see also ch. 33 on remission of sin by drinking Christ's blood, or *On the Psalms* 49.3–6, where he argues that mankind is redeemed from the sins of Adam and Eve through the Eucharist.

192   *byting of an appul smale*. A reference to the story of Adam and Eve's eating of the forbidden fruit in the Garden of Eden.

193   Latin marginalia: *Ambrosius*.

194   *langage laureate*. Lerer (*Chaucer and His Readers*, pp. 47–48), noting Lydgate's tendency to use the French proclitic article before vowels (e.g., *Lenvoy*), suggests that sometimes *laureate* is probably *l'aureate* and that here the phrase should be *langage aureate*.

196–200   See Ambrose's *De sacramentis*, *Patrologia Latina* 16.

201   Marginalia: *Maistre of storyes* [i.e., the French theological writer Peter Comestor (died c. 1178), author of the *Historia scholastica*, an important source of biblical history and Christian legend; see Harley MS 1704 (Halliwell, *Selection from the Minor Poems*, p. 268, note to p. 102)].

204   *pytee pleyning*. The lines suggest that the host contains within it a pietà, or image of the Virgin Mary lamenting the death of her son.

209   Latin marginalia: *Thomas de Alquino*.

218   *By divers likenesses you to doo plesaunce.* While arguing that "shewed" (line 217)
        need mean nothing more than "presented" or "demonstrated," Clopper, *Drama,*
        Play, and Game, pp. 164–65, admits that "diuers likenesses" may suggest
        "something more tangible."

220   *This bred of lyfe.* I.e., the Eucharistic wafer.

SOTELTES AT THE CORONATION BANQUET OF HENRY VI

Sometime before November 6, 1429, Lydgate was apparently commissioned to write verses to accompany the subtleties served at the coronation banquet of Henry VI. Although the verses are not attributed to Lydgate in the surviving manuscripts, MacCracken thinks they are "certainly" by Lydgate, although he dates them to 1432 (*MP*, 1:xxviii and 2:623) on the grounds that they fit with the other poems Lydgate wrote for the coronation (the *Prayer for King, Queen, and People*; the *Roundel for the Coronation of Henry VI*; and the *Ballade to King Henry VI upon His Coronation*). There were three subtleties (miniature pageants made of confectionary) at the banquet: the first showed Saints Edward and Louis with Henry VI between them; the second featured Henry VI kneeling before Emperor Sigismund and Henry V; the third depicted the Virgin with child, holding a crown in her hand, flanked by Saints George and Denis, who present the kneeling king to her. Lydgate's verses probably accompanied each subtlety as a written text to explain the meaning of the image; A. Lancashire thinks the verses would probably also have been recited aloud so that everyone in the hall could hear them (*London Civic Theatre*, p. 125; for a subtlety with dialogue, at Ely in 1479, see I. Lancashire, *Dramatic Texts and Records*, no. 642). Lydgate's verses seem to have been special expansions on the short "reasons" that typically accompanied subtleties, and were perhaps requested to enhance the effect, given the importance of the occasion. It is possible that Lydgate was responsible for the design of the subtleties (the "device"), but Kipling believes someone else decided on the emblematic subject matter that the artisans and cooks created and Lydgate was merely assigned the task of writing the accompanying verses or "scriptures" ("Poet as Deviser," p. 83).

While the occasion was royal, civic and religious leaders would have been present for the banquet (according to one chronicler, Queen Catherine's coronation banquet in 1421 was "opyn to alle pepull" [*The Brut*, p. 427]), and Lydgate's verses touch on themes that would be of concern to all, particularly the vexed issue of the legitimacy of the dual monarchy (see McKenna, "Henry VI of England and the Dual Monarchy," p. 157) and Henry's youth. Lydgate stresses the king's French heritage and his father's friendship with Emperor Sigismund, which as Griffiths notes was a reminder of "the Lancastrian *imperium* into which Henry VI was now entering" (*Reign of King Henry VI*, p. 190), while also advocating a tough line against heretics and invoking various protectors for the young king, including the patron saints of England and France.

Soteltes survives in six manuscripts and in an altered version in Fabyan's *New Chronicles* (1516). BL MS Cotton Julius B.i., fols. 79r–80r is the base text for this edition (*MP*, 2:623–24), collated (Lydgate's stanzas only) with BL MS Lansdowne 285, fols. 5v–7v.

headnote   This manuscript version is a chronicle that preserves the description of the
           courses and subtleties as well as Lydgate's eight-line verses. John Russell, who
           was usher to Humphrey, duke of Gloucester, in his *Boke of Nurture* (lines 719–94)
           describes how to serve meals that include subtleties. Subtleties were presumably

meant to be eaten: at Windsor in May of 1416, during the visit of Emperor Sigismund, three elaborate subtleties were served to Henry V and the emperor, while the other lords were served subtleties suited to their rank (see BL MS Cotton Julius B.i, fol. 39a). See the recent discussion of the verses and banquet by Epstein, "Eating."

2   The appearance of the monarch-saints Edward and Louis underscores Henry VI's supposed hereditary right to the thrones of both England and France. Compare Lydgate's "Title and Pedigree" (*MP* 2:613–22).

5   The claim that Henry VI is the inheritor of the fleur-de-lys is an attempt to assert the legitimacy of his rule over France.

11   Lansdowne 285 (1450–75) substitutes "N" (presumably for the Latin word "nomen") for the name of Henry VI in this line and for Henry V in line 20, possibly as a way of recycling the verses for other use. Compare the *Prayer for King, Queen, and People*, which in some manuscript versions has been altered to use for Edward IV (*MP* 1:215).

9–13   The reference is to Sigismund's actions against the Hussites and to Henry V's against the Oldcastle Lollard plot of of 1413, both instances in which heterodox threats were suppressed. Also see the *Ballade to King Henry VI on His Coronation*, lines 81–88, for the use of the same figures and theme. For Lydgate's attitude towards heretics, see Brie, "Mittelalter und Antike bei Lydgate," p. 275.

18–19   Saints George and Denis were the patron saints of England and France, respectively. During the first course, Philip Dymmock rode into the hall costumed like St. George and declared himself the king's champion (see *PPC*, 3:6–7, and *Historical Collections of a Citizen of London*, p. 168).

22   *His tendre yougth*. Henry was barely eight years old at his coronation.

23–24   The last lines stress Henry VI's claim by birth and "title of right" to rule over England and France.

 **TEXTUAL NOTES**

ABBREVIATIONS: A: Additional 29729 (Stow's copy of R.3.20); **B**: Bodley Ashmole 59, copy text for the *Mumming at Bishopswood*; **Bo**: Bodley 2527 (Bodley 686); **C**: Trinity R.3.19; **CC**: Cotton Cleopatra C.iv; **F**: Bodley Fairfax 16; **H**: Harley 2251; **Ha**: Harley 565; **Hb**: Harley 2255; **Ji**: Cotton Julius B.i, copy text for the *Soteltes*; **Jii**: Cotton Julius B.ii, copy text for *King Henry VI's Triumphal Entry into London* ; **L**: Lansdowne 285; **M**: MacCracken's 1934 edition; **R**: Trinity R.3.21, copy text for the *Pageant of Knowledge*; **T**: Trinity R.3.20, copy text for all of the disguisings and mummings except *Bishopswood*, and for *Bycorne and Chychevache,* the *Procession of Corpus Christi,* and *Of the Sodein Fall of Princes*.

BYCORNE AND CHYCHEVACHE

headnote	Omitted in C and H; headings of stanzas omitted in C and poem is untitled, but is laid out with indented stanzas and marginal notes supplied by Stow. M claims that C contains the running titles *the couronne of disguysinges contrived by Daun Iohan Lidegate / The maner of straunge desguysinges, the gyse of a mummynge,* but no such titles are visible on the manuscript today.
5	C and H omit *of* in phrase *of theyre stryves.*
6	*derrain.* C reads *durayne.*
8–21	T transposes these two stanzas, but uses *a* and *b* notation in the margin to indicate that they should be in the order shown here and in M. C also transposes the two stanzas, without noting any correction.
10	*us.* Omitted in C; *here.* Omitted in H.
	to forne. C reads *beforne* and H, *beforn.*
13	*sentence.* M's emendation; T reads *setence.*
14	*or thorughe.* C reads *and thorough.*
15	*For.* C reads *Furst.*
16	*Wil noon other.* C reads *Wyll have noon.*
17	*men.* M claims H reads *husks,* but the manuscript omits *men* and inserts above the line something that may be *husbandes.*
20	*Be.* C reads *Byn.*
	not. M erroneously claims T omits.
21	*lak.* M's emendation, as well as the reading in C and H; T reads *luk.*
28	*nat.* M's emendation; T omits.
33	*I beshrewe.* C reads *I theym beshrew.*

35	*nought.* C reads *nat to.*
36	*foode.* M's emendation; T reads *foote.*
37	*not tarye.* C and H read *nat to tarye.*
38	*whiche ther living.* C reads *whyche beth here lyvyng.*
46	*no gayne.* C reads *nothing.*
	us may. C and H read *may us.*
48	*which theyre lyves.* C reads *of her lyfes.*
67	*no maner.* C and H read *in no maner.*
75	*voydethe.* C reads *and voyde.*
76	*Or.* C reads *For.*
79	*sklendre.* M erroneously says that H reads *tendre,* but it is C.
91	*Amorowe.* C reads *To morow.*
97	*sought.* C omits and inserts *goo* above the line.
98	*yit oone.* C reads *oone lyke.*
100	*go.* C and H read *ago.*
102	*no more.* C reads *any more.*
109	*beest.* C omits.
111	*a.* C reads *another.*
114	*ful.* C reads *suche.*
115	*of.* C reads *by.*
116	In T, a later hand inserts *forever* before *Pacyence.* H reads *forever pacience.*
118	*fayle.* C reads *to fayle.*
120	*longe.* C reads *full long.*
132	*bytwixen.* M's emendation; T reads *bytwix.*
133	*Lynkeld.* C reads *lynked.*
explicit	After the explicit, C includes the note: *Compilyd by John Ludgate monke of berye at the request of a worthye cyttesyne of London to be paynted in a parlor* (fol. 159r).

DISGUISING AT HERTFORD

Before 1, s.d.	*compleyning.* M reads *compleynyng.*
5	*vigyle.* A reads *begyninge.*
6	*froward of ther chere.* Missing from T (torn leaf); M supplies from A.
7	*fallen on ther kne.* Missing from T (torn leaf); M supplies from A.
11	*endured.* A reads *endued.*
14	*unremuwable.* A reads *vuneriable.*
17	*yonge.* M's emendation; T reads *yong.*
35	*hungry.* A reads *hugely.*
42	*hir.* A reads *his.*
43	*hir.* A reads *he.*
53	*bloode.* M's transcription; T reads *blood.*
63	*felt.* M reads *felte.*
116	*wyres.* A reads *wynes.*

133	*dotardes.* A reads *dastardes.*
157	*Seothe.* A reads *Soth.*
166	*darrein.* Not clear in A.
169	*or.* M's emendation based on A; T reads *of.*
184	*strowtethe.* A reads *straweth.*
186	*bakoun.* M claims that A reads *babeenu,* but it looks like *bakoun* to me.
195	*sory.* A reads *sorowe.*
215	*mooste.* M reads *moost.*
223	*stryf.* M reads *stryffe.*
239	*nexste.* M's emendation; T reads *nexst.*
rubric	*herde, the kyng givethe.* A reads *hard the kynge and gave.*

DISGUISING AT LONDON

11	*pleyne.* A reads *pleynly.*
30	*fordoothe.* A reads *for dereth.*
86	*manny.* M's emendation; T and A read *mannys.*
102	*eeke of.* A reads *of all.*
115	*was.* Omitted in T and A; added by M.
118	*his pruyde.* T and A read: *hir pruyde.*
169	*at.* Omitted in T and A; added by M.
170	*hir.* M's emendation; T and A read *his.*
178	*al kyns meede.* A reads *all hines nede.*
183	*yore agoone.* A reads *thor agone.*
190	*bothen.* A reads *boden.*
261	*chaumpyounes.* M's emendation; T and A read *chaumpyouns.*
266	*I.* M's emendation; T and A read *In.*
278	*not.* A reads *it.*

HENRY VI'S TRIUMPHAL ENTRY INTO LONDON

headnote	Omitted in Ha; CC reads *Pur le Roy. Ordynauncez.*
2	*eronne.* Ha reads *ronne* (not noted by M); CC reads *croune.*
6	*shewed.* Ha reads *shed.*
8	*reyne.* Ha reads *reynes.*
	hevynesse. CC reads *highnes.*
9	*olde.* Omitted in Ha.
12	*dissent.* Ha reads *assent.*
13	*hevene.* Ha reads *even.*
19	*eyre.* Ha reads *erthe.*
26	*the.* CC and Ha read *this.*
32	*colour.* Ha reads *colour of.*
34	*well.* Ha reads *were wel.*
	made. Ha reads *and mad.*

40	*dyde.* M's emendation; Jii reads *dyd.*
45	*the.* Omitted in CC and Ha.
46	*gladde.* Ha reads *clad.*
55	*theire.* Ha reads *the.*
56	*the kyng.* Omitted in CC.
62	*konnyngly abrayde.* CC reads *knouyngly abbarayd.*
prose	*God.* Ha reads *Almyghty god.*
	arenyng. Ha reads *athenyng.*
	Beseching. Ha reads *besechynge of;* not noted by M.
65–66	These lines are reversed in Jii.
66	*dyvers.* Jii reads *dyverser.*
69	*shall yt.* Ha reads *it schal.*
71	*he passed was.* Ha reads *they passyd* (M: *passed*) *was.*
72	*town.* M's emendation as well as the reading in Ha; Jii reads *Citee.*
82	*a scripture.* Ha reads *a long scripture.*
84	Some of the marginal rubrics are positioned above stanzas in Ha.
85	*Alle tho that ben.* CC reads *Also that beth.*
91	*of the.* Ha reads *of this.*
96	*and.* Ha reads *and all.*
97	*mow ryde or.* Ha reads *myghte ryden and;* CC reads *mowgh ride and.*
102	*yitt.* M's emendation; Jii reads *yutt.*
103	*velvettes.* CC reads *welvettes.* Ha reads *velvetty.*
106	*beauté.* M mistakenly claims that Ha reads *Benygne.*
109	*here.* Ha reads *his.*
111	*gaf.* Jii reads *yaf.*
113	*called was.* Ha reads *was callyd.*
116–17	These lines are transposed in Jii; M mistakenly claims they are transposed in Ha.
119	*komyth.* Ha reads *com.*
120	*of grete.* CC reads *of the grete.*
123	*to.* M mistakenly claims omitted in CC.
124	*holdeth.* CC reads *haldith;* Ha reads *halt.*
127	*shulde.* Ha reads *shal.*
	contune. M's emendation, following Ha; Jii reads *continue.* MacCracken notes that *contune* is Lydgate's regular spelling (see "King Henry's Triumphal Entry," p. 83n4).
130	*Apperyng to hym.* CC reads *To apperyng him;* M claims Ha reads *Tokyne aperyng,* but it actually reads *To hym aperyng.*
132	*Grace lyst to.* Ha reads *lust.*
134 ff.	Rubrics in left margin in Jii not noted by M: *Nature / Grace and / Fortune.*
137	*hyhnesse.* Ha reads *hignesse.*
138	*termyne.* Ha reads *determyne.*
144	*this.* Omitted in CC.
146	*joyfully.* So Jii. M emends to *ioyfully.*

148	*undirstonde*. Ha reads *understondith*.
155	*thes emperesses*. CC reads *this Empresse*.
158	*cornall*. Ha reads *crownall*.
164	*an*. CC reads *in*.
168	*at komyng of*. Ha reads *at the comyng*; CC reads *at comyn*.
169	*of*. Ha reads *on*.
172	*theym thouht*. Ha reads *thei thought*.
	unto hem. Ha reads *to hem*.
175	*include*. Ha reads *includyd*.
	thes giftes. Ha reads *the gyftes*.
183	*unto thy moste vaylle*. Ha reads *to thi moost availe*.
185	*of strenth*. CC reads *a strength*.
186	*and*. Ha reads *and of*.
192	*attendaunce*. CC reads *attendaunt*.
196	*theire*. CC reads *thre*.
198	*septre*. Ha reads *a septre*.
199	*swerde*. Ha reads *sheld*.
	myht. Ha reads *right*.
202	*encrees*. CC reads *encreses*.
206	*othir*. CC reads *ther*; Ha reads *here*.
216	*of herte*. CC reads *offte hert*.
217	*ye be*. Ha reads *oure joye*.
219	*now*. Ha reads *newe*.
222	Line omitted in Ha, but indicated in margin by the words *Soverayn Lord*.
232	*callyd*. Omitted in CC.
236	*hire*. Ha reads *his*.
240	*hire*. Ha reads *here ek*.
241	*moste clerkely*. Ha reads *so clerkly*.
244	*voyde*. Ha reads *royde*.
248	*scolers*. Ha reads *clerkes*.
249	*eke*. Ha reads *we*.
250	*at komyng of the*. Ha reads *at the comynge of oure*.
255	*stode*. CC reads *tooke*.
258	*called*. Ha reads *callyd dame*.
270	*hyh*. Ha reads *highe*.
273	*upon*. M's emendation; Jii reads *on*.
279	*figured*. Ha reads *asgnyd*.
281	*shall nat feyne*. CC reads *schuld not fayle*.
283	*Clemens*. CC reads *clennes*.
287	*kepyn*. CC reads *kepyng*.
288	*kepte*. Ha reads *kepit*.
291	*sayde*. Omitted in Ha.
292	*prosperytee*. Ha reads *felicite*.
293	*afore*. Ha reads *afore also*.

297–98   M's emendation following Ha; Jii and CC read *Honour of kyng which I shall expresse / With this scripture in every mannes siht*. Ha omits *I*; CC transposes 297–98.

301   *geve*. Ha reads *gif us*.

302   *and thy*. M claims H inserts *and thi*, but H follows Jii.

303   *The*. Ha reads *To the*.
        his. M's emendation; Jii reads *hie*.

306   *in lawe*. CC reads *in the lawe*.

307   *Chepe*. M's emendation, following Ha; Jii and CC read *into Chepe*.
        anoon. Omitted in CC.

309   *the*. CC reads *to*.

313   *was*. CC and Ha read *were*.

314   *that*. Omitted in CC.

315   *welle*. CC reads *well*.

316   *Bachus*. CC reads *bochous*.

320   *Shewed*. Ha and CC read *shedde*.

321   *of recreacioun*. M's emendation, following Ha; Jii reads *of grete recreacioun*.

322   *alle*. Omitted in Ha.

323   *Unto the Kyng of famous and hyh*. Ha reads *Into the kyngges famous high*.
        and. CC reads *of*.

324   *us*. Omitted in CC and Ha.

329   *wyn up*. CC reads *of wyne up*; Ha reads *up wynes of*.

332   *hire*. CC reads *the*.

335   *by*. Ha reads *of*.

337   *cristallyne*. M's emendation, following CC (as he notes in "King Henry's Triumphal Entry," p. 90n1); Jii reads *cristall*.

339   *blymsith*. CC reads *blemeshith* (M transcribes CC's reading as *blemishith*).

340   *Convenable*. Ha reads *Conable*.

342   *take*. Ha reads *tok*.

350   *of yeer*. Ha reads *of the yeer*.

356   *the fruytes which*. Ha reads *othere frutis whiche* (M transcribes as *whice*).

357   *and*. MacCracken notes that CC reads *etiam* (abbreviated), perhaps pointing to a copy of this list in Latin, which Lydgate used ("King Henry's Triumphal Entry," p. 90n2); note, however, that elsewhere CC employs the same abbreviation for *and*.

364   *Alle*. CC reads *And*.

366   *of*. Omitted in Ha.

372   *in*. Ha reads *on*.

373   *that*. Omitted in Ha.

378   *Seyde well devoutly*. Ha reads *wel devoutly seyde*.

380   *in erthe levyng*. Ha reads *in erthe here*.

382   *specially*. Ha reads *special*.

384   *at fronteur*. Ha reads *at the frontour*.

388	*curen.* M claims that CC reads *ouryn*, but it appears to me to be *curen.*
	langour. CC reads *langures.*
390	*avoydyng.* M's emendation; Jii reads *avoydoying.*
392	*clene.* Ha reads *clere.*
396	*notable.* CC reads *noble.*
397	*This.* Ha reads *The.*
398	*upriht.* M emends to *up-[a]riht.*
401	*by lynes.* Omitted in Ha.
402	*and.* Omitted in Ha.
405	*pedegree.* M's emendation, following Ha; Jii reads *degree.*
412	*on the tothir.* CC reads *unto the thoder.*
415	*crounyd first.* Ha reads *first crounyd.*
416	*myht.* So Jii. M emends to *myhte.* Ha reads *myghte.*
417	*in.* Omitted in Ha.
423	*of.* CC reads *be.*
424	*to excuse.* Ha reads *for to excuse.*
428	*Conduyt a liht.* Ha reads *the conduyt he light*; CC reads *a lytell.*
432	*wern.* Ha reads *was*; CC reads *were.*
433	*goven.* Jii reads *yoven.*
434	*Wrete.* M claims that Ha reads *Wrethe*, but it is actually *Wreten.*
	hyhe. M's emendation; Jii reads *hyh*; Ha reads *highe* (M transcribes as *hize*).
436	M, following Ha and CC, inserts *sure* after *kyng*; omitted in Jii.
438	*sprede and shyne.* Ha reads *shyne and sprede.*
439	*And.* Omitted in Ha.
	his. CC reads *these.*
440	CC contains the Latin marginalia: *Longitudinorem repletem et ostendet illi saltare imem* (not noted by M).
442	M, following Ha, inserts *many* after *lengthe off.*
445	*And.* Omitted in Ha.
446	*thurh.* CC reads *thorow oute*; Ha reads *thorough out.*
448	*pees.* CC reads *Pees and.*
450	*contune.* M's emendation; Jii reads *cotune.*
451	*Meire.* CC reads *mayer*; Ha reads *mair.*
453	*With how good will.* M's emendation, following Ha; Jii reads *Heer good wille*; CC reads *Here god woll.*
455	*Entryng.* CC reads *Entered.*
463	CC reads *For of dewete* (M misnumbers the line [to 462] and mistakenly claims that CC reads *dew os*).
475	*alle.* M's emendation; Jii deletes *al.*
478	*septre.* Ha reads *scripture.*
479	*it.* Ha reads *he.*
481	*the Kyng.* CC reads *he.*
483	*Tyl.* Ha reads *Til that.*

485	*the.* Ha reads *all the.*
486	*Thanked.* Ha reads *Thankynge.*
489	*this ys.* Ha reads *this it; the* omitted in Ha.
491	M, following Ha, inserts *anon* after *kyng.*
494	*this.* Ha reads *this thing.*
499	*Kyng.* So Jii. M emends to *King.*
500	*theire asking.* Ha reads *there a thyng.*
502	*to.* Omitted in CC and Ha.
505	*yclosyd.* CC and Ha read *closyd.*
prose	*otherwyse cleped.* Ha reads *otherwise callid.*
	to youre. CC reads *unto youre.*
	a goode wille. Ha reads *as good awille.*
	of trouthe. of omitted in Ha.
510	In margin of CC and Ha: *Verba translatoris.*
514	*thy.* Ha reads *the.*
517	*nevere.* CC reads *nat;* omitted in Ha.
518	*surplusage.* M's emendation; Jii and Ha read *surpluage.*
522	*the.* Ha reads *his;* omitted in CC.
530	*thee.* CC reads *it.*
530a	*L'envoye.* Omitted in CC.
531	*unto.* Ha reads *into.*
532	*to.* Ha reads *unto.*
536	*in.* Ha reads *in the.*
537	*yow.* Omitted in Ha.
	There is no colophon in Jii. CC reads *Deo gracias;* Ha reads *Here endith the makyng of the comynge of the kyng out of fraunce to London, Be the monk of Bery. Deo Gracias.*

THE LEGEND OF ST. GEORGE

headnote	R lacks headnote and line *The poete first declarethe* (an omission not noted by M). T reads *thee poete.*
1	*yee folk that heer present be.* R reads *Ye folke all whyche here in presence;* Bo reads *folkes.*
2	*story shal.* R reads *history shull.*
4–5	These lines are transposed in R.
4	*His.* R reads *Of hys.*
	and his. R reads *and of hys.*
	passyoun. M reads *passyon.*
5	*is.* R reads *ys oure.*
7	*Englisshe.* R reads *englysshe.*
8	*sithen goon ful yoore.* Bo reads *sithen gon ful yoore;* T reads *goon sithen ful yoore;* R reads *syth ago* (M: *agon*) *nat full yore.*
10	*b'assent.* Bo reads *by assent;* R reads *by lordys assent.*

	Wyndesore. R reads *Wyndsore*.
11	*th'ordre*. Bo reads *the ordre*; R reads *the Ordre*.
	first. Omitted in R.
	gartier. R reads *Gartere*.
12	*ay*. R reads *euer*; Bo reads *fro*.
13	*Foure and twenty*. Bo reads *xxiiii*^*te*.
14	*ther*. Bo reads *the*; R reads *hys*.
15	*interpretacioun*. Bo reads *interupcioun*.
16	*Is sayde*. M's emendation; Bo reads *Is seid*; R reads *Ys seyde*; T omits *Is*.
	of tweyne. R reads *for tweyne*.
	the first. M's emendation, following Bo; *the* omitted in T and R.
17	*And the secound*. Bo reads *So the secound*; R reads *The secund*. M mistakenly claims T reads *And of secound*.
18	*As*. R reads *And as*.
	that. Bo reads *one*; M mistakenly claims R reads *one*.
	for. Omitted in Bo and R.
19	*feond*. Bo reads *devel*; R reads *devyll*.
	manhoode. R inserts *hys* before *manhoode*; Bo reads *maydynhode*.
20	*Crystes*. R reads *hys*; Bo reads *kristes*.
	knyght. M reads *knight*.
21	*bright*. R inserts *full* before *bryght*.
23	*story*. R reads *history*.
	to. Omitted in Bo.
	endyte. R reads *endure*.
24	*to*. Bo reads *in*.
25	*And*. R reads *And he*.
	he gaf. R reads *gan* (M, mistakenly: *gaf*); Bo reads *he gan*.
	himself. R omits *self*.
26	*Frome*. Bo reads *Fro*.
27	*so gynnyng*. R reads *he gan*.
31	*noblesse*. Bo reads *nobelnesse*; R reads *nobyles*.
34	*swerd*. R reads *the swerd*.
35	*The*. Omitted in Bo.
	and of. Bo reads *and*.
rubric	At the top of p. 315 in R is written in Stow's hand: *The lyfe of saynt gorge compyled by John ludgate monke of bery at the request of the armerers of london to peynt about ther haulle.*
36	*aventure is falle*. Bo reads *adventure is byfalle*.
38	*whiche*. Bo reads *which that*.
	Lybye. R reads *lyby*; Bo reads *lybie*.
39	*a*. R reads *the*.
	Lysseene. R reads *lysene*; Bo reads *lessene*.
41	*monstruous*. Bo reads *monstrous*.
43	*qweene*. M reads *queene*.

	taken. M's emendation, following the reading in Bo. T and R read *takyng*.
44	*sodeyne wooful*. Bo reads *sodeyne ooful*; R reads *wofull and sodayne*.
	aventure. R reads *adventure*.
45	*fellen*. Bo reads *fallyng*; R reads *fyll*.
46	*that*. Omitted in Bo and R.
	stonde. Bo reads *stode*; R reads *stood*.
47	*As*. R reads *And*.
	not. Omitted in R.
48	*assaute*. Bo reads *the assent*.
	felle. R reads *foule*.
49	*theyre*. R reads *that*.
50	*But*. R reads *Then*.
	theyre. Bo and R read *the*.
51	*that*. Omitted in Bo and R.
53	*this beest foule and abhomynable*. R reads *thys foule beest that was so abhomynable*.
54	*staunche*. R reads *withdrawe*.
	which. M reads *whiche*.
	which was. Omitted in R.
56	*nuwe*. R reads *nede*.
	more. Bo and R read *for more*.
57	*ne*. Bo reads *nor*.
59	*Thane*. Bo reads *When*.
	tooke. Bo reads *token*.
	other. Bo and R read *or*.
60–61	These lines are transposed in R.
61	*Lyche*. Bo and R read *Like*.
	by. Bo reads *ther*.
	chaunce. M claims T reads *launce* and so emends following Bo, but T actually reads *chaunce*.
62	*to*. Omitted in R.
63	*that citee*. R reads *the cyte*.
66	*Touchant*. Bo reads *Touching*; R reads *Towchyng*.
	that foule. R omits *that*.
67	*Eche*. Bo and R read *Every*.
	maner. Omitted in R.
68	*devowred*. M reads *devoured*.
69	*at the last*. Bo reads *atte last*.
70	*right*. Omitted in Bo and R.
71	*she*. M reads *sche*.
	nexst. Omitted in Bo and R.
72	*so*. Omitted in Bo and R.
	helpe. Bo reads *ther helpe*; R reads *ther help*. M reads *helpe*.

73	*But to beo sent.* R reads *And by oon assent.*
	to. Omitted in Bo.
74	*quakyng.* R reads *stondyng.*
	hir. R reads *gret.*
75	*Upon.* R reads *In.*
	shee did. R reads *dyd she.*
76	*hir.* R reads *and hir.*
77	*so.* Omitted in Bo and R.
78	*oute goyng.* R reads *goyng out.*
79	*al.* Omitted in R.
80	*In.* Bo reads *with.*
	with stoones. R reads *with preciouse stoones.*
81	*ful sheene.* Omitted in R.
83	*frome.* Bo reads *fro.*
	In R this line reads *Brought thedyr by god for her defence* (M transcribes as *hyr diffence*).
84	*Ageynst.* Bo reads *Agayn*; R reads *Agayne.*
85	*owen.* Omitted in R.
	knight. M reads *knyght.*
86	*a ryal.* Bo reads *ariol.*
87	*Which.* R reads *The whyche.*
	mayde. M reads *mayden.*
88	*Of.* R reads *With gret.*
	grete. M's emendation, following the reading in Bo; T reads *gret.*
89	*quod.* R reads *seyde.*
	takethe. Bo reads *toke*; R reads *tooke.*
90	*And.* Omitted in Bo and R.
	fleen. R reads *fle in hast.*
	hir. Bo reads *his.*
93	*eeke.* Omitted in Bo; R reads *gret.*
95	*cheekys.* Bo reads *chekyns.*
	reyne and royle adowne. R reads *royall and so ren a downe.*
96	*Thought.* R reads *And thought.*
	beon. Bo and R read *be.*
97	*nor.* R reads *ne*; Bo reads *for.*
	to. Omitted in Bo and R.
98	*jupart.* R reads *gepart*; Bo reads *iuparte.*
99	*smote on.* M's interpolation from Bo and R; T is indeciperable.
101	*And towardes.* R reads *Then toward.*
102	*with outen.* Bo reads *withoute.*
103	*Avysyly of witt he tooke.* R reads *Avysydly with all wyt and toke.*
104	*kene.* R reads *kenely.*
	egrounde. Bo and R read *grounde.*
105	*the body.* Bo reads *his body.*

the feonde. M's interpolation from Bo and R; *the* is faded in T.

107   *maked.* Bo and R read *makyng.*

109   *debonayre.* Bo and R read *a benyngne.*

112   *in thyn hande.* Bo reads *on the grounde.*

115   *she gan.* Bo reads *gan she.*

116   *ouggely.* Bo reads *Owgle.*

       For this line R reads *With thys vyle monstre whyche durst nat abrey.*

117   *mayden.* Bo and R read *mayde.*

       gan. R reads *dyd.*

118   *That whane.* R reads *Of the whyche.*

       hade. Bo reads *hed.*

119   *banner.* Bo reads *laurer.*

       goothe. Bo and R read *goth a.*

120   *Giving.* T reads *Yiving.*

       him. Bo reads *hem.*

       the. Omitted in R.

       of this. Bo reads *of his*; R reads *and the.*

122   *his.* R reads *theyre.*

123   *a swerde.* Bo reads *aswere.*

124   *alwey taking ful goode heed.* R reads *awayted and sawe thys gret dede.*

       goode. M reads *good.*

126   *thorughe.* Bo reads *thorgh.*

129   *hem.* Omitted in R.

131   *th'errour.* Bo reads *there erroure*; R reads *errour.*

       conversyoun. R reads *conversacioune.*

132   *hem.* R reads *theym.*

       the kyng and the cyté. R reads *kyng and cyte.*

134   *in honnour.* Bo reads *in the honnour.*

137   *and.* Omitted in R.

138   For this line, Bo reads *Mydde of the which ther sprong up anon right*; R
          reads *Mydde of the churche there sprang anon right.*

       up. M's emendation from Bo; omitted from T and R.

140   *seek.* Bo reads *sike.*

       For this line, R reads *Every day to her servyce whych ys dyvyne.*

141   *thanne.* Omitted in Bo.

       gan the. R reads *gan then.*

143   *above al other.* Bo and R read *over al.*

144   *have ever.* Bo reads *have*; R reads *to have.*

146   *on poore, and first.* R reads *the poore and furst.*

       first. Omitted in T; M's emendation, following Bo's reading.

147   For this line, Bo and R read *Every day to here service which is devyne.*

       here. M's emendation, following the readings in Bo and R; T reads *hir.*

148   *This.* Bo and R read *The.*

       telle. Bo and R read *tell.*

149	*Ageynst*. Bo reads *Agayn*.
150	*Theodacyan*. R reads *Aras Dacian*; Bo reads *Dacian*.
151–52	These lines are transposed in T.
151	*paynyme*. R reads *paynyms*.
	a. Omitted in R.
152	*to*. Omitted in Bo.
153	*Cryst*. R reads *the churche*.
	his. R reads *the*.
154	*With*. R reads *By*.
	his. Omitted in R.
155	*that*. Omitted in Bo and R.
	hereof. R reads *therof*.
157	*of*. Omitted in T and Bo; M's emendation, following R.
	knightly. R reads *knightes*.
160	*he*. Omitted in Bo.
161	*Oon*. Bo reads *O*.
	on. Bo reads *on thi*.
162	*false*. M's emendation, following R; T and Bo read *fals*.
163	*Comaunded*. M reads *Commaunded*.
	hathe. Omitted in R.
	be. R reads *were*.
164	*broughte*. M reads *brought*.
165	*that*. Omitted in Bo.
166	*he ne liste noo delayes maake*. R reads *he lyst nat any delayes to make*.
	liste. M's emendation, following Bo; T reads *list*.
167	*Aunswerd*. R reads *Assuryd*.
168	*lawe*. R reads *feythe*.
	declyne. M's emendation, following Bo and R; T reads *enclyne*.
171	*upon*. Bo and R read *on*.
172	*scowrges beet*. Bo reads *skorged*; R reads *be scourged*.
	ful feele. R reads *foule*.
174	*sydes*. M reads *sides*.
	not hees. R reads *with*.
	hees. M reads *hes*.
175	*opende*. Bo reads *open*; R omits (M mistakenly claims R reads *our*).
	salt. R reads *with salt*.
176	For this line, Bo reads *The nyght after criste dede him appere* and R reads *The nyght after cryst dyd to him appere*.
177	*to*. Omitted in R.
	coumfort. R reads *recomforte*.
178	*And beed*. Bo reads *Bad*; R reads *Bade*.
	with goode. Bo reads *with ful gode*.
180	*victor*. R reads *vyctory*.
	schal. R reads *shuld*.

	report. Bo reads *resorte*.
181	*and*. Omitted in R.
	wynnen. R reads *wynnyng*.
184	*venyme*. R reads *poyson*.
	b'enchauntement. Bo reads *by ente*; R reads *by enchauntement*.
188	*Saughe ageyne*. R reads *Sy that ayenst*.
190	*Axethe*. Bo reads *And axeth*; R reads *And askyd*.
191	*bytwix*. Bo and R read *betwyxt*.
192	*false*. M's emendation, following R; T and Bo read *fals*.
	voyde. Bo reads *fals*.
193	*shuld*. M's emendation, following R; omitted in Bo and T.
194	*roose*. M's emendation. T reads *roos*; R reads *roose*; Bo reads *ros*.
196	*that*. R reads *whyche*.
197	*cruwel*. R reads *full cruell*.
198	For this line, R reads *Thought hym on a new wyse in Angor and tene*.
199	*Reysed*. R reads *And reysed*.
	aloft. Bo reads *on lofte*.
200	*grounden*. Bo reads *grounde*; omitted in R.
201	*moost*. R reads *ful*.
202	*Tourned*. R reads *Was turnyd*.
	that. R reads *theyr*.
	rage. T reads *raige*?
203	*tobraake*. R reads *braste*.
204	*Eeke*. R reads *Also*.
205	*eplounged*. Bo reads *plunched*; R reads *ploungyd*.
206	*withouten*. R reads *without*; Bo reads *withoute*.
208	This line is omitted in T; M's interpolation, following Bo and R.
	liche. R reads *lyke*; Bo reads *lych*.
	bath. R reads *bathe*
	consolacioun. Bo reads *consulacioun*.
210	*al*. R reads *that*.
211	*eeke*. Omitted in R.
	the story. R reads *as the hystory*.
213	*Of*. R reads *And of*.
	have. Omitted in R.
214	*theyre*. Bo reads *hir*.
	can. Bo reads *hath*; R reads *dyd*.
215	*oure*. R reads *youre*.
216	*frome*. Bo reads *of*.
217	*till*. Bo and R read *to*.
220	*Alexandrea*. Bo and R read *Alexandria*.
	of. Omitted in R.
221	*al hir fals creaunce*. R reads *all myscreaunce*.
224	*starf*. R reads *hyng*.

225   *thanne.* Omitted in R.

           by ful mortal. Bo reads *a ful mortal*; R reads *by a mortall.*

227   *be.* M's emendation, following Bo and R; T reads *he.*

229   Line omitted in T.

           He to ben heveded. R reads *For to behedyd.*

           cruwel. Bo reads *cruel.*

230   *thus.* Bo reads *this.*

231   *hem.* R reads *theym.*

232   Bo contains the marginal note *Qualiter Georgius oravit.*

           quod. R reads *quoth.*

           thou. Omitted in Bo and R.

233   *unto thee.* R reads *to thy.*

234   *That alle.* R reads *All the* (M: *tho*); Bo reads *That alle the.*

238   *Al.* Omitted from Bo and R.

240   *frome.* Bo reads *fro.* M reads *from.*

           the hye. Omitted in R.

241   *that.* Omitted in Bo and R.

244   *unwarly by.* R reads *merveloulsy by a.*

245   *hoome.* R reads *hem.*

           Colophon in Bo reads *Here endeth the lyfe of seynt George*; in R it reads *Explicit vita sancti Georgii Martiris.* In T: *Explicit.*

MESURE IS TRESOUR

3   *lyfe.* M's emendation. Hb reads *lyf.*

6   *hyh.* M reads *hyll.*

21   *with cost.* Hb reads *with with cost.*

24   *there.* M reads *ther.*

25   *emperours.* M's emendation; Hb reads *empours.*

45   *devisioun.* M reads *divisioun.*

50   *folk.* M reads *folke.*

55   *bryngen.* M's emendation; Hb reads *brynge.*

91   *hom.* M's emendation; Hb reads *hem.*

131   *Isaak.* M reads *Isaac.*

132   *shepperdys.* M reads *shepperdws.*

MUMMING AT BISHOPSWOOD

2   *hast.* Stow silently emends to *hath* (*Survey*, p. 100); Norton-Smith (*John Lydgate: Poems*, p. 124) notes that Shirley has misread þ in his exemplar as long *st*, on the assumption that Flora is in the vocative and the verb should thus be second person singular.

4   *sonne.* M's emendation; B reads *sonnes.*

10   *trascende*. Norton-Smith (*John Lydgate: Poems*, p. 124), emends to
        transcend, on the assumption that B has omitted the stroke over the
        a, and following Stow (*Survey*, 100), who silently expands to
        "transcends." Under *transcenden* v., the *MED* lists *trascender* as a
        variant form and suggests that "it may show the influence of ME
        ascenden," but since *Bishopswood* is the sole example it cites, Norton-
        Smith's conjecture may be correct.

23   *payne*. M prints as *payne*, but B reads *peyne*, as Norton-Smith (*John
        Lydgate: Poems*, p. 7), agrees.

24   *sugre*. Norton-Smith (*John Lydgate: Poems*, p. 7) emends to *sugred*, a
        favorite past participial adjective of Lydgate's, on the grounds that
        if *sugre* is correct, this attributive use of the noun would be unique
        (125). But the MED cites several examples of the adjectival use of
        sugre, as here (see *sugre*, n. [i]).

27   *morwenyng*. M's emendation; B reads *morowneydge*.

44   *Flowres*. M's emendation; B reads *fowers*.

46   *blosme*. M's emendation; omitted in B.

53   *constreynen*. M's emendation; B reads *consteynen*.

55   *beo*. Norton-Smith (*John Lydgate: Poems*, p. 125) emends to *have* to suit
        the sense of the line that judges protect the commons.

58   *parseveraunce*. M's emendation; erasure in B.

59   *vertue*. M's emendation; B repeats *parseveraunce* from the preceding line,
        with something written over it that seems to end in [*tu*]; Norton-
        Smith (*John Lydgate: Poems*, p. 8) emends to *hir [vertu]*.

70   *Represse the derknesse*. Norton-Smith (*John Lydgate: Poems*, p. 8) omits *the*.

73   *hert*. Norton-Smith (*John Lydgate: Poems*, p. 9) emends to *herte*.

87   *And foolis*. Norton-Smith (*John Lydgate: Poems*, p. 9), inserts *[smale]*
        before *foolis*.

88   *ermonye*. My emendation; M follows B's reading of *enemye*, which is
        written over an erasure. Norton-Smith (*John Lydgate: Poems*, p. 125)
        also emends to *ermonye*, reasoning that Shirley's exemplar probably
        read "ermonye" but that the contraction for *r* disappeared from the
        first *e*, the second *e* is a misreading of *o*, and *m* and *n* have been
        transposed.

91   *shoures*. M's emendation; B repeats *odoures* from the preceding line.

92   *Topyted*. Norton-Smith (*John Lydgate: Poems*, p.125) emends to *Tapyted*;
        compare *Troy Book* 1659 ff. and 1.2611, where Lydgate imitates
        Chaucer (see the *Book of the Duchess*, 258 ff.). The MED cites this line
        from *Bishopswood* as the sole example under the verb *topiten*.

95   *And*. Norton-Smith (*John Lydgate: Poems*, p.10) emends to *Whan*, and
        prints the whole line as: *Whan firy Tytan shews h[i]s tresses sheene*.

104   *heos*. Norton-Smith (*John Lydgate: Poems*, p. 10) prints as *h[i]s*.

MUMMING AT ELTHAM

13	*youre*. M reads *Houre*.
14	*with*. A reads *and*.
16	*Gaf*. A reads *of* (the G is struck through).
23	*lordshipethe*. A reads *lorshipe*.
25	*stint*. A reads *stinte*.
28	*and*. A reads *with*.
45	*hir*. A reads his.
	A miscopies line 48 here, strikes it out, and renumbers lines in correct order; not noted by M.
	T reads *This God, this Goddesse, also theyre gyfftes dresse / In goodely wyse of entent ful goode*, marked by *b* and *a* corrections indicating the phrases should be transposed; not noted by M. A copies the incorrect version, then corrects.
57	*theyre*. A reads *gyve*; not noted by M.
60	*remuwe*. M's emendation; T reads *renuwe* and A reads *renewe*.
	hir. A reads *ther*; not noted by M.
65	T reads *texyle al hevynesse awaye*, with a superscript *b* after *texyle* and superscript *a* after *hevynesse*, indicating that the two words should be reversed. A reads *texyle*.
	awaye. Not noted by M.
66	*eeke*. Not in T or A; added by M.
68	*grounded in*. Now missing in T (torn leaf), but supplied by A (from another manuscript, according to M).
69	*refrete, yif yowe list*. Missing in T (torn leaf), but supplied by A (from another manuscript, according to M).
70	*encresse joye and gladnesse of hert*. Missing in T (torn leaf), but supplied by A (from another manuscript, according to M).
76	*yif yee*. A reads *give*.
77	*and*. Omitted in T and A; added by M.
82	*Ceres*. T reads *Cerces*.
84	*and*. Omitted in T and A; added by M.

MUMMING AT WINDSOR

5	*mescreaunce*. A reads *mestraunce*.
23	*wacche*. A reads *wacchinge*; not noted by M.
53	*Whas*. A reads *was*.
71	*Th'aumpolle*. M reads *Þampolle*.
78	*yit*. A reads *ther*.

MUMMING FOR THE GOLDSMITHS OF LONDON

headnote	In A, the headnote reads: *Here folowythe a lettar made by John Lidgat for a momanynge, whiche the goldsmythes of london shewyd before Eestfyld the mayr on candylmas* [M: *Condylmas*] *day at nyght. this letar was presentyd by an harold callyd fortune.*
3	*the bookes.* A reads *as boks.*
10	*Fro.* M's emendation; T reads *for.*
27	*eure.* A reads *ende.*
68	*citeseyns.* A reads *shreves*; not noted by M.
87	*as.* A reads *at*; not noted by M.
96	*awey.* A reads *all ways*; not noted by M.

MUMMING FOR THE MERCERS OF LONDON

headnote	*And now.* A reads *Here*; not noted by M. A has marginalia as in T, but Stow also notes that William Estfeld was mayor in 1430 and 1478. *Daun Iohan.* A reads *daun John Lydgat.* *poursuyvaunt.* M reads *poursuyaunt.*
4	*swyft.* A reads *swyfte.*
6	*coosteying.* A reads *costynge.*
42	*Europe.* A reads *erope.*
67	*currant.* T reads *curraat.*
71	*thilk sakk.* A reads *that lakk.*
88	*til.* A reads *to*; not noted by M.
91	*And.* T and A lack *nd*; added by M.

OF THE SODEIN FAL OF PRINCES IN OURE DAYES

headnote	Omitted in H; A includes same marginalia as in T. *folowen.* A reads *foloweth*
15	In the margin of A next to stanza three: *Kynge Charlles* (M: *Charlle*).
23	M's note to this line is confusing; H follows T's reading.
25	*yong hert thought.* M emends to *yonge herte thoughte*; A follows T's reading.
27	*assent.* M emends to *assente.*
28	*he in Parys.* H reads *he in parice*; A reads *themferys.*
31	*was.* T and A read *it was.*
33	*that.* H reads *and that.*
42	*th'Ermynakes.* H reads *the Armynakes.*
44	*he ledde.* M claims H reads *he edde*, but it actually reads *he ledde.*
46	*i. laumerrane* (in margin). Omitted in H; A reads *loomcerean.*
49	*banned.* A reads *bourned*; M claims H reads *dlanned*, but it actually reads *banned.*

PAGEANT OF KNOWLEDGE

2	*Prynces*. M's emendation; R reads *Prynce*.
	the. Missing from R; added by M.
5	*fyghte*. M's emendation; R reads *fyght*.
	shal the. M's emendation; R reads *shalbe*.
17	*Thynges*. Blank space left in R for large *T*.
21	R omits entire line; supplied by M.
56	*fynden*. M's emendation; R reads *fynde*.
64	*herte*. M's emendation; R reads *hert*.
66	*Jubal*. Blank space left in R for large *J*.
69	*Jubal*. M's emendation; R reads *Tubal*.
84	*longe*. M's emendation; R reads *long*.
115	*Of*. Blank space left in R for large *O*.
131	*Saturne*. Blank space left in R for large *S*.
139	*Aries*. Blank space left in R for large *A*.
	coleryk. M's emendation; R reads *coloryk*.
157	*longer*. M's emendation; R reads *long*.
161	*The*. Blank space left in R for large *T*.
	sely. R reads *ӡely*.
176	*naturally*. M's emendation; R reads *naturall*.
180	*than be stable*. M's emendation; R reads *than stable*.
196	*The*. Blank space left in R for large *T*.
204	*coleryk*. M's emendation; R reads *coloryk*.
218	*sentement*. M's emendation; R reads *centement*.
220	*Man*. Blank space left in R for large *M*.
226	*man than be*. M's emendation; R reads *man be*.
242	*maner*. M's emendation; R reads *man*.
248	*The*. Blank space left in R for large *T*.
251	*valeys*. M's emendation; R reads *valeyce*.
261	*All*. M's emendation; R reads *All*.
266	*with*. M's emendation; R reads *whyche*.
274	*hardy*. M's emendation; R reads *harde*.
280	*unto the hevyn*. M's emendation; R reads *unto hevyn*.
283	*palace*. M's emendation; R reads *place*.

A PROCESSION OF CORPUS CHRISTI

1	*nowe for to magnefye*. In T, *nowe* is missing but there is an insertion mark for it; A reads *for to magnefye nowe*; H omits *nowe*.
2	*Feste*. H reads *Now fest*.
3	*guye*. M's emendation, following A; T reads *guyde*; H reads *guy*.
5	*t'enlumyne*. H reads *to enlumyne*.
7	*many*. H reads *many an*.

9	*more*. H reads *the more*.
21	*er*. H reads *that*.
23	*takethe hereof*. H reads *take herof*.
27	*that*. Omitted in H.
30	*Sette*. M reads *Set*.
33	*Yssake*. H reads *Isaac*; A reads *Ysake*.
35	*and*. M transcribes as *aud*.
36	*the Olly*. H reads *the holy*; A reads *holly*.
37	*Gesse*. H reads *Iesse*.
40	*Whos*. M's emendation; H reads *Whas*.
45	*eseyne*. H reads *I seyne*; A reads *esene*.
62	*Crists*. M reads *Cristes*.
68	*and*. H reads *that*.
	venqwysshed. M's emendation; H reads *venqwysshde*.
70	*victorie of*. H reads *victor with*.
71	*Philisteys*. H reads *the Philistes*.
79	M mistakenly claims H reads *falseth*.
82	*B'avisyoun*. H reads *Be avisyoun*.
	hevenly. H reads *hevenly and*.
89	*Ysayes*. H reads *Isaye* (M: *I saye*).
91	*that*. Omitted in H.
96	*oure*. M reads *our*.
	were. H reads *was*.
102	*lenkethe*. H reads *length*.
104	*strenkethe*. H reads *strength*.
106	*swoote*. M's emendation, following H; T and A read *swete*.
107	This line follows line 112 in T, but the lines are correctly numbered a b d e f g h c; H and A follow the order of T; A adds the renumbering, but H omits it.
119	*stinten*. H reads *stynte*.
120	*oure*. M reads *our*.
126	*O*. H reads *On*; M's note "of the S." (which suggests that an unnamed manuscript S has the variant *of the*) is unclear to me.
133	*ful blessed*. H reads *blisful*.
139	*holy*. Omitted in A.
141	*nuwe*. H and A read *the newe*.
142	*shal*. M reads *schal*.
157	*doome*. H reads *brede*.
158	*I mene*; M adds *I*, following H; *I* omitted in T and A.
175	*This*. H reads *This is*.
176	*circumcyded*. A reads *circumsised*.
177–84	In T, written a b e f g h c d and so lettered; A corrects according to the lettering, while H does not.
183	Omitted in H.

	medisyn. In a later hand in T.
185–92	In T, written a b c e f d g h and so lettered; A corrects, but H does not.
190	*ternal*. H reads *eternal*.
198	*Recounseylling*. H reads *Reconsilyng*.
199	*mathe us mighty*. H reads *makith us myght*.
201	*Maistre*. H reads *Maister*; A reads *Master*.
	notable. A reads *notabell*.
202	*Holding*. A reads *holdinge*; H reads *holdyng*.
	chalys. H reads *chalice*.
	sonne. A reads *sone*.
	clere. H reads *cliere*.
203	*Ooste*. H reads *host*; A reads *oste*.
	aloft. A reads *alofte*.
	gloryous. H reads *glorious*.
	comendable. A reads *comendabell*.
204	*pytee*. H reads *pitee*; A reads *pite*.
	pleyning. H reads *playeng*; A reads *pleyninge*.
	cheere. H reads *chiere*.
205	*caste*. A reads *cast*.
	shewing. H reads *shewyng*; A reads *shewinge*.
206	*compleynte*. A reads *compleynt*.
	pytous. H reads *pitous*.
207	*dethe*. H reads *deth*.
	deere. H and A read *dere*.
209	*hoolly*. H reads *holy*; A reads *holly*.
	called. H reads *callid*.
210	*hie*. H reads *high*; A reads *hye*.
	sawghe. A reads *sawethe*; H reads *sawgh*.
211	*ooste*. H reads *ost*; A reads *hoste*.
	sunne. A reads *sune*; H reads *sonne*.
	about. A reads *aboute*.
212	*oon*. A reads *one*.
	parfyte. H reads *parfite*.
	unytee. H reads *unite* (M: *uynite*); A reads *uynte*.
213	*gloryous*. H reads *glorious*; A reads *gloryus*.
	liknesse. A reads *likenesse*.
	Trynitee. H reads *Trynite*; A reads *Trinite*.
214	*Gracyous*. H reads *Gracious*; A reads *Gracyus*.
	beo. H and A read *be*.
	comended. H reads *commendid*.
215	*feyth*. A reads *faythe*.
	parfyte. H reads *parfite*.
	charitee. H reads *charite*; A reads *charyte*.
216	*byleeve*. H reads *beleeve*; A reads *beleve*.

	comprehended. H reads *comprehendid.*
217	*theos.* H reads *there*; A reads *thos.*
	figures. A reads *fygures.*
218	*likenesses.* H and A read *liknesse.*
	doo. H and A read *do.*
219	*Resceivethe.* H reads *Receyvith.*
	devoute. H reads *devout.*
220	*This.* A reads *Thys.*
	bred. H reads *brede.*
	lyfe. H reads *lyf.*
221	*Egipte.* H reads *Egipt.*
	worldely. H and A read *worldly.*
222	*Youre.* A reads *Your.*
	restoratyf. A reads *restoratyffe.*
	celestyal. H and A read *celestial.*
223	*graunt.* A reads *graunte.*
	suffysaunce. H reads *suffisaunce.*
224	*aungels.* A reads *angelles.*
	sing. H reads *syng*; A reads *singe.*
	everlasting. H and A read *everlastyng.*
Colophon	*of.* H reads *for.*

SOTELTES AT THE CORONATION BANQUET OF HENRY VI

L simply lists in two columns the dishes served in each of the three courses.

3	*see.* Omitted in L.
4	*moost sovereigne of price.* L reads *of moost soveraigne prynce.*
6	*help of.* Omitted in L.
	Crist. L reads *grace.*
7	*sixt Henry.* L reads *seide harry.*
8	*hem.* Omitted in L.
9	*Ageinst.* L reads *Geyn.*
10	*which is.* L reads *with his.*
11	*Sithen Henry the Fifth.* L reads *And with N.*
14	*that succede.* L reads *that shulde succede.*
18	*that.* Omitted in L.
	art. Omitted in L.
20	*The.* L reads *To.*
	Henry. L reads *N.*
	your. L reads *oure.*
21	*of grace on hym.* L reads *on hym of grace.*
23	*by title.* L omits *by.*
24	*in Fraunce.* L omits *in.*

 **APPENDIX**

MUMMING OF THE SEVEN PHILOSOPHERS

Robbins (*Secular Lyrics*, pp. 110–13) prints the verses from Trinity R.3.19, fols. 1r–1v, which are unattributed. According to a headnote, they were written for "Festum Natalis Domini" and address the "kyng of Crystmas" (line 11), who is later invoked as "noble prince" (line 78). In the course of the mumming, the seven philosophers appear, each speaking a verse of conventional advice (rule your body, be generous, balance work with leisure, imitate good examples, don't do anything you can't handle, etc.) in order to help the Christmas king rule properly. The last verse is spoken by a messenger, who advises the king to heed their advice as he grows up and who ushers in a song by the seven mummers. Although it has gone virtually unnoticed, the poem has recently been discussed by Mortimer in his study of *The Fall of Princes* (*Lydgate's Fall of Princes*, pp. 225–26). It is the first item in Trinity College MS R.3.19, a manuscript produced in the London area c. 1478–83, and is in the hand of the same scribe who wrote fols. 1r–45v and 55r–213r (*Manuscript Trinity R.3.19*, pp. xv and xxvi). It stands at the beginning of a number of extracts from Lydgate's *Fall of Princes* and other Chaucerian and pseudo-Chaucerian texts; at the top of fol. 1r, written in a later hand is the note "Poemata of daun Jaun Anglice Lidgati." The verses seem designed for a Christmas entertainment at court or in a school, perhaps an inversionary one similar to boy bishops' ceremonies. While there is no evidence linking the verses to Henry VI's court, the advice offered by the seven philosophers would be consistent with the advisory agenda adopted by Humphrey, duke of Gloucester, in the early 1430s; much of its advice could have been culled from a number of places in *The Fall of Princes*, as Mortimer notes (p. 225), and would have been appropriate for Henry at any point in the late 1420s and 1430s. The verses below follow Robbins' edition, checked against the manuscript.

[*Festum Natalis Domini*

Tronos celorum continens,
Whos byrthe thys day reiterate,
Bothe god and man in exystens,
Borne of a mayde immaculate;
5   Preserve your dygne and high estate,
Syth ye preferre thys most high feste,
In quo Redemptor natus est.

Senek the sage that kyng ys of desert,
Regent and rewler of all wyldernesse,

10   Sendeth gretyng with all entier hert
        Unto yow hys brother, kyng of Crystmas;
        Lettyng yow wete with hertly tendyrnes
        What longeth now unto youre astate royall
        That ye be now to so sodenly call.

15   Hyt ys perteynyng to every prynce and kyng
        That pepyll shall have under governaunce,
        That he have prudent and wyse counselyng,
        And to her counseyll geve attendaunce;
        And that your reame shall nat fall perchaunce
20   Unto rewen for defaute of good counsell,
        Take hede herto, hit mayest avayle.

        For oute of olde feldes, as men sayth,
        Cometh all these new cornes from yere to yere;
        So oute of olde expert men in feyth
25   Cometh all these good rules, as ye shall here;
        And by theire age they have in thys matere
        The good rewle of verrey experience,
        Wherefore he sendeth hem to your hygh presence.

        [*Primus Philosophus*

        Attempt nothyng surmountyng your myght,
30   Ne that to finissh that passeth your power;
        For than ye stand foule in youre owne lyght,
        And whoso doth, hymsylf shall foule a-dere
        With shame, and therefore thys wysdom ye lere:
        That hyt ys foly a man suche to begyn
35   Which to performe hys wyttes be to thyn.

        [*Secundus*

        When that tyme ys of grete and large expence,
        Beware of waste and spende ay be mesure;
        Who at suche tyme can fynde no dyfference,
        Hys goodes may nat with hym long endure;
40   The olde ys that "Mesure ys tresure,"
        For in short tyme the good may slyp away
        That was gotyn in many a sondry day.

        [*Tercius*

        Of elther men ye shall your myrrour make,
        Conforme yow to that that may most yow avayle,
45   What ye shall do and what shall forsake;

A bettyr thyng ne may ye not contryve
Than to other mennys dedys to releve;
To all that perteyneth yow eny thyng,
Make other men rule of your levyng.

[*Quartus*

50   Take good hede to youre owne estate,
         To rule your body with a good diete;
         Loke with tyme be nat at debate,
         Though thurgh youre owne mysrule and surfete
         Sekenes or sorow have yevyn yow an hete,
55   The tyme ys good, and no dysemable there ys,
         But men hit make for they do amys.

[*Quintus*

         To preve youresylf take deliberacion
         Be lycly conjectour what may betyde;
         Advertyse and here thys informacion
60   How soone owre lord can set a state asyde;
         Folowe hym, therfore, and let hym be your gyde
         That all thyng hath in hys regement,
         Future and past and youre estate present.

[*Sextus*

         Into a gret age when ye be crept,
65   Havyng gret ryches and habundaunce,
         Be lyberall of the good that ye have kept;
         Thynke that ye have ynough and suffisaunce;
         Let nat youre good of yow have governanuce,
         But governe hit and part hit with your frende;
70   When ye go hens hit may nat with yow wende.

[*Septimus*

         Who that lakketh rest may nat long endure;
         Therefore among take your ease and dysport,
         Delyte yow never in besynes ne cure
         But that other whyle ye may eft resort
75   To play, recreacion, and comfort;
         Ye may the better labour at the long,
         When ye have myrthe your besynes among.

[*Nuncius*

> Lo, noble prince, ye here the counseyll
> Of the vii phylosophyrs sage,
80 Whyche to advertyse hit may hap to avayle
> To let these wysdoms grow up in your age,
> And in your presence afore her passage,
> They purpos all afore yow for to syng,
> Yef to your hyghnes hit myght be plesyng.

[*Explicit.*

MARGARET OF ANJOU'S ENTRY INTO LONDON, 1445

On May 28, 1445, Henry VI's new wife, Margaret of Anjou, entered London in preparation for her coronation at Westminster two days later. As she made her way through the city from Southwark, she was greeted by eight pageants that emphasized peace and the hope that the Anglo-French conflict would soon end. The verses for the pageants, which are no longer attributed to Lydgate, were probably the work of someone hired by Mayor John Chichele and London's city council. Kipling ("London Pageants for Margaret of Anjou," p. 6) believes that Lydgate's way of describing the scriptures for the 1432 entry, which recast written texts as spoken, may have given the devisers of the 1445 entry the idea to use actual speech for the first recorded time in English entries. MacCracken omitted the 1445 entry from his edition of Lydgate's minor poems on the grounds that it was not by Lydgate, who in 1445 was apparently in retirement in Bury. Griffiths (*Reign of King Henry VI*, pp. 487–89) discusses the Entry as well as the wedding ceremonies. An imperfect version of the verses has been printed by Brown, and in even less complete form in Withington, "Lydgate's Verses." Kipling ("London Pageants for Margaret of Anjou") has reconstructed the verses from a manuscript (Harley 3869) of Gower's *Confessio Amantis*, where they were copied onto some blank leaves at the front of the manuscript, and presents a strong argument against Lydgate's authorship of them. The verses, following Kipling's reconstruction and checked against the manuscript, are as follows.

[*Atte the Brigge foot in Suthwerke*

[*Pees and Plenté*

> Moost Cristen Princesse, by influence of Grace[1]
> Doughter of Jherusalem, oure plesaunce
> And joie, welcome as evere princesse was,
> With hert entier and hool affiaunce,
5 Causer of welth, joie, and abundaunce,
> Youre cite, youre poeple, youre subgites alle,

---

[1] *Ingredimini et replete terram* (Genesis 8:17)

With herte, with worde, with dede at youre entraunce,
"Welcome, welcome, welcome" unto you calle!

[*Pees*

So trusteth youre poeple, with affiaunce,
10   Through youre grace and highe benignité,
Twixt the reawmes two, Englande and Fraunce,
Pees shal approche, rest and unité,
Mars sette aside, with alle hys cruelté,
Whiche to longe hath troubled the reawmes tweyne,
15   Bydynge youre coumfort in this adversité,
Moost Cristen Princesse, oure lady sovereyne.

[*At Noes Shippe upon the [Draught] Brigge*

[*Expositor:*]

Moost Cristen Princesse, oure lady sovereyne,
Right as whilom, by Goddes myght and Grace,
Noe this Arke didde forge and ordeyne,
20   Wherein he and hys myght escape and passe
The flood of vengeaunce caused by trespasse,
Conveied aboute, as God liste hym to gye,[1]
By moiean of mercy founde a restyng place
After the Flood uppon this Armonie.

25   Unto the Dove that brought the braunche of pees
Resemblynge youre symplenesse columbyne,
Tokyn and signe the Flood shulde cesse;
Conducte by Grace and Pure Divine,
Sonne of comfort gynneth faire to shyne
30   By youre presence, wherto we synge and seyne,
Welcome of joie, right extendet lyne,
Moost Cristen Princesses, oure lady sovereyne.

[*At Leden Halle*

[*Madame Grace, Chauncelere de Dieu*

Oure benigne Princesse and lady sovereyne,
Grace conveie you forthe and be youre gide
35   In good life longe, prosperously to reyne.

---

[1] *Iam non ultra irascar super terram* (Genesis 8:21)

Trouth and Mercy togedre ben allied,[1]
Justice and Pees; these sustres schal provide
Twixt reawmes tweyn stedfast love to sette.
God and Grace the parties han applied.
40   Now the sustres have hem kiste and mette.

Prenostike of pees, ferme and infenite,
Dame Grace, Goddes Vicarie Generalle,
Foure patentes, faire, fressh, and legible,
Conteynyng iiii preceptes imperialle,
45   Sealles impressed for memorialle,
To these sustres foure thus be directe,
Whiche as mynystres further proclamen shalle,
T'encresen pees, werres to correcte.

Clergie, Knyghthode, the Lawes commendable
50   Assentyng all this matere to ratefie,
Conseile of Grace, haldyng ferme and stable;
George and Dionise for here poeple crie
Uppon the Lorde that alle schall justefie
This tyme of Grace. Thus wolde the storie seyne,
55   Trustynge that pees schall floure and fructifie
By you, Pryncesse and lady sovereyne.

[*At the Tonne in Cornehille*

[*Expositor*:]

"Aungeles of pees shall have dominacioun,"
Sentence yeven from the hevenes highe,
Siewed by Grace and good mediacioun,
60   Pees graunted to growe and multeplie,
Exiled th'angeles of wrecched tirannye,
Werre proscribed, pees shal have hys place;
Blesside be Margarete makyng this purchace.

Conveie of Grace, Virgyne most benigne,
65   Oo blessid Martir, holy Margarete,
Maugre the myght of spirites maligne
To God above hire praier pure and swete
Maketh now for rest, pees, and quiete,
Shewed here pleynly in this storie,
70   Oure Queene Margarete to signifie.

---

[1] *Misericordia et veritas obviaverunt sibi; Iustitia et pax osculate sunt* (Psalm 84:11)

God in hevene comaundynge abstinence,
Noo wicked aungel schall do more grevaunce;
Erthe, see, and trees shal ben in existence
Obeisant to mannes wille and plesaunce,
75   Desired pees bitwixt Englande and Fraunce,
This tyme of Grace by mene of Margarete,
We triste to God to lyven in quiete.

[*At the Grete Conduite in Chepe*

[*Expositor*:]

Grace in this lyf and aftirwarde Glorie,[1]
David in the psalme he saith thus expresse,
80   "How plesaunt be thy tabernacles highe,
Lorde," he saith; this psalme by short processe
Of oure Lorde concludeth high goodnesse:
Noo man to lacke reward when he goth hens
That lyveth here in parfite innocens.

85   Ensaumpled pleynly by faire parable:[2]
Ten virgynes ayens the Spouse they yede,
Fyve necligent refused, founde unable;
And of the Spouse five prudent had mede
For contynence in thoght, worde, and dede.
90   Noo mannes laude sechyng in thaire entent
To serve the Spouse hire hertes onely brent.

The Spouse is sought; Sponsus with hire is mette.
After laboure He wille she take hire rest,[3]
So moche He hath Hys herte uppon hire sette.
95   Now hath the turtle founde a plesaunt nest.
"Come on," she saith, "I wil yeve thee my brest.[4]
Who seketh rest with feithfull, trewe corage
Shalle dwelle atte last in Goddes heritage.

Sponsus Pees the Kynge will make hys feste;
100   Alle thing is redy; plentie and suffisaunce.
Praied for to come, gestes moost and leste,
Unto the Spouses, full of hevenly purveaunce.
Milke and honye flowyng in habundaunce

---

[1] *Gratiam et gloriam dabit Dominus. Non privabit bonis eso qui ambulant in innocentia* (Psalm 83:12–13)

[2] *Parabola decem virginum* (Matthew 25:1–13)

[3] *Quaesivi quem diligit anima mea* (Canticles 3:1)

[4] *Dabo tibi ubera mea* (Canticles 7:12)

Aboute the londe whither He hath us brought;
105   Right ferre and wide gestes clept and sought.

"Eteth and dryncketh, my frendes, of the beste,
Moost chered frendes, dryncketh inwardly;
After the feste take ye youre reste,"
Thus seith the Spouse, Hys feste to magnifie.
110   This joious Canticle dothe signifie
A pees shall be where as now trouble is,
After this lyfe, endely in blys.

[*At the Crosse in Chepe*

[*The angels sing*:] *Sacris solempniis iuncta sunt gaudia, etc.*

[*Expositor*:]

Oo blissful psalme and song celestialle,
"Letatus sum;" for thynges that I here,[1]
115   Noon erthely joie compared nor egalle
May ben here to this blys, may not dispeire,
But schyneth amydde the hevenly spere,
Th'orient Sonne, that noon eclipse may fade;
To Goddes house now schall we goo right glade.

120   Many mansioun bilt in that paleis
Of that Cité, thynges right gloriouse
Been saide. O Lorde, who can Thy paleis preise
So is it faire and inly speciouse.
All holynesse besemeth the Lordes house;
125   Sanctus is songe in every Ierarchie,
Praisyng the Lorde of eternall Glorie.

Oo declared Pryncesse, unto youre noble Grace,
How God hath made this conducte and conveye
Thus throgh youre Cité from place to place,
130   More hertly welcom then youre folk can seie,
Enioieng entierly youre highe nobleye,
This pagent wold mene, youre Excellence,
That ther is ioie in verrey existence.

Where is rejoiced all felicité
135   Withouten ende eternally t'endure,
Contemplacioun of the Deité,

_____

[1] *Laetatus sum in his quae dicta sunt mihi: In domum Dominum ibimus* (Psalm 121:1)

Which noon erthely langage may discure,
God behalden of hys creature,
Whiche aperteneth to gostly suffisaunce,
140 Whan from the worlde is made disseveraunce.

From vertu to vertu men shall up ascende;
Than shall God be seyn in the Mount Sion.[1]
Thus you gide unto youre lyves ende,
We praie the Lorde that gideth al alloon,
145 So that with yow we may atteigne ecchon
To the faire Cite of Iherusalem,
Bisette aboute with many a precious gemme.

   [At Seynt Michaeles in Querne

[*Expositor*:]

Assumpt above the hevely Ierarchie,
Cristes Modre, Virgyn immaculate,
150 God Hys tabernacle to sanctifie
Of sterres xii the croune hath preparate,[2]
Emprise, Queene, and Lady Laureate.
Praie for oure Queene that Crist will here governe
Long here on lyve in hire noble astate,
155 Aftirward crowne here in blisse eterne.

This storie to your Highnes wolde expresse
The grete Resureccioun generall,
Wherof oure feith bereth pleyn witnesse:
The ferefull sowne of Trumpe Judiciall
160 Uppon the poeple yt sodeynly shall calle,
Eche man to make acompte and rekenynge
Right as hys consciencie bewreien shalle,
All be it Pope, Emperour, or Kynge.

Who hath wel doon, to lyf predestinate:
165 What joie, what blis, how greet felicité
Unto the saved of God is ordinate,
Noo tunge can telle, noon erthly igh may see.
Joie, laude, rest, pees, and parfite unité,
Triumphes of eternalle victorie,

---

[1] *Ibunt de virtute in virtutem, / Videbitur Deus deorum in Sion* (Psalm 83:8)

[2] *Signum magnum apparuit in caelol mulier amicta sole, et luna sub pedibus eius, et in capite eius corona stellarum duodecim* (Apocalypse 12:1)

170   With fruicioun of the Trynite,
       By contemplacioun of Hys Glorie.

       [*Deos Gracias Amen.*

 **BIBLIOGRAPHY**

MANUSCRIPTS

Bycorne and Chychevache. Cambridge, Trinity College Library, MS R.3.20; Cambridge, Trinity College Library, MS R.3.19; London, British Library MS Harley 2251.

Disguising at Hertford. Cambridge, Trinity College Library, MS R.3.20; London, British Library, MS Additional 29729.

Disguising at London. Cambridge, Trinity College Library, MS R.3.20; London, British Library, MS Additional 29729.

Henry VI's Triumphal Entry into London. London, British Library MS Cotton Cleopatra C.iv; London, British Library MS Cotton Julius B.ii.; London, British Library, MS Harley 565; London, Guildhall, MS 3313; Longleat House 257, at end of MS (stanzas 1–23 only); Rome, English College Library, MS1306 (also numbered 127 and A.347). Printed by Pynson, 1516.

Legend of St. George. Oxford, Bodleian Library MS Bodley 686; Cambridge, Trinity College Library, MS R.3.20; Cambridge, Trinity College Library, MS R.3.21; Manchester, Chetham Library MS 6709.

Mesure Is Tresour. London, British Library, MS Harley 2255.

Mumming at Bishopswood. Oxford, Bodleian Library, MS Ashmole 59.

Mumming at Eltham. Cambridge, Trinity College Library, MS R.3.20; London, British Library, MS Additional 29729.

Mumming at Windsor. Cambridge, Trinity College Library, MS R.3.20; London, British Library, MS Additional 29729.

Mumming for the Goldsmiths. Cambridge, Trinity College Library, MS R.3.20; London, British Library, MS Additional 29729.

Mumming for the Mercers. Cambridge, Trinity College Library, MS R.3.20. London, British Library, MS Additional 29729.

Of the Sodein Fal of Princes in Oure Dayes. Cambridge, Trinity College Library, MS R.3.20; London, British Library MS Harley 2251; London, British Library MS Additional 29729.

Pageant of Knowledge. Cambridge, Trinity College Library, MS R.3.21; extracts, not meant for performance, in several other manuscripts.

Procession of Corpus Christi. Cambridge, Trinity College Library, MS R.3.20; London, British Library MS Harley 2251; London, British Library MS Additional 29729.

Soteltes at the Coronation Banquet of Henry VI. Oxford, St John's College Library, MS 57; London, British Library, MS Cotton Julius B.i.; London, British Library, MS Lansdowne 285; London, British Library, MS Egerton 1995; London, Guildhall, MS 3313; New York, Pierpont Morgan Library, MS M.775.

In Appendix:

Margaret of Anjou's Entry into London, 1445. London, British Library, MS Harley 3869. Transcribed by Stow, British Library, MS Harley 542.

Mumming of the Seven Philosophers. Cambridge, Trinity College Library, MS R.3.19.

SOURCES AND CONTEMPORARY WORKS

Amundesham, John. *Annales monasterii S. Albani, 1421–40*. Ed. Henry Thomas Riley. 2 vols. London: Longmans, Green, and Company, 1870–71.

Annales Londiniensis. In *Chronicles of the Reigns of Edward I and Edward II*. Ed. Williams Stubbs. 2 vols. London: Longman, 1882–83. 1:1–251.

The Anonimalle Chronicle: 1333 to 1381, From a Manuscript Written at St. Mary's Abbey, York. Ed. V. H. Galbraith. Manchester: Manchester University Press, 1927.

Augustine. *De civitate Dei*. Ed. and trans. P. G. Walsh. Oxford: Oxbow, 2005.

Ausonius, Decimus Magnus. *Works*. Ed. R. P. H. Green. Oxford: Clarendon, 1991.

Boethius. *De Consolatione*. With a trans. by S. J. Tester. Loeb Classical Library 74. Cambridge, MA: Harvard University Press, 1973.

The Book of Brome. New Haven, Yale University Library, MS 365.

The Brut. Ed. Friedrich W. D. Brie. 2 vols. EETS o.s. 131, 136. London: Kegan Paul, Trench, and Trübner, 1906–08.

Charles d'Orléans. *Poésies*. Ed. Pierre Champion. 2 vols. Paris: H. Champion, 1923–24.

Chaucer, Geoffrey. "A Treatise on the Astrolabe." In *The Riverside Chaucer*. Pp. 661–83.

———. "The Book of the Duchess." In *The Riverside Chaucer*. Pp. 329–46.

———. "The Canterbury Tales." In *The Riverside Chaucer*. Pp. 3–328.

———. "The House of Fame." In *The Riverside Chaucer*. Pp. 347–73.

———. *The Riverside Chaucer*. Ed. Larry D. Benson. 3rd ed. Boston: Houghton Mifflin, 1987.

———. "Troilus and Criseyde." In *The Riverside Chaucer*. Pp. 471–585.

A Chronicle of London from 1089 to 1483. Ed. Nicholas H. Nicolas and Edward Tyrrell. London: Longman, Rees, Orme, Brown, and Green, 1827.

Chronicles of London. Ed. Charles Lethbridge Kingsford. Oxford: Clarendon, 1905.

Fabyan, Robert. *The New Chronicles of England and France*. Ed. Henry Ellis. London: F., C., and J. Rivington, 1811.

Foedera. Ed. Thomas Rymer. 10 vols. The Hague: Joannem Neulme, 1739–45.

Gesta Henrici Quinti: The Deeds of Henry the Fifth. Trans. Frank Taylor and John S. Roskell. Oxford: Clarendon, 1975.

Godfrey of Viterbo. *Pantheon, sive, Uniuersitatis*. Basil: Iacobi Parci, 1559.

Gower, John. *Confessio Amantis*. Ed. Russell A. Peck, with Latin translations by Andrew Galloway. 3 vols. Kalamazoo, MI: Medieval Institute Publications, 2000–06.

Guillaume de Lorris and Jean de Meun. *Le Roman de la Rose*. Ed. Félix Lecoy. 3 vols. Paris: H. Champion, 1965.

The Historical Collections of a Citizen of London in the Fifteenth Century. Ed. James Gairdner. Westminster: Camden Society, 1876.

Hoccleve, Thomas. *The Regiment of Princes*. Ed. Charles R. Blyth. Kalamazoo, MI: Medieval Institute Publications, 1999.

Isidore of Seville. *Etymologiae sive originum*. Ed. W. M. Lindsay. Oxford: Oxford University Press, 1911.

———. *Liber de ortu et obitu patriarcharum*. Ed. J. Carracedo Fraga. Turnholt: Brepols, 1996.

John of Salisbury. *Policraticus: Of the Frivolities of Courtiers and the Footprints of Philosophers*. Ed. and trans. Cary J. Nederman. Cambridge: Cambridge University Press, 1990.

Jubinal, Achille, ed. *Mystères inédits du quinzième siècle*. 2 vols. Paris: Téchener, 1837.

Lambert, John J. *Records of the Skinners of London, Edward I. to James I*. London: The Company, 1933.

Langland, William. *Piers Plowman. A Parallel-Text Edition of the A, B, C and Z Versions. Volume I. Text*. Ed. A. V. C. Schmidt. London: Longman, 1995.

Lydgate, John. *The Dance of Death, Edited from MSS. Ellesmere 26/A.13 and B.M. Lansdowne 699, Collated with the Other Extant MSS*. Ed. Florence Warren. EETS o.s. 181. London: Oxford University Press, 1931.

———. "A Dietary, and a Doctrine for Pestilence." In *The Minor Poems of John Lydgate*. Pp. 702–07.

———. *Fall of Princes*. Ed. Henry Bergen. 4 vols. EETS e.s. 121–24. London: Oxford University Press, 1924–27.

———. *The Minor Poems of John Lydgate: Edited from All Available Manuscripts, with an Attempt to Establish the Lydgate Canon. Part II: Secular Poems*. Ed. Henry Noble MacCracken. EETS o.s. 192. London: Oxford University Press, 1934.

———. *The Serpent of Division*. [See p. 101, note to lines 517–23.]

———. "Stans puer ad mensam." In *The Minor Poems of John Lydgate*. Pp. 739–44.

———. "Title and Pedigree of Henry VI." In *The Minor Poems of John Lydgate*. Pp. 613–22.

———. *Troy Book: Selections*. Ed. Robert R. Edwards. Kalamazoo, MI: Medieval Institute Publications, 1998.

Manuscript Trinity R.3.19, Trinity College, Cambridge: A Facsimile. Intro. Bradford Y. Fletcher. Norman, OK: Pilgrim Books, 1987.

Munimenta Gildhallae Londoniensis: Liber Albus, Liber Custumarum, et Liber Horn. Ed. Henry Thomas Riley. 4 vols. London: Longman, Brown, Green, Longmans, and Roberts, 1859–62.

The N-Town Plays. Ed. Douglas Sugano. With assistance by Victor I. Scherb. Kalamazoo, MI: Medieval Institute Publications, 2007.

Ovid. *Metamorphoses*. Trans. Frank Justus Miller. 2 vols. Cambridge, MA: Harvard University Press, 1976–77.

A Parisian Journal: 1405–1449. Trans. Janet Shirley. Oxford: Clarendon, 1968.

Plato. *The Republic*. Trans. R. E. Allen. New Haven: Yale University Press, 2006.

Proceedings and Ordinances of the Privy Council of England. Ed. Harris Nicholas. 7 vols. London: Eyre and Spottiswoode, 1834–37.

Promptorium parvulorum sive clericorum. Ed. Albert Way. 3 vols. London: Camden Society, 1843–65.

Recueil de farces françaises inédites du XVᵉ Siècle. Ed. Gustave Cohen. Cambridge, MA: Medieval Academy of America, 1949.

Redman, Robert. *Vita Henrici Quinti*. In *Memorials of Henry the Fifth, King of England*. Ed. Charles Augustus Cole. London: Longman, Brown, Green, Longmans, and Roberts, 1858. Pp. 1–59.

Rotuli Parliamentorum. 6 vols. London, 1767–77.

Russell, John. *The Boke of Nurture*. Bungay: J. Childs, 1867.

St. Erkenwald. Ed. Ruth Morse. Cambridge: D. S. Brewer, 1975.

Stow, John. *Annales, or a Generall Chronicle of England*. London: Ralfe Newbery, 1592.

———. *A Survey of London: Reprinted from the Text of 1603*. Ed. Charles Lethbridge Kingsford. 2 vols. Oxford: Clarendon, 1908.

A Tretise of Miraclis Pleyinge. Ed. Clifford Davidson. Kalamazoo, MI: Medieval Institute Publications, 1993.

Vatican Mythographers I and II. *Mythographi Vaticani I et II*. Ed. Péter Kulcsár. Turnholt: Brepols, 1987.

Walsingham, Thomas. *Historia anglicana*. Ed. Henry Thomas Riley. 2 vols. London: Longman, Green, Longman, Roberts, and Green, 1863–64.

Wardens' Accounts and Court Minute Books of the Goldsmiths' Mistery of London, 1334–1446. Ed. Lisa Jefferson. Woodbridge: Boydell, 2003.

The Westminster Chronicle, 1381–1394. Ed. and trans. L. C. Hector and Barbara F. Harvey. Oxford: Clarendon, 1982.

EDITIONS

Brown, Carleton. "Lydgate's Verses on Queen Margaret's Entry into London." *Modern Language Review* 7 (1912): 225–31. [*Margaret's Entry*]

Dodsley, Robert. *A Select Collection of Old Plays*. 2nd ed. Ed. Isaac Reed. 12 vols. London: H. Hughs, 1780. [*Bycorne*]

Forbes, Derek. *Lydgate's Disguising at Hertford Castle: The First Secular Comedy in the English Language*. West Sussex: Blot Publishing, 1998. [*Hertford*]

Halliwell, James Orchard, ed. *A Selection from the Minor Poems of Dan John Lydgate*. London: C. Richards for the Percy Society, 1840. [*Bycorne*; *Henry VI's Entry*; *Mesure is Tresour*; *Procession of Corpus Christi*]

Kingsford, Charles L., ed. *Chronicles of London*. Oxford: Clarendon, 1905. [*Entry*]

Kipling, Gordon. "The London Pageants for Margaret of Anjou: A Medieval Script Restored." *Medieval English Theatre* 4 (1982): 5–27. [*Margaret's Entry*]

The Minor Poems of John Lydgate. Ed. Henry Noble MacCracken. 2 vols. EETS o.s. 192, e.s. 107. London: Oxford University Press, 1911–34. [Vol. 2 contains all but *Bishopswood, Margaret's Entry, St. George*, and *Seven Philosophers*]

Malcolm, James P. *Londinium Redivivum, or an Antient History and Modern Description*. London: J. Nicholas, 1803. [modernization of *Entry*]

Nicolas, N. H., and Edward Tyrrell, eds. *A Chronicle of London, from 1089 to 1483*. London: Longman, 1827. [*Entry*]

Norton-Smith, John, ed. *John Lydgate: Poems*. Oxford: Clarendon, 1966. [*Bishopswood*]

Robbins, Rossell Hope. *Historical Poems of the XIVth and XVth Centuries*. New York: Columbia University Press, 1959. [*Sodein Fal*]

———. *Secular Lyrics of the XIVth and XVth Centuries*. Oxford: Clarendon, 1955. [*Seven Philosophers*]

BIBLIOGRAPHICAL SOURCES

Edwards, A. S. G. "Additions and Corrections to the Bibliography of John Lydgate." *Notes and Queries* 230 (1985): 450–52.

———. "A Lydgate Bibliography, 1926–68." *Bulletin of Bibliography and Magazine Notes* 27 (1970): 95–98.

———. "Lydgate Scholarship: Progress and Prospects." *Fifteenth-Century Studies: Recent Essays*. Ed. Robert F. Yaeger. Hamden, CT: Archon Books, 1984. Pp. 29–47.

Lee, Sidney. "Lydgate." In *Dictionary of National Biography*. Ed. Leslie Stephen and Sidney Lee. London: Oxford University Press, 1921–22. Pp. 306–16.

Reimer, Stephen R. "The Lydgate Canon: A Project Description." *Literary and Linguistic Computing* 5 (1990): 248–49.

Renoir, Alain, and C. David Benson. "John Lydgate." In *A Manual of the Writings in Middle English, 1050–1500*. Ed. J. Burke Severs, Albert E. Hartung, and Peter G. Beidler. 11 vols. to date. New Haven: Connecticut Academy of Arts and Sciences, 1967– . 6:1809–1920, 2071–2175.

SELECTED CRITICISM

Anglo, Sydney. "The Evolution of the Early Tudor Disguising, Pageant, and Mask." *Renaissance Drama* n.s. 1 (1968): 3–44.

———. *Spectacle, Pageantry, and Early Tudor Policy*. Oxford: Clarendon, 1969.

Aston, Margaret. "Corpus Christi and Corpus Regni: Heresy and the Peasants' Revolt." *Past and Present* 143 (1994): 3–47.

Barney, Stephen A. "The Plowshare of the Tongue: The Progress of a Symbol from the Bible to *Piers Plowman*." *Medieval Studies* 35 (1973): 261–93.

Barron, Caroline M. *London in the Later Middle Ages: Government and People, 1200–1500*. Oxford: Oxford University Press, 2004.

———. *The Medieval Guildhall of London*. London: Corporation of London, 1974.

———. "The Quarrel of Richard II with London 1392–7." In *The Reign of Richard II: Essays in Honour of May McKisack*. Ed. F. R. H. Du Boulay and Caroline M. Barron. London: Athlone Press, 1971. Pp. 173–201.

Beadle, Richard. *The Cambridge Companion to Medieval English Theatre*. Cambridge: Cambridge University Press, 1994.

Bennett, H. S. *Chaucer and the Fifteenth Century*. Oxford: Clarendon, 1947.

Benson, C. David. "Civic Lydgate: The Poet and London." In Scanlon and Simpson, pp. 147–68.

Bergeron, David M. *English Civic Pageantry 1558–1642*. Columbia: University of South Carolina Press, 1971.

Binski, Paul. *The Painted Chamber at Westminster*. London: Society of Antiquaries, 1986.

Boffey, Julia. "Lydgate's Lyrics and Women Readers." In *Women, the Book and the Worldly: Selected Proceedings of the St. Hilda's Conference, 1993*. Ed. Lesley Smith and Jane H. M. Taylor. Cambridge: D. S. Brewer, 1995. Pp. 139–49.

———. "Short Texts in Manuscript Anthologies: The Minor Poems of John Lydgate in Two Fifteenth-Century Collections." In *The Whole Book: Cultural Perspectives on the Medieval Miscellany*. Ed. Stephen G. Nichols and Siegfried Wenzel. Ann Arbor: University of Michigan Press, 1996. Pp. 69–82.

Brie, Friedrich. "Mittelalter und Antike bei Lydgate." *Englische Studien* 64 (1929): 261–301.

Brotanek, Rudolf. *Die Englischen Maskenspiele*. Vienna: Wilhelm Braunmüller, 1902.

Brown, Carleton. "Lydgate's Verses on Queen Margaret's Entry into London." *Modern Language Review* 7 (1912): 225–34.

Brusendorff, Aage. *The Chaucer Tradition*. London: Oxford University Press, 1925.

Bryant, Lawrence M. "Configurations of the Community in Late Medieval Spectacles: Paris and London during the Dual Monarchy." In *City and Spectacle in Medieval Europe*. Ed. Barbara A. Hanawalt and Kathryn L. Reyerson. Minneapolis: University of Minnesota Press, 1994. Pp. 3–33.

Bühler, Curt. "Lydgate's *Horse, Sheep and Goose* and Huntington MS. HM 144." *Modern Language Notes* 55 (1940): 563–70.

Bunt, Gerrit H. V. *Alexander the Great in the Literature of Medieval Britain*. Groningen: Egbert Forsten, 1994.

Cary, George. *The Medieval Alexander*. Cambridge: Cambridge University Press, 1956.

Chambers, E. K. *The Mediaeval Stage*. 2 vols. Oxford: Oxford University Press, 1903.

Christie, Mabel E. *Henry VI*. Boston: Houghton Mifflin, 1922.

Clopper, Lawrence M. *Drama, Play, and Game: English Festive Culture in the Medieval and Early Modern Period*. Chicago: University of Chicago Press, 2001.

Coldewey, John C. "Plays and 'Play' in Early English Drama." *Research Opportunities in Renaissance Drama* 28 (1985): 181–88.

Connolly, Margaret. *John Shirley: Book Production and the Noble Household in Fifteenth-Century England*. Aldershot: Ashgate, 1998.

Cornell, Christine. "'Purtreture' and 'Holsom Stories': John Lydgate's Accomodation of Image and Text in Three Religious Lyrics." *Florilegium* 10 (1988–91): 167–78.

Crane, Susan. *The Performance of Self: Ritual, Clothing, and Identity during the Hundred Years War*. Philadelphia: University of Pennsylvania Press, 2002.

Crow, Brian. "Lydgate's 1445 Pageant for Margaret of Anjou." *English Language Notes* 18 (1980–81): 170–74.

Davidson, Clifford. *Technology, Guilds, and Early English Drama*. Kalamazoo, MI: Medieval Institute Publications, 1996.

Denny-Brown, Andrea. "Lydgate's Golden Cows: Appetite and Avarice in Lydgate's *Byrcorne and Chychevache*." In *Lydgate Matters: Poetry and Material Culture in the Fifteenth Century*. Ed. Lisa H. Cooper and Andrea Denny-Brown. New York: Palgrave Macmillan, 2008. Pp. 35–56.

DeVries, David N. "And Away Go Troubles Down the Drain: Late Medieval London and the Politics of Urban Renewal." *Exemplaria* 8 (1996): 401–18.

Dobson, R. B. "The Religious Orders, 1370–1540." In *Late Medieval Oxford*. Ed. J. I. Catto and Ralph Evans. Oxford: Clarendon, 1992. Pp. 539–79.

Doyle, A. I. "Book Production by the Monastic Orders in England (*c.* 1375–1530): Assessing the Evidence." In *Medieval Book Production: Assessing the Evidence*. Ed. Linda L. Brownrigg. Los Altos Hills, CA: Anderson-Lovelace, 1990. Pp. 1–19.

———. "More Light on John Shirley." *Medium Aevum* 30 (1961): 93–101.

Duschl, Joseph. *Das Sprichwort bei Lydgate nebst Quellen und Parallelen*. Weiden: Nickl, 1912.

Ebin, Lois A. *Illuminator, Makar, Vates: Visions of Poetry in the Fifteenth Century*. Lincoln: University of Nebraska Press, 1988.

———. *John Lydgate*. Boston: Twayne, 1985.

Edwards, A. S. G. "John Lydgate, Medieval Antifeminism and Harley 2251." *Annuale Mediaevale* 13 (1972): 32–44.

———. "John Shirley and the Emulation of Courtly Culture." In *The Court and Cultural Diversity: Selected Papers from the Eighth Triennial Congress of the International Courtly Literature Society, The Queen's University of Belfast, 26 July–1 August 1995*. Ed. Evelyn Mullally and John Thompson. Cambridge: D. S. Brewer, 1997. Pp. 309–17.

———. "Lydgate Manuscripts: Some Directions for Future Research." In *Manuscripts and Readers in Fifteenth-Century England: The Literary Implications of Manuscript Study*. Ed. Derek Pearsall. Cambridge: D. S. Brewer, 1983. Pp. 15–26.

———. "Lydgate's Attitudes to Women." *English Studies* 51 (1970): 436–37.

———. "Middle English Pageant 'Picture'?" *Notes and Queries* 237 (1992): 25–26.

Edwards, A. S. G., and Carol M. Meale. "The Marketing of Printed Books in Late Medieval England." *The Library*, sixth series, 15 (1993): 95–124.

Enders, Jody. *Rhetoric and the Origins of Medieval Drama*. Ithaca, NY: Cornell University Press, 1992.

Epstein, Robert. "Eating Their Words: Food and Text in the Coronation Banquet of Henry VI." *Journal of Medieval and Early Modern Studies* 36 (2006): 355–77.

———. "Lydgate's Mummings and the Aristocratic Resistance to Drama." *Comparative Drama* 36 (2002): 337–58.

Fisher, John H. "A Language Policy for Lancastrian England." *PMLA* 107 (1992): 1168–80.

Floyd, Jennifer. "St. George and the 'Steyned Halle': Lydgate's Verse for the London Armourers." In *Lydgate Matters: Poetry and Material Culture in the Fifteenth Century*. Ed. Lisa H. Cooper and Andrea Denny-Brown. New York: Palgrave Macmillan, 2008. Pp. 139–64.

Forbes, Derek. *Lydgate's Disguising at Hertford Castle, the First Secular Comedy in the English Language: A Translation and Study*. Pulborough: Blot Publishing, 1998.

Freehafer, John. "John Warburton's Lost Plays." *Studies in Bibliography* 23 (1970): 154–64.

Ganim, John M. "The Experience of Modernity in Late Medieval Literature: Urbanism, Experience and Rhetoric in Some Early Descriptions of London." In *The Performance of Middle English Culture: Essays on Chaucer and the Drama in Honor of Martin Stevens*. Ed. James J. Paxson, Lawrence M. Clopper, and Sylvia Tomasch. Cambridge: D. S. Brewer, 1998. Pp. 76–96.

Gattinger, E. *Die Lyrik Lydgates*. Vienna: Wilhelm Braumüller, 1896.

Gerould, Gordon H. "Legends of St. Wulfhad and St. Ruffin at Stone Priory." *PMLA* 32 (1917): 323–37.

Gibson, Gail McMurray. "Bury St. Edmunds, Lydgate, and the *N-Town Cycle*." *Speculum* 56 (1981): 56–90.

Gillespie, James L. "Ladies of the Fraternity of Saint George and of the Society of the Garter." *Albion* 17 (1985): 259–78.

Green, Richard Firth. *Poets and Princepleasers: Literature and the English Court in the Late Middle Ages*. Toronto: University of Toronto Press, 1980.

———. "Three Fifteenth-Century Notes." *English Language Notes* 14 (1976): 14–17.

Griffiths, Ralph A. *The Reign of King Henry VI: The Exercise of Royal Authority, 1422–1461*. Berkeley: University of California Press, 1981.

Hammond, Eleanor Prescott. "Ashmole 59 and Other Shirley Manuscripts." *Anglia* 30 (1907): 320–48.

———. *English Verse Between Chaucer and Surrey*. Durham, NC: Duke University Press, 1927.

———. "Lydgate's Mumming at Hertford." *Anglia* 22 (1899): 364–74.

———. "A Reproof to Lydgate." *Modern Language Notes* 26 (1911): 74–76.

———. "Two British Museum Manuscripts (Harley 2251 and Add. 34360): A Contribution to the Bibliography of John Lydgate." *Anglia* 28 (1905): 1–28.

———. "Two Tapestry Poems by Lydgate: The *Life of St. George* and the *Falls of Seven Princes*." *Englische Studien* 43 (1910–11): 10–26.

Hanna, Ralph, III. "Some Norfolk Women and Their Books, ca. 1390–1440." In *The Cultural Patronage of Medieval Women*. Ed. June Hall McCash. Athens: University of Georgia Press, 1996. Pp. 288–305.

Hardman, Phillipa. "Lydgate's Uneasy Syntax." In Scanlon and Simpson, pp. 12–35.

Harriss, G. L. *Cardinal Beaufort: A Study of Lancastrian Ascendancy and Decline*. Oxford: Clarendon, 1988.

Hasted, Edward. *The History and Topographical Survey of the County of Kent*. 12 vols. Canterbury: W. Bristow, 1797–1801.

Herbert, William. *The History of the Twelve Great Livery Companies of London*. 2 vols. London: J. and C. Adlard, 1836–37.

Horrox, Rosemary. "Urban Patronage and Patrons in the Fifteenth Century." In *Patronage, the Crown and the Provinces in Later Medieval England*. Ed. Ralph A. Griffiths. Gloucester: Alan Sutton, 1981. Pp. 145–66.

Imray, Jean. *The Mercers' Hall*. London: Mercers' Company, 1991.

Jacob, E. F. *The Fifteenth Century: 1399–1485*. Oxford: Clarendon, 1961.

James, Mervyn. "Ritual, Drama and Social Body in the Late Medieval English Town." *Past and Present* 98 (1983): 4–29.

James, M. R. "Bury St. Edmunds Manuscripts." *English Historical Review* 41 (1926): 251–60.

Kipling, Gordon. *Enter the King: Theatre, Liturgy, and Ritual in the Medieval Civic Triumph*. Oxford: Clarendon, 1998.

———. "'Grace in this Lyf and Aftirwarde Glorie': Margaret of Anjou's Royal Entry into London." *Research Opportunities in Renaissance Drama* 29 (1986–87): 77–84.

———. "The London Pageants for Margaret of Anjou: A Medieval Script Restored." *Medieval English Theatre* 4 (1982): 5–27.

———. "Lydgate: The Poet as Deviser." In *Chaucer and the Challenges of Medievalism: Studies in Honor of H. A. Kelly*. Ed. Donka Minkova and Theresa Tinkle. Frankfurt am Main: Peter Lang, 2003. Pp. 73–101.

Lancashire, Anne. *London Civic Theatre: City Drama and Pageantry from Roman Times to 1558*. Cambridge: Cambridge University Press, 2002.

Lancashire, Ian. *Dramatic Texts and Records of Britain: A Chronological Topography to 1558*. Toronto: University of Toronto Press, 1984.

Lawton, David. "Dullness and the Fifteenth Century." *ELH* 54 (1987): 761–99.

Lerer, Seth. *Chaucer and His Readers: Imagining the Author in Late Medieval England*. Princeton, NJ: Princeton University Press, 1993.

MacCracken, Henry Noble. "King Henry's Triumphal Entry into London, Lydgate's Poem, and Carpenter's Letter." *Archiv* 126 (1911): 75–102.

McFarlane, K. B. *Lancastrian Kings and Lollard Knights*. Oxford: Clarendon, 1972.

McKenna, J. W. "Henry VI of England and the Dual Monarchy: Aspects of Royal Political Propaganda, 1422–1432." *Journal of the Warburg and Courtauld Institutes* 28 (1965): 145–62.

McLaren, Mary-Rose. *The London Chronicles of the Fifteenth Century: A Revolution in English Writing, with an Annotated Edition of Bradford, West Yorkshire Archives MS 32D86/42*. Cambridge: D. S. Brewer, 2002.

McNamer, Sarah. "Female Authors, Provincial Setting: The Re-Versing of Courtly Love in the Findern Manuscript." *Viator* 22 (1991): 279–310.

Menner, Robert J. "Bycorne-Bygorne, Husband of Chichevache." *Modern Language Notes* 44 (1929): 455–57.

Middleton, Anne. "The Idea of Public Poetry in the Reign of Richard II." *Speculum* 53 (1978): 94–114.

Mooney, Linne R. "John Shirley's Heirs." *Yearbook of English Studies* 33 (2003): 182–98.

———. "Scribes and Booklets of Trinity College, Cambridge, Manuscripts R.3.19 and R.3.21." In *Middle English Poetry: Texts and Traditions: Essays in Honour of Derek Pearsall*. Ed. A. J. Minnis. York: The University of York, 2001. Pp. 241–66.

Mortimer, Nigel. *John Lydgate's Fall of Princes: Narrative Tragedy in Its Literary and Political Contexts*. Oxford: Clarendon, 2005.

Nolan, Maura. *John Lydgate and the Making of Public Culture*. Cambridge: Cambridge University Press, 2005.

Oppenheimer, Francis. *The Legend of the Ste. Ampoule*. London: Faber and Faber, 1953.

Ord, C. "Account of the Entertainment of King Henry the Sixth at the Abbey of Bury St. Edmund's." *Archaeologia* 15 (1806): 65–71.

Osberg, Richard H. "The Goldsmiths' 'Chastell' of 1377." *Theatre Survey* 27 (1986): 1–15.

———. "The Jesse Tree in the 1432 London Entry of Henry VI: Messianic Kingship and the Rule of Justice." *Journal of Medieval and Renaissance Studies* 16 (1986): 213–32.

———. "The Lambeth Palace Library Manuscript Account of Henry VI's 1432 London Entry." *Mediaeval Studies* 52 (1990): 255–67.

Pantin, William Abel, ed. *Documents Illustrating the Activities of the General and Provincial Chapters of the English Black Monks 1215–1540*. 3 vols. London: Camden Society, 1931–37.

Parry, P. H. "On the Continuity of English Civic Pageantry: A Study of John Lydgate and the Tudor Pageant." *Forum for Modern Language Studies* 15 (1979): 222–36.

Patch, Howard R. *The Goddess Fortuna in Mediaeval Literature*. Cambridge, MA: Harvard University Press, 1927.

Patterson, Lee. "Making Identities in Fifteenth-Century England: Henry V and John Lydgate." In *New Historical Literary Study: Essays on Reproducing Texts, Representing History*. Ed. Jeffrey N. Cox and Larry J. Reynolds. Princeton, NJ: Princeton University Press, 1993. Pp. 69–107.

Pearsall, Derek. *John Lydgate*. London: Routledge and Kegan Paul, 1970.

———. *John Lydgate (1371–1449): A Bio-Bibliography*. Victoria: University of Victoria, 1997.

Rastall, Richard. *Music in Early English Religious Drama*. 2 vols. Cambridge: D. S. Brewer, 1996–2001.

Reddaway, T. F., and Lorna E. M. Walker. *The Early History of the Goldsmiths' Company, 1327–1509, Including The Book of Ordinances 1475–83*. London: Edward Arnold, 1975.

Renoir, Alain. "On the Date of John Lydgate's *Mumming at Hertford*." *Archiv für das Studium der Neueren Sprachen und Literaturen* 198 (1961): 32–33.

———. *The Poetry of John Lydgate*. London: Routledge and Kegan Paul, 1967.

Reyher, Paul. *Les masques Anglais: étude sur les ballets et la vie de cour en Angleterre (1512–1640)*. Paris: Hachette, 1909.

Robbins, Rossell Hope. *Secular Lyrics of the XIVth and XVth Centuries*. Oxford: Clarendon, 1959.

Robertson, Jean, and D. J. Gordon, eds. "A Calendar of Dramatic Records in the Books of the Livery Companies of London, 1485–1640." *Collections III*. London: Malone Society, 1954.

Samuel, Irene. "Semiramis in the Middle Ages: The History of a Legend." *Medievalia et Humanistica* 2 (1944): 32–44.

Saygin, Susanne. *Humphrey, Duke of Gloucester (1390–1447) and the Italian Humanists*. Leiden: Brill, 2002.

Scanlon, Larry, and James Simpson, eds. *John Lydgate: Poetry, Culture, and Lancastrian England*. Notre Dame, IN: University of Notre Dame Press, 2006.

Scattergood, V. J. *Politics and Poetry in the Fifteenth Century*. London: Blandford Press, 1971.

Schirmer, Walter F. *John Lydgate: A Study in the Culture of the XVth Century*. Trans. Ann E. Keep. London: Methuen, 1961.

Scott, Kathleen L. *Later Gothic Manuscripts: 1390–1490*. 2 vols. London: Harvey Miller, 1996.

Sponsler, Claire. "Alien Nation: London's Aliens and Lydgate's Mummings for the Mercers and Goldsmiths." In *The Postcolonial Middle Ages*. Ed. Jeffrey Jerome Cohen. New York: St. Martin's Press, 2000. Pp. 229–42.

———. "Drama in the Archives: Recognizing Medieval Plays." In *Redefining British Theatre History*. Ed. Stephen Orgel and Peter Holland. New York: Palgrave, 2004. Pp. 111–30.

Straker, Scott-Morgan. "Propaganda, Intentionality, and the Lancastrian Lydgate." In Scanlon and Simpson, pp. 98–128.

Streitberger, W. R. *Court Revels, 1485–1559*. Toronto: University of Toronto Press, 1994.

Strohm, Paul. *Hochon's Arrow: The Social Imagination of Fourteenth-Century Texts*. Princeton, NJ: Princeton University Press, 1992.

Thomson, R. M. "The Library of Bury St. Edmunds Abbey in the Eleventh and Twelfth Centuries." *Speculum* 47 (1972): 617–45.

Tiner, Elza, Shirley Carnahan, and Anne Fjestad Peterson. "'Euer aftir to be rad & song': Lydgate's Texts in Performance [Parts I and II]." *Early Drama, Art and Music Review* 19.1 (1996): 41–52; 19.2 (1997): 85–92.

Trapp, J. B. "Verses by Lydgate at Long Melford." *Review of English Studies* n.s. 6 (1955): 1–11.

Tuve, Rosemond. *Allegorical Imagery: Some Mediaeval Books and Their Posterity*. Princeton, NJ: Princeton University Press, 1966.

Twycross, Meg, and Sarah Carpenter. *Masks and Masking in Medieval and Early Tudor England*. Aldershot: Ashgate, 2002.

Watts, John. *Henry VI and the Politics of Kingship*. Cambridge: Cambridge University Press, 1996.

Welsford, Enid. *The Court Masque: A Study in the Relationship Between Poetry and the Revels*. Cambridge: Cambridge University Press, 1927.

Westfall, Suzanne R. *Patrons and Performance: Early Tudor Household Revels*. Oxford: Clarendon, 1990.

Whiting, Bartlett Jere, with the collaboration of Helen Wescott Whiting. *Proverbs, Sentences, and Proverbial Phrases: From English Writings Mainly before 1500*. Cambridge, MA: Belknap Press, 1968.

Wickham, Glynne. *Early English Stages 1300–1600*. 3 vols. London: Routledge and Kegan Paul, 1959–81.

Withington, Robert. *English Pageantry: An Historical Outline*. 2 vols. Cambridge, MA: Harvard University Press, 1918–20.

———. "Queen Margaret's Entry into London, 1445." *Modern Philology* 13 (1915–16): 53–57.

Wolffe, Bertram. *Henry VI*. London: Eyre Methuen, 1981.

Wylie, James Hamilton, and William Templeton Waugh. *The Reign of Henry the Fifth*. 3 vols. Cambridge: Cambridge University Press, 1914–29.

🌿 GLOSSARY

aboode *delay*
accoye *soothe*
acorde *accord, agreement*
advert *attend to; notice*
advertence *attention*
aforne *before*
agens *against*
ageyne *again*
agoon *ago*
alight *descended*
almesse *charity*
ampoulle *phial*
apperteyning *pertaining*
appul *apple*
armes *warfare, weapons*
armonye *harmony*
armys *arms*
arsmetrike *arithmetic*
artificer *craftsman*
asselen *approve*
attempre *temperate*
auctor *author*
auctorysed *honored*
avaunce *increase, enhance*
avayle *be helpful, benefit, help*
aventure *fortune, chance*
avisyoun *vision, prophetic dream*
avoydinge *avoiding*
avysely *carefully, shrewdly*
awter *altar*
ay *ever*

b'assente *by assent*
batayll *battle*
bating *beating*
bawm *balm*
be(e)mys *beams*

beestis *beasts*
beheestes *commands*
benignely *graciously*
benignytee *grace, good will*
beo *is, are*
beshrew *curse*
blenchethe *flinches; turns aside*
bodekyns *daggers*
borde *table*
bountee *virtue, goodness*
bour *cottage*
bowes *boughs*
breche *breeches*
bridde *bird*
bulted *sifted*
byforne *before, previously*
byleeve *belief*

cas *fate, fortune*
cely *saintly or virtuous; unfortunate*
cesse *cease*
chaumbre *chamber, room*
chaumpartye *battle, contest*
chawf *warm*
cheer *look; face, mien*
chefe *chief*
cherisshing *nourishment*
circumsyde *exterminate, purge*
citeseyn *citizen*
citrine *yellowish*
clene *pure*
clepen *call*
clere *bright*
clerk *member of the clergy; scholar,*
    university student; writer
clouten *strike*
colorik *choleric, quick tempered*

colver *dove*
compaignye *company*
comune *common*
condycyouns *dispositions*
consaylle *counsel*
consistorye *consistory, court*
contune *contain*
conversacyoun *manner of life*
coosteying *coasting, going past*
coroune *crown*
co(u)rage *heart, feelings; sexual desire*
coustume *custom*
crabbed *spiteful*
creance *doctrine, belief*
crepaudes *heraldic toads*
Cristen *Christian*
cronycles *chronicles, histories*
cruwel *cruel*
cruweltee *cruelty*
cuntree *country*
cyte(e) *city*

darrein (derrein) *decide the outcome of*
debate *dispute*
debonaire *courteous*
deeme *judge*
defye *scorn*
delite *delight*
demayne *domain*
departed *multicolored*
depeynted *painted, decorated*
derknesse *darkness*
descryve *describe*
desguysee *decked out; disguised*
desobeyssaunce *disobedience*
desteined *stained*
devoyre *duty*
devynayle *meaning*
devyne *divine*
devyse *plan*
devysyoun *dissent*
difer *defer*
digne *worthy*
discent *descent*
disrewyld *disobedient*
doome *justice, judgment*
double *deceitful*

doute *uncertainty, fear*
dreed, drede *dread, fear, apprehension*
dresse *direct to; offer*
dured *lasted; resided*
dyamandes *diamonds*
dyspence *spending*
dyssevable *deceitful*
dytes *verses*

eche *each*
echoon *each one*
eek(e) *also*
elate *exalted*
emperesse *empress*
encresse *increase, intensify, grow*
enfourmen *instruct*
enhaunce *advance; exalt*
enlumyne *illumine*
en(m)pryses *deeds*
ennoyt *annointed*
ensaumple *example*
entent(e) *intent*
entier *entire, complete; perfect*
envyroun *around, round about*
ere *plow*
ermonye *harmony*
erst *earlier, before*
eschuwing *avoiding*
esse *ease, comfort*
estate *rank, social group; condition*
eure *fortune*
evermoore *always*
eyeghe *eye*

fade *withered, faded*
fader *father*
fayre (feyre) *pleasant, attractive*
felicytee *happiness*
felle *evil*
felnesse *treachery*
feonde *devil, fiend*
fer(re) *far, remote*
fest *feast*
feyth *faith*
filowethe *follows*
flaterye *flattery*
fleete *overflow*

flitten *go*
floure *flower*
floure de lys *fleur de lys*
flytting *changeable; fleeting*
foo *foe*
foole *bird, fowl*
for *because*
forsooke *forsook*
foule *wickedly*
foulsome *plentiful*
foulsomenesse *satiety*
fraunchise *freedom*
fredame *freedom*
fressh(e) *young, unfaded, vigorous*
fresshly *afresh, with continued vigor*
fro *from*
frowarde *unruly*
ful(ly) *fully, completely*
fury *fiery*

gadre *gather*
geaunt *giant*
gentilesse *gentility, nobility*
gere *fickle*
geve *gave*
gif *give*
glade *jolly, happy*
glene *sheaf*
glose *gloss*
goostely *spiritual*
gramer *grammar*
greable *suitable*
gre(e)t(e) *great*
gruchche *complain*
guye *guide*

haboundance *plenty, abundance*
happe *good fortune, luck*
hardy *bold, daring*
heet *heat*
helthe *health*
hem *them; themselves*
herp *harp*
hert *heart*
heven *heaven*
hevynesse *sluggishness; sadness*
hir *her; their*

honurable *honorable*
hool *whole, complete*
hoolde *building; stronghold, castle*
ho(o)lsome *wholesome, healthful*
howsyll *good luck*
hure *fortune*
hyeghe, hye *high, lofty, noble; divine*
hyenesse *high rank, highness*

ilke *same*
imaginatyf *imagination*
importable *unbearable*
in *on*
inbringethe *ushers in*
indifferent *impartial*
innosentes *innocent people*

joustely *justly, by right*
juparten *put at risk*

kan *can*
konnyng *knowledge*
kynde *kind; nature; race; disposition*
kynrede *kindred*

lak *lack*
large *generous*
lat *let, permit*
laurier *laurel*
lawde *praise*
leere *teach*
leete *let, permitted*
lene *lean*
lengest *longest*
lenkethe *length*
L'envoye *epilogue*
lesing *lying*
letting *hindrance*
lettres *writings*
leven *flash, lightning bolt*
lieges *subjects*
list *desire, wish*
loke *look*
lond *land*
longen *belong*
loore *lure*
lordshipethe *rules over*

lousty *lusty, pleasant, mirthful, vigorous*
lowly *humbly*
lowlyhede *humility, humbleness*
lowten *bow*
lustynesse *pleasure*
lyche *like*
lyf *life*
lykour *liquid, sap*
lynaage *lineage*

magnefye *magnify, increase*
makes *mates*
manase *threaten*
manly *manly, nobly*
marchandes *merchants*
mater *reason*
maugrey *despite*
mawmetrye *idolatry*
mayde *virgin*
maystre *master*
maystrye *mastery*
mede *meadow*
medegatyf *palliative*
meede *profit, reward*
meene *companionship*
meete *pleasant; fitting*
mene *mean, intend, signify*
merciable *merciful*
meryte *merit*
meschaunce *misfortune*
meschef *affliction; misfortune*
mescreaunce *unbelief*
mescreauntes *pagans, heathens*
mette *dreamed*
miche *much*
mischefe *misfortune*
moder *mother*
momyng *mumming, dumbshow*
mone *moon*
moo *more*
mo(o)ste *most, greatest*
morwenyng *morning*
mourdre *murder*
mynistre *administer*
myrour *mirror*
nature *nature, natural instinct, character*
ner *nor*

nesshe *soft*
neven *name*
newfangylnes *changeability*
noblesse *nobility, highness*
noisaunce *annoyance*
nolle *head*
noman *no one*
noon *not*
noone *no*
notable *remarkable*
nuwe *new*
nys *is not*

obeyssance *homage*
of *of, with, about*
oon *one, one and the same*
oonys *once*
ordenaunce *plan*
orysouns *prayers*
ougly *ugly*
outrage *excess; act of violence, criminal act*
outraien *banish*

paganymes *pagans*
paleys *palace*
parayllous *perilous*
parfyt (perfite) *perfect*
parfytnesse *perfection, perfect life*
parllement *assembly*
passing *excellent*
payne (peyne) *pain*
paynyme (paganim) *pagan, heathen*
pees *peace*
peisen *consider, ponder*
perseveraunt *steadfast, continued*
pertourbe *harm*
perturbaunce *disturbance*
plein (pleyne) *full*
pleinly *fully*
plenté *abundance*
plesaunce *pleasure*
pleynethe *complains*
pourayle *poor people*
poursy(v)ant *messenger*
powstee *power*
practyk *craft; method*

predicacioun *preaching*
prees *crowd*
preost *priest*
prescyence *foreknowledge*
prouesse *might, courage*
prowe *benefit*
proygne *preen*
pruyde *pride*
prys *fame; nobility*
puissance *power*
purveiaunce *providence*

qweeme *satisfy, please*
qweene *queen*
qwytt *repay*

reaume *realm, kingdom*
recure *regain*
recuvre *recover*
rede *wisdom*
reed *red*
refeccion *refreshment*
refrete *donation*
regallye *power; royalty; sovereignty*
rejoye *rejoyce*
reklesse *heedless of rules*
remevable *changeable*
remission *forgiveness*
remuve *remove*
renommed *renowned*
renoun *fame, renown*
repayre *return*
resemblable *similar*
resoun *sentiment; statement*
restoratyf *medicine*
rethorycyens *rhetoricians*
revelucyoun *revelation*
richesse *riches, wealth*
rightwys *righteous*
rightwysnesse *righteousness*
roche *rock*
rote *root*
roundel *short poem, often meant to be sung*
routhe *pity*
rude *rough, crude*
ruwe *consider*

ryal *royal*
ryallych *royally*
ryche *rich, splendid*
ryte *rite*

sad *sober*
salve *greet*
sapyence *wisdom*
sate *sat*
sayle *sail*
sayso(u)n *season*
see *seat, throne, kingdom*
seke *sick*
semblabully *similarly*
sentence *meaning; precept*
serche *search*
sette *put, placed*
seylen *to sail*
shadde *shed*
shadwe *cover*
sheene *bright, brightly*
shent *exhausted; harmed*
shew *show, demonstrate, display*
shoures *showers*
sikernesse (sekerness) *security*
sith(en) *since, afterwards*
sklendre *slender*
smote *struck*
so *such*
socour *relief*
sodeynly *suddenly*
some *some, a certain*
somwhile *sometimes*
sondes *sands*
sondry *different, varied*
sonne *sun*
soore *soar*
sort *lot, chance; turn*
soteltes *subtleties (confectionary decorations)*
souffisaunce *sufficiency*
soustene *sustain*
soveraine *excellent, superior*
spede *protection*
stabulnesse *stability*
steede *war horse*
ste(e)(r)re *star*

ston *jewel*

straunge *exotic, strange, unknown, foreign*

strenkethe *strength*

strif *quarrel, strife*

stronde *shore*

stynt *stopped*

substance *substance; essence*

subtyle *cunning*

suen *follow*

suffisaunce *sufficiency*

surquydous *haughty*

sustre *sister*

swaged *assuaged*

swerd *sword*

sweynes *commoners, rustics*

swo(o)te *sweet*

tabyde *to abide*

ta(e)rrage *taste; quality, characteristic*

tebreken *break apart*

teene *pain*

temperd *harmonious*

texyle *takes*

thilke *the same*

thridde *third*

thyes *thighs*

til *to*

tofore *before*

toforne *first; ahead*

tonnys *casks*

toun *town*

trascende *ascend, rise up*

tresore *treasure*

tretable *reasonable*

trouthe *truth*

trowe *trust, believe*

unccyoun *consecration*

underfong *undertake*

unkouthe *unknown*

unremuwable *unremovable*

unto *for*

unytee *unity*

varyaynce *fickleness, change, mutability*

venery *hunting*

vengeable *vindictive, vengeful*

verray *genuine*

vertu *power, ability; moral excellence*

victayle (vitaille) *food, provisions*

wacche *watch, vigil*

wastour *spendthrift*

weder *weather*

weede *clothes*

weel *well*

weene *hope*

wende *believed*

werre *war*

wex *increase*

whame *whom*

whane *when*

wheoche *which*

wherfore *therefore, for which reason*

whoo so *whoever, whomever*

whylom *formerly; once*

wellis *springs*

werke *deed*

will *wish, desire*

withseien *resist*

wol *will*

wone *custom*

wont *accustomed*

wo(o)d(e) *angry, mad*

woodness *madness*

wynnen *conquer*

wyse *manner*

ydooles *idols*

yf *if*

yit *yet*

yoore *long ago, formerly*

Stanzaic Guy of Warwick, edited by Alison Wiggins (2004)

Saints' Lives in Middle English Collections, edited by E. Gordon Whatley, with Anne B. Thompson and Robert K. Upchurch (2004)

Siege of Jerusalem, edited by Michael Livingston (2004)

The Kingis Quair and Other Prison Poems, edited by Linne R. Mooney and Mary-Jo Arn (2005)

The Chaucerian Apocrypha: A Selection, edited by Kathleen Forni (2005)

John Gower, *The Minor Latin Works*, edited and translated by R. F. Yeager, with *In Praise of Peace*, edited by Michael Livingston (2005)

Sentimental and Humorous Romances: Floris and Blanchefl our, Sir Degrevant, The Squire of Low Degree, The Tournament of Tottenham, and The Feast of Tottenham, edited by Erik Kooper (2006)

The Dicts and Sayings of the Philosophers, edited by John William Sutton (2006)

"Everyman" and Its Dutch Original, "Elckerlijc," edited by Clifford Davidson, Martin W. Walsh, and Ton J. Broos (2007)

The N-Town Plays, edited by Douglas Sugano, with assistance by Victor I. Scherb (2007)

The Book of John Mandeville, edited by Tamarah Kohanski and C. David Benson (2007)

John Lydgate, *The Temple of Glas*, edited by J. Allan Mitchell (2007)

The Northern Homily Cycle, edited by Anne B. Thompson (2008)

Codex Ashmole 61: A Compilation of Popular Middle English Verse, edited by George Shuffelton (2008)

Chaucer and the Poems of "Ch," edited by James I. Wimsatt (revised edition 2009)

William Caxton, *The Game and Playe of the Chesse*, edited by Jenny Adams (2009)

John the Blind Audelay, *Poems and Carols*, edited by Susanna Fein (2009)

Two Moral Interludes: "The Pride of Life" and "Wisdom," edited by David Klausner (2009)

COMMENTARY SERIES

Haimo of Auxerre, *Commentary on the Book of Jonah*, translated with an introduction and notes by Deborah Everhart (1993)

Medieval Exegesis in Translation: Commentaries on the Book of Ruth, translated with an introduction and notes by Lesley Smith (1996)

Nicholas of Lyra's Apocalypse Commentary, translated with an introduction and notes by Philip D. W. Krey (1997)

Rabbi Ezra Ben Solomon of Gerona, *Commentary on the Song of Songs and Other Kabbalistic Commentaries*, selected, translated, and annotated by Seth Brody (1999)

John Wyclif, *On the Truth of Holy Scripture*, translated with an introduction and notes by Ian Christopher Levy (2001)

Second Thessalonians: Two Early Medieval Apocalyptic Commentaries, introduced and translated by Steven R. Cartwright and Kevin L. Hughes (2001)

The "Glossa Ordinaria" on the Song of Songs, translated with an introduction and notes by Mary Dove (2004)

The Seven Seals of the Apocalypse: Medieval Texts in Translation, translated with an introduction and notes by Francis X. Gumerlock (2009)

DOCUMENTS OF PRACTICE SERIES

Love and Marriage in Late Medieval London, selected, translated, and introduced by Shannon McSheffrey (1995)

Sources for the History of Medicine in Late Medieval England, selected, introduced, and translated by Carole Rawcliffe (1995)

A Slice of Life: Selected Documents of Medieval English Peasant Experience, edited, translated, and with an introduction by Edwin Brezette DeWindt (1996)

Regular Life: Monastic, Canonical, and Mendicant "Rules," selected and introduced by Douglas J. McMillan and Kathryn Smith Fladenmuller (1997); second edition, selected and introduced by Daniel Marcel La Corte and Douglas J. McMillan (2004)

Women and Monasticism in Medieval Europe: Sisters and Patrons of the Cistercian Reform, selected, translated, and with an introduction by Constance H. Berman (2002)

Medieval Notaries and Their Acts: The 1327–1328 Register of Jean Holanie, introduced, edited, and translated by Kathryn L. Reyerson and Debra A. Salata (2004)

✐ Medieval German Texts in Bilingual Editions Series

Sovereignty and Salvation in the Vernacular, 1050–1150, introduction, translations, and notes by James A. Schultz (2000)

Ava's New Testament Narratives: "When the Old Law Passed Away," introduction, translation, and notes by James A. Rushing, Jr. (2003)

History as Literature: German World Chronicles of the Thirteenth Century in Verse, introduction, translation, and notes by R. Graeme Dunphy (2003)

Thomasin von Zirclaria, *Der Welsche Gast (The Italian Guest)*, translated by Marion Gibbs and Winder McConnell (2009)

✐ Varia

The Study of Chivalry: Resources and Approaches, edited by Howell Chickering and Thomas H. Seiler (1988)

Studies in the Harley Manuscript: The Scribes, Contents, and Social Contexts of British Library MS Harley 2253, edited by Susanna Fein (2000)

The Liturgy of the Medieval Church, edited by Thomas J. Heffernan and E. Ann Matter (2001; second edition 2005)

✐ To Order Please Contact:

Medieval Institute Publications
Western Michigan University
Kalamazoo, MI 49008-5432
Phone (269) 387-8755
FAX (269) 387-8750
http://www.wmich.edu/medieval/mip/index.html

Typeset in 10/13 New Baskerville
and Golden Cockerel Ornaments display
Designed by Linda K. Judy
Manufactured by Cushing-Malloy, Inc.

Medieval Institute Publications
College of Arts and Sciences
Western Michigan University
1903 W. Michigan Avenue
Kalamazoo, MI 49008-5432
http:/ /www.wmich.edu/medieval/mip

 WESTERN MICHIGAN UNIVERSITY